PRAISE FOR

Music and the Idea of a World

"Many people write about the meaning of music, but few can do it as well as Peter Kalkavage does in this marvelous, winsome, and often hauntingly beautiful book. We all know that the language of music overflows with meaning, profound meaning, both in the way it gives an expressive shape to the flow of our inner life, and in the way it models the transcendent grandeur of the cosmos, and even gives us a glimpse of the eternal. But the language of music resists translation into words. Kalkavage is equal to the challenge, however, and takes us on a deep dive into the philosophical dimensions of music, through a series of connected essays that demonstrate again and again the ways in which music is intimately connected to the most important questions we wrestle with, about the nature of time, space, and the human condition. It is a book of great learning, but one also brimming over with enthusiasm and love for its subject, a combination that readers will find irresistible."

—**Dr. Wilfred M. McClay, Professor of History, Hillsdale College**

"This book is a compilation of treasures from Peter Kalkavage, one of the most perceptive music theoreticians and practitioners. He is deeply grounded in first principles, knows the Greek classics and, most importantly, knows modernity in light of them. The relationship between music and the world was one of the most important to the ancient Greeks. Have we lost the enriching idea that the universe is musically constituted, as they thought? This book delves deeply into what music is and what it does. Is it its own world, or is it *the* world? Kalkavage lays before the reader various answers, ancient and modern. This is a profound work that needs to be read and then meditated upon."

—**Robert R. Reilly, author of** *Surprised by Beauty:*
A Listener's Guide to the Recovery of Modern Music

"Music is the language of the cosmos and of the human soul, and inevitably reflects—and inculcates—a vision of reality as a whole. The ancients and medievals honored it as one of the seven liberal arts, keys for opening the doors to wisdom. Peter Kalkavage patiently and beautifully unfolds neglected but profound truths about this mysterious art, as he shares with readers the fruit of decades of teaching the Great Books and leading students into the mysteries of tones, rhythms, and harmonies. Illustrating his themes with aptly-chosen composers and works, Kalkavage treats his subject with an eloquence and authority that make *Music and the Idea of a World* a sheer joy to read."

—**Dr. Peter A. Kwasniewski, author of** *Good Music,*
Sacred Music, and Silence

"In this lovely book, Peter Kalkavage has given us some flowers and fruit from the seed sown by Plato in his *Timaeus*, cultivated by composers like Bach and Wagner, and wondered at by thinkers who attended to Cosmos and Soul. The prose is lucid and sensitive to roots, the details of analysis, for such a short book, surprisingly accessible to intelligent readers, and the whole book food for heart and mind. Read it. It will nourish you."

—**Dr. Richard Ferrier, Thomas Aquinas College**

Music and the Idea of a World

Music *and the* Idea *of a* World

PETER KALKAVAGE

PAUL DRY BOOKS
Philadelphia 2024

First Paul Dry Books Edition, 2024

Paul Dry Books, Inc.
Philadelphia, Pennsylvania
www.pauldrybooks.com

ISBN: 978-1-58988-186-0

Printed in the United States of America

LCCN 2023950792

Where should this music be?
I'th'air or th'earth?

Shakespeare, *The Tempest*

Contents

Preface

This book is intended for philosophic-minded readers who are fascinated by music and music lovers who enjoy thinking about the philosophic questions that music raises. My theme is the bond between music and world. World, here, has several meanings. It is the external world or cosmos, the inner world of thought and feeling, world history, and the autonomous tonal world that Paul Valéry called "the musical universe." It also refers to the worlds of individual musical works, especially those of arias and operas.

The title of the book and of its inaugural chapter was inspired by Wallace Stevens's *The Idea of Order at Key West*. The poem celebrates music's transformative power, embodied in a solitary singer—a She—over the unformed and blustering immensities of mere nature, symbolized by the Sea:

> She was the single artificer of the world
> In which she sang. And when she sang, the sea,
> Whatever self it had, became the self
> That was her song, for she was the maker.

The book's seven chapters form a journey that takes the reader from the musical-mathematical cosmos of the Pythagorean Greeks to the music and world of the first half of the twentieth century. I begin with a contrast between the cosmological optimism of the "likely story" in Plato's *Timaeus* and the corresponding pessimism of Schopenhauer's *The World as Will and Representation*. In a brief coda, I discuss music and world in the context of the Bible, with reference to Renaissance polyphony and a motet by Palestrina.

The second chapter, on Victor Zuckerkandl's *Sound and Symbol*, is an extended reflection on force, motion, time, and space in tonal harmony. It explores the author's provocative claim that music, far from being confined to our subjectivity, is a window into the inner truth and soul of external nature. The chapter takes up the connection between Zuckerkandl's affirmation of tone as tension or force and Schopenhauer's doctrine of a cosmic will.

In the third and fourth chapters, I put Zuckerkandl's tonal dynamism to work by examining the worlds of two love songs. The first is a song of divine love from Bach's *St. Matthew Passion* ("*Aus Liebe will mein Heiland sterben*"), the second a song of earthly love from Mozart's *Magic Flute* ("*Dies Bildnis ist bezaubernd schön*"). Crucial to these chapters are the following questions: What is the relation between the world of words and the world of tones? What can tones do, by way of meaning, that words cannot?

The fifth chapter examines the Schopenhauer-inspired world of Wagner's *Tristan and Isolde* and the bond between Love and Death. In this work, Wagner pushes the tonal world to its furthest limits. The chapter continues the inquiry into music and love from the previous two chapters. It takes us from love aimed at marriage (love as depicted in the *Magic Flute*) to forbidden love and the ravages and ecstasies of erotic striving.

The sixth chapter takes us to the twelve-tone world of Arnold Schoenberg and his students. In this musical universe, the hierarchical rule of a tonic or key is replaced by a fixed row of equal-valued pitches. After a brief summary of the principles of twelve-tone composition, the chapter reflects on how the music-haunted Thomas Mann uses this compositional method in his novel *Doctor Faustus* to symbolize the diabolic spirit of music and of the Third Reich.

The seventh and final chapter takes up the resurgence of tonality in the twentieth century. My exemplar is Francis Poulenc's opera, *Dialogues of the Carmelites*. This resplendent and frequently performed work, with its close ties to Bach's *St. Matthew Passion*, brings us back to a theme from the first and third chapters: music and world in the context of the Bible. Set against the backdrop of the French Reign of Terror, Poulenc's opera, which is based on an historical event, is a musical depiction of the psychology of fear and the mysteries of grace.

It will be obvious from this summary that my focus is *vocal* music—the union of words and tones in the musical dramas of oratorio and opera. The topic of *instrumental* music and the idea of a world must await a separate inquiry.

Readers who are innocent of music theory will find the book difficult at times, especially the chapters on Bach, Mozart, and Poulenc. 1 have tried to make the technical elements of music as lucid and interesting as possible in the hope of enticing readers not familiar with such things to learn some music theory. This reflects my goal for the book as a whole: to invite readers to look closely at the texts and musical works to which the chapters are devoted and, more broadly, to incorporate music into their thinking about life, world, and being.

The book began as an assemblage of four lectures on music given over the last two decades: "The Power of Song in Bach's *St. Matthew Passion*" (Magdalen College [2002] and Thomas Aquinas College [2004]), "The Musical Universe and Mozart's *Magic Flute*" (Thomas Aquinas College [2011] and St. John's College in Annapolis [2012]; published in *The St. John's Review*, Vol. 53, Number 2, 2012, under the title "Passion and Perception in Mozart's *Magic Flute*"), "Music and the Idea of a World" (The Catholic University of America [2014] and St. John's College in Annapolis [2015]; published in *The St. John's Review*, Vol. 57, Number 2, 2016), and "Schopenhauer's Will and Wagner's Eros" (the Wagner Society in Washington DC [2016]; published in *Kronos Philosophical Journal*, Vol. 16, 2017). These lectures were revised as chapters for the present edition. They were supplemented by recently composed chapters on Zuckerkandl, Mann, and Poulenc.

This book has had a very long gestation period. It would not have seen the light without much help from many sources. I must first thank St. John's College for giving me the opportunity to study music by teaching it, to become acquainted with the musical works discussed in the book, and to conduct the St. John's Chorus. I also wish to thank the many students and colleagues who offered their generous encouragement.

I am immensely grateful to my friend and colleague, Eric Salem, who read drafts of the book with his usual thoughtfulness and attention to detail. The book owes much to his insights, questions, and encouragement. I must also thank another friend and colleague, Eva Brann, who for years has encouraged me to write a book on music. My thanks also go to St. John's graduate Timothy Creighton for his keen reader's eye, astute suggestions, and personal support. I also wish to thank Keith Whitaker for his critical comments on Chapter Two.

I am indebted to Joseph Padgett, another St. John's graduate, for his meticulous work on the musical inserts and diagrams that appear in the book. I am also grateful for his lively interest in my project.

A special thanks goes to my friend and publisher Paul Dry, who waited patiently, spurred me on, and offered needful prodding.

My deepest thanks go to my wife, Christine, who believed in me and in the book. Over the years, we have had many conversations about the shape of a music book that was yet to be. She, too, read drafts of the chapters and offered invaluable suggestions regarding style and substance. My debt to her is beyond measure.

Music and the Idea of a World

CHAPTER ONE

Music and the Idea of a World

And he spoke to them, propounding to them themes
of music; and they sang before him, and he was glad.

J. R. R. Tolkien, *The Silmarillion*

In this opening chapter, I explore the differences between two
perspectives on music: one ancient, one modern. The texts I have
chosen are Plato's *Timaeus* and Schopenhauer's *The World as Will
and Representation*. Each presents an all-embracing account of the
world—a cosmology—that highlights the bond between world and
music. I hope that my study in contrast will lead us to a deeper
understanding of music as it relates to the whole of all things, our
human condition, and our highest good. I also hope that it will
show why music is the most comprehensive of the liberal arts,
and why it is the case that to speak about music is to speak about
everything.

My inquiry has three parts. In the first, I focus on the central
role that music plays in the cosmological optimism of Plato's character, Timaeus. According to Timaeus, the world of Becoming is
a beautiful work of art ruled by the supreme goodness of intelligent divinity. As the ancient counterpart and precursor of Leibniz,
Timaeus is at pains to depict the cosmos as "the best of possible worlds." In the second part, I turn to Arthur Schopenhauer's
cosmological pessimism, according to which the world is not the
shining forth of intelligent purpose but the work of a blind urge
that Schopenhauer calls *will*. Music, for Schopenhauer, is the most

3

potent and truthful of the arts because it is a "copy [*Abbild*] of the will itself." In the third part I conclude, by way of a coda, with some thoughts on music and world in the context of the Bible.

Rootedness and Musicality

The *Timaeus* is Plato's most overtly musical work. Music, to be sure, is prominent in other dialogues, notably in the *Republic* and *Laws*. In the *Phaedo*, Socrates describes philosophy as "the greatest music" (61A) and comports himself on this, his last day on earth, with a grace that can only be called musical. But music is so much a part of the form and substance of the *Timaeus* that the dialogue may be said to be all about music—music as the mathematical harmonization of the various elements that constitute the visible, touchable cosmos.

The projected drama of the *Timaeus* is a performance by three illustrious political men, whose task is to entertain Socrates with a feast of speech: Timaeus of Italy, Hermocrates of Sicily, and Critias of Athens. A fourth was supposed to have joined them, but he is a no-show. The men who did show up form a trio of poet-rhetoricians, who have agreed to gratify Socrates' desire to behold his best city (which he had described on the previous day) engaged in the words and deeds of war (19B–20C). The star of the show is officially Critias, who boasts about how he will harmonize the particulars of Socrates's city in speech with those of an ancient unsung Athens. This Athens of old, Critias claims, really existed once upon a time and nobly fought against the insolent kings of Atlantis. But Timaeus upstages Critias with his long speech about the cosmos and proves the superior poet. How can one top a magnificent, richly detailed speech about the whole of all things—*the* cosmology that is the archetype of all cosmologies to come?

Early in the *Timaeus*, we hear about the importance of music in human communal life, as Critias recollects what his great-grandfather and namesake experienced when he was a young boy. This Critias joined other boys in a music contest in which they sang poems recently composed by the lawgiver Solon (21B). The contest was part of the boys' initiation into their family tribe and took place during a festival in honor of Dionysus, the god of intoxication. It depicts the very moment in which impressionable youths are officially rooted in their tribe and by extension their city. Through the act of singing, the opinions of Solon take root in these young souls and become authoritative. They become things not merely heard and obeyed but imbibed, incorporated, and cherished. A similar ritual enrooting is at work, as we shall see, in the grand cosmological speech of Timaeus.

We know from the *Republic* that music, which for the Greeks includes poetry, is not just important to human life but dangerous. Because music has the power to shape the soul for good or ill, to make the psychic regime orderly or disorderly, an account of the best regime must include a critique of music as one of its prime components. At one point Socrates tells us why:

> So, Glaucon . . . isn't this why nurture in music is most sovereign? Because rhythm and concord most of all sink down into the inmost part of the soul and cling to her most vigorously, bringing gracefulness with them; and they make a man graceful if he's nurtured correctly, if not, then the opposite. [3.401D5–E1][1]

The passage underscores the tremendous power of music and shows why music is vital to moral-political education. This idea is further developed in the final book of Aristotle's *Politics*, where Aristotle treats the musical education of those who are to become free human beings and good citizens.

Plato and Aristotle remind us that we are on intimate terms with music. The intimacy verges on the supernatural, since music seems to be a kind of magic that causes the listener to be held and spellbound. Music, like Orpheus, enthralls. And while Aristotle observes at the beginning of his *Metaphysics* that sight is the privileged sense, the one that we hold most dear and that most reveals the differences and articulation of things, musical hearing can lay claim to another kind of privilege. Music has an intense personal inwardness, an immediate emotional effect, and a power to form our character, opinions, and way of life. In moving our affections, it shapes our whole being. This is the ground of the danger that music poses. In music, there is no safe distance, as there is in sight, between perceiver and perceived, subject and object. There is also no refuge. We cannot turn away from music as we can from a painting, since music is not spatially bounded but sounds everywhere. Moreover, in listening to a piece of music, we are not free to survey its parts at will, as we can with an object that is seen, but must wait for a moment to sound.[2] The tones come when they want to. And yet, listening to music is more than mere passivity, for music affects us by virtue of its forms and structures. Musical listening, in other words, is an act which we do not just feel but perceive and attend to. This is the paradox that is music, which can overwhelm our reason and self-control but always through the order and precision of its tones and rhythms. It is, after all, not the mere sound of drums but their rhythmic pattern that stirs us.

As I mentioned earlier, Timaeus's speech—or, as he calls it, his "likely story" (29D)—is an effort to put the visible, touchable world of Becoming in the best possible light by making the world into music. It is an *apologia* or defence of Becoming and body in response to Socrates's indictment in the *Republic*. In that dialogue, we hear that genuine education turns the soul away from Becoming or flux and toward the changeless realm of Being (7.518C). It leads the potential philosopher out of the cave of opinion and up into the sunlight of truth. The likely story of Timaeus takes us in the opposite direction, from Being down to Becoming. It tells us how an ingenious craftsman-god, who is without envy and who gazed on archetypal Being, brought order to the primordial chaos through a combination of forethought and the beautiful structures of mathematics.[3]

Timaeus calls his speech at various times a *mythos* (story) and a *logos* (account). Socrates calls it, even more provocatively, a *nomos*, which in Greek means both law and song, as well as custom and convention (29D). The implied close connection between politics and music is perfectly captured in a famous saying of the Greek music theorist, Damon: "For never are the ways [*tropoi*] of music changed without the greatest political laws being changed."[4] The word *nomos* suggests that Timaeus's cosmology is a form of qua-si-political music that establishes our right relation to the cosmic whole, whose offspring we are. It makes us law-abiding citizens of the world—good cosmopolitans. By playfully re-enacting the birth of the cosmos, Timaeus attempts to persuade his listeners, especially Socrates, that the world of body and flux, properly under-stood, is worthy of our serious attention, emulation, and praise. All the mathematical constructions and stories are songs that commemorate the Great Founding. By singing these songs of law and order in thought and speech, we celebrate our cosmic roots. Moreover, since the world for Timaeus is a god (34B), physics as the study of the cosmos becomes the highest act of piety.

Musical references abound in the likely story. The primor-dial chaos is said to be unmusical or out of tune (30A), and the movement of the stars resembles a choric dance (40C). The elu-sive receptacle or matrix—the cosmic "mother" who shakes the four elemental bodies into their proper places when they wander like wayward children—gives the world a rhythmic sway (52C–53A). The cosmic sway is evident in all cyclic movement: in our heartbeat, breathing and walking, in the vibrating string and the motions of the pendulum, swings, and cradles, and the undulat-ing surface of the sea. The construction of the regular geometric solids is also music. Here Timaeus ingeniously harmonizes these beautiful sphere-like shapes—tetrahedron, octahedron, icosahe-dron, and cube—with the observable properties and behaviour of the four elements: fire, air, water, and earth (53D–E). To be sure, it is not music that one can hear but an intellectual, hermetic music that is inscribed in the nature of things.[5]

The greatest musical moment in the story is the construction of the musical scale out of ratios of whole numbers (35A–36B). Like everything in the likely story, it has the character of a celebratory re-enactment and ritual. As such, it embodies a kind of playful solemnity. The construction is musically allusive, since Timaeus does not say explicitly that his mathematical construction has anything to do with music. The inference is left to the educated listener (or reader). The construction is based on the momentous Pythagorean discovery that the intervals that make up melody— octave, perfect fifth, perfect fourth, whole tone—are produced by string-lengths that are in the smallest whole-number ratios: 2:1 for the octave, 3:2 for the perfect fifth, 4:3 for the perfect fourth, and 9:8 for the whole tone. These ratios (*logoi*) function as laws of nature. They are no mere empirical facts but norms that govern the motions of the whole.[6]

Much can be said about the artist-god's act of scale building with respect to the problem it solves, namely, the mathematical incompatibility of some intervals with others. Here, I must rest content with a brief summary of how the god constructs the world soul.[7] Timaeus's craftsman builds this soul out of musical ratios, having first mixed together forms of Being, Same, and Other. He then cuts and bends the scale-strip to form the rotation of the celestial sphere and the orbits of the planets (36B). These periodic movements, the ensemble of which constitutes time, are not only the music in the outer sky but also the inner, musically moving circuits of divine thought, whose image we carry around in our sphere-shaped heads.

For Timaeus, musicality is the core of human virtue and the ground of our happiness. By musicality I mean the adjustment and tuning of all our actions to the regular, periodic movements of the heavens. To be virtuous and happy is to conform to the cosmic *nomos* and to move in sync with the music of the whole. It is to live a life that is in every respect well timed, symmetrical, and balanced—the life of a star. We achieve balance when, for example, in

devoting ourselves to study, we also make sure we get enough rest
and physical exercise (88A). The most essential human musicality comes from astronomy, not because the beauty of the whole is
most apparent in the visible heavens, but because the heavens are
the home of thought in its healthiest, most regular form. To think
the heavenly motions, to discern the ratios in the sky, is to be one
with that heavenly condition of intellectual health and consummate musicality enjoyed perpetually by the world soul.

I have said that the likely story is a form of music, a law-song
or *nomos* that celebrates our cosmic roots. But it is also the story
of a fall. In Genesis, there is creation and fall; in the *Timaeus* creation *is* fall. As I noted earlier, world-building starts at the top and
goes down, just like a Greek musical scale. It goes from Being to
Becoming and from the best things in the world to the worst. The
lower, subhuman animals are generated by an intellectual devolu-
tion that ultimately completes and beautifies the whole by giving
the world its full complement of living kinds. This is the process in
which human beings lose their divine intelligence by having lived
an acosmic, unmusical life and must re-enter Becoming in an animal form suited to their moral and intellectual degradation. The
likely story begins with the heavens and ends with shellfish, creatures that contain the souls of humans who in their previous lives
exhibited what Timaeus calls a "total lack of musicality" (92B).[8]
But even these lowest beings enhance the beauty of the whole,
since without them the cosmic scale of life would lack its lowest
notes and be incomplete.

According to Timaeus, our souls originated as pure intellects,
each living in its own star. In being born, we become profoundly
disordered. We leave off being star-children and degenerate into
mindless, inarticulate *babies*, incapable of controlling any of our
movements. That is why education is necessary—because, as
fallen stars, we must recover "the form of [our] first and best condition" (42D). Mathematical astronomy is the most important part
of education because it is the means by which we humans, whom

Timaeus calls "heavenly plants," return to our roots in the sky (90A). It is also the highest form of therapy. By engaging in astronomy, the human intellect, which grew ill at birth, comes to itself and recovers its circular movement, former health, and proper functioning as the guide and navigator of daily life. We study astronomy so that by "imitating the utterly unwandering circuits of the god [Cosmos], we might stabilize the wander-stricken circuits in ourselves" (47C). Music that is heard and felt plays a similarly therapeutic role. The gods gave us music "not for the purpose of irrational pleasure . . . but as an ally to the circuit of the soul within us when it's become untuned, for the purpose of bringing the soul into arrangement and concord with herself" (47D–E).

On this note of music as therapy, I conclude the first part of this chapter. I now turn to a very different account of music and world.

From Divine Circles to the Wheel of Ixion:
Music in a World of Woe

The first and main volume of *The World as Will and Representation* is divided into four books.[9] In his essay on Schopenhauer, Thomas Mann, the philosopher's greatest admirer in the twentieth century, called the work "a symphony in four movements."[10] Mann, himself a cosmological pessimist, was keenly sensitive to the role that music plays in the work. In the same passage, he observes that Schopenhauer, who was very musical, "celebrates music as no thinker has ever done" by making music metaphysically significant. Mann proceeds to speculate: "Schopenhauer did not love music because he ascribed such a metaphysical significance to her, but rather he did this because he loved her."[11] For Mann, will rather than intellect is the source of Schopenhauer's metaphysics of music, where will signifies everything in us born of love, passion, and feeling. The supremacy of will over intellect is the most important respect in which the world of Schopenhauer differs from the world of Timaeus.

As its title indicates, *The World as Will and Representation* depicts the world as having two distinct sides or aspects. One side, representation, is the topic of Book One. As representation or *Vorstellung*, the world is everything that is *vorgestellt*, that is, "placed before" us and made present in the daylight of consciousness. Although a more accurate rendering of the word would be "presentation," which suggests original coming-to-presence as opposed to derivative imitation, I have chosen to keep the traditional term. Representation is the realm of perceived objects, finite determinate things and all their properties, which appear in space and time and interact according to the principle of sufficient reason, that is, the relation of cause and effect. Representation, *Vorstellung*, is the world as a well-ordered surface. It is what most of us would call the world simply.

Schopenhauer turns to the other, inner aspect of the world in Book Two. He uses terms from Kant's *Critique of Pure Reason*: whereas representation is the world as appearance or *phenomenon*, will is the world as thing-in-itself or *noumenon*. Will, here, is not a psychic faculty. It is not my will or your will, or God's will, since for Schopenhauer there is no God. Will is the universal, cosmic force and infinite striving that underlies all things and rises to self-awareness in man. Schopenhauer calls the will "eternal becoming, endless flux" (164). As the world's "innermost being" and "kernel" (30–31), will is the source of meaning (98–99).[12] Will reminds us that life is more than the cool perception of objects; it is also feeling and care. Objects of representation are vessels of my care. They are meaningful, important to me, in all sorts of ways. This object I desire and strive to possess, that one I avoid. This event I hope for, that one I dread. This human being I love, that one I despise. My body, which is mere appearance, is the embodiment of my care. It is the seemingly concrete reality to which I am intimately joined and which I care about in a thousand ways. My living body reminds me that I am constantly in the condition of seeking to preserve my life and to stave off harm, pain, frus-

tration, and death. My being and my life consist in striving to be
and to live. I cannot escape striving, not even when I sleep, for it is
more obvious in dreams even than in waking life that representations matter to me and are the creatures of my care. Dreams are
my hopes, fears, anxieties, and desires made into a private movie,
often a surreal one. It goes without saying that as a human being
with a certain nature I am subject to this care. But Schopenhauer
goes further. For him, I am this care, this infinite striving to be
and to live as *this* individual with *this* body. The identification of
human care with individuality is Schopenhauer's tragic version of
Leibniz's *principium individuationis*.

Dreams are to desire what the whole phenomenal realm is
to the noumenal will. Schopenhauer reminds us repeatedly that
what we call life is a dream—a worldview that Nietzsche appropri-
ated in his *Birth of Tragedy*. The will is not the cause of the world,
since causality operates only within the dream world of phenomena. There is no intelligible principle or intelligent god, as there
is for Timaeus, that is responsible for the natural order. Nature
is unaccountably there, just as human beings are unaccountably
there—"thrown," to use Heidegger's term, into existence. The will,
then, does not cause nature but rather objectifies itself as nature,
just as our care objectifies itself in dreams. Hence the phrase,
"the world *as* will and representation." The self-objectification
of the will is the basis of Schopenhauer's cosmology. Will objectifies itself in a fourfold way: as inorganic nature, plant life, animal life, and human life. Schopenhauer constructs an ingenious
isomorphism between these four grades of nature and the tones
that make up the major triad with its octave (153). The work of the
will is especially noteworthy in the case of our bodily parts, which
are so many ways in which the will objectifies itself: "Teeth, gullet,
and intestinal canal are objectified hunger; the genitals are objectified sexual impulse; grasping hands and nimble feet correspond
to the more indirect strivings of the will which they represent"
(108). This graphic rendition of the human body is a counterpart

to Timaeus's ingenious stories about our bodily parts, which are mythically represented as manifesting and ministering to our souls.[13] But whereas Timaeus is tongue-in-cheek, Schopenhauer is in deadly earnest.

The identity of will and meaning shows why music is metaphysically significant. As Schopenhauer writes in another work, music—especially melody—"speaks not of things but simply of weal and woe [*Wohl und Weh*] as being for the *will* the sole realities."[14] From the standpoint of the will, being is meaning. Music is unique among the arts because it depicts the inner world of care—pure subjective meaning apart from all objectivity. It represents not the rational world soul but the passionate world heart.[15] Music, moreover, is not an elitist Pythagorean who speaks only to her learned inner circle but rather the "universal language" that is "instantly understood by everyone," intuitively and without the aid of concepts (256).[16]

In my account of the *Timaeus*, I highlighted the therapeutic function of astronomy and music, both of which minister to fallen man. These two arts are a corrective to the cosmic necessity of our having been born as mortal beings subject to mortal flux and mindless desire (42A ff.). Being born, for Timaeus, is a gift—the gift of organic life. But it is also, for the reasons I mentioned earlier, our burden and our fate. Being born is a mixed blessing. For Schopenhauer, it is an outright curse. To be born is to become an egocentric individual afflicted with insatiable desire, in particular sexual desire. To be is to be subject to "the miserable pressure of the will" (196).[17] The will, as I noted earlier, is infinite striving—striving with no ultimate good or end. Moments of contentment and joy appear, but only as passing tones, ripples in a sea of frustration, ennui, and renewed desire. To live is to suffer. Schopenhauer here reveals the hard edge of his pessimism and his tragic sense of life.[18] He approvingly cites poets like Calderón, who defines original sin as "the guilt of existence itself," and affirms that it would be better never to have been born.[19]

Schopenhauer's recurring image of life as suffering is the wheel of Ixion. Ixion was King of the Lapiths. After being shown hospitality by Zeus, he lusted after Hera and tried to seduce her. For this attempted outrage Zeus bound Ixion on a wheel of fire and consigned him to Tartarus. Only once did the wheel of torment stop: when Orpheus descended to the Underworld and charmed its inhabitants with his song.[20] This, for Schopenhauer, is the human therapy that all fine art offers, most especially the art of music. Music represents the will as thing-in-itself, meaning apart from all things and pictures. That is why music is metaphysically significant. But music also gives us momentary relief from the fiery wheel on which we are bound, the wheel of infinite longing. In music, as in all aesthetic contemplation, we are no longer self-interested individuals but "pure, will-less subject[s] of knowing," subjects who are "lost in the object" (209). In art, as Schopenhauer puts it, "We celebrate the Sabbath of the penal servitude of willing; the wheel of Ixion stands still" (196).

The third part of Schopenhauer's book is devoted to the arts, which, although manifesting order and precision, are beyond the reach of the principle of sufficient reason. This is evident in music, where tones, though tightly connected, have no causal relation to each other. For example, the opening phrase of Beethoven's Fifth Symphony,

does not cause the second,

[21]

Unconcerned with causality and inference, art is the intuitive apprehension of the Ideas, which Schopenhauer takes from Plato, for the most part from the *Timaeus*. The Ideas are the eternal archetypes of nature, the four grades of the will's self-objectification that I mentioned earlier (inorganic nature, plant life, animal life, and human life). In the human realm, they are the universals of experience. Shakespeare's plays, for example, are a distillation of what is eternally true of human life.[22] In the ambition of Macbeth, jealousy of Othello, and brooding of Hamlet, we behold archetypes of will at its highest grade.[23] Art is therapeutic because, as the purely aesthetic contemplation of universal Ideas, art detaches us from the objects of our care. To behold the sufferings of Oedipus or Lear is precisely to be taken away from our own. That is why we take pleasure even in the saddest music, which calls upon us not to weep but to listen and recognize: to hear and intuitively know what is there.

Art, however, is powerless to provide enduring release from Ixion's wheel and offers only "occasional consolation" (267). The fourth part of Schopenhauer's book takes us from the artist to the saint, who alone is truly happy—if, that is, one can call resignation happiness. The saint has neutralized the will to be and to live through the gnosis of nothingness,[24] the knowledge that objects of care are nothing but illusion (451). He needs no artworks. This neutralization of the will makes the saint good. In the obliteration of his ego, he is released from his private suffering, especially from erotic longing, and free to feel compassion for the suffering of other human beings and even for that of animals (372).

Schopenhauer's metaphysics of music appears in both volumes of *The World as Will and Representation*: in Chapter 52 of Volume One and in Chapter 39 of Volume Two. These chapters contain one of the most fascinating discussions of music ever written. They are an attempt to identify music as a source of truth, indeed the deepest truth: "The composer reveals the profoundest wisdom in a language that his reasoning faculty does not understand, just as a magnetic somnambulist gives information about things of which she has no conception when she is awake" (260). Music reveals the world as thing-in-itself, as will, which includes "the feelings, passions, and emotions of the hearer" (Vol. 2, 448).

In a Timaean-Pythagorean vein, the scientifically-minded Leibniz had asserted (correctly, for Schopenhauer) that listening to music was "an unconscious exercise in arithmetic in which the mind does not know it is counting" (256).[25] But in Schopenhauer's view, which goes to the depths of the world rather than remains at its surface, musical listening is "an unconscious exercise in metaphysics in which the mind does not know it is philosophizing" (264).

Schopenhauer illustrates his general ideas with many references to specific musical phenomena. I shall address only a few of them. I begin with music as imitation. According to Plato and Aristotle, music, in its tones and rhythms, imitates the dispositions and passions of the soul. As Aristotle observes in the *Politics*, melodies and rhythms are "likenesses of the true natures of anger and gentleness, and also of courage and moderation and all the opposites of these and the other states of character" (8.5).[26] Aristotle is referring to the Greek musical modes—Dorian, Phrygian, Mixolydian, etc., which achieve their different effects and capture different psychic dispositions through a different placement of half steps in their scales. The Dorian mode, Aristotle says, gives the soul "a moderate and settled condition," whereas the Phrygian "inspires." A difference in mode can be heard in our familiar opposition of "bright" major and "dark" minor. This consequential musical difference hinges on no more than whether there is a whole step or a half between the second and third degrees of the scale. It is gratifying to hear Schopenhauer, a philosopher, respond to this fact with fitting amazement (261).

What Timaeus and Schopenhauer add to the imitative relation between music and soul is the connection between music and world. We are responsive to music because the so-called external world has an interior, as do we, and is always already music-imbued. For Timaeus, music in the form of the diatonic pattern—the recurring order of whole and half steps—is woven into the fabric of the cosmic soul, of which our souls partake. That is why we respond so strongly to the diatonic modes. We look with longing at the stars because that is where our souls come from, and we take delight in identifying Same and Other in the things of the world because our souls are made of Same and Other. So too, we welcome music into our souls because we detect in it the inflections of our psychic modalities, our various soul-possibilities. Where there is music and listener, music calls to music. It is, for Timaeus, a case of sympathetic vibration grounded in the nature of the ensouled cosmos.

Schopenhauer, we must note, differs from Timaeus in his understanding of interiority. He rejects the soul as a principle of being on the grounds that it makes real what is in fact illusory, namely, our individuality.[27] In general, the principle of individuation, like that of sufficient reason, applies only to the world of phenomena, which Schopenhauer regularly calls the "veil of Maya" or illusion. In listening to music, we suspend our individuality and are in touch with will as process rather than with a stable mode of soul and character.

From a musical standpoint, Schopenhauer differs from Timaeus by going beyond the Pythagorean idea of interval as sensed ratio and treats music as the embodiment of *tension* or *force*. This modern concept of force, also known as *conatus* or endeavour, is prominent in the physics of Newton and Leibniz and was introduced into natural science by Hobbes, who, like Schopenhauer, rejects a highest good and depicts desire as an infinite striving "that ceaseth only in death."[28] Dissonance in music is the exemplar of tonal tension or force. As the vector-like impulse to move in a definite direction, it is the tonal analogue of desire. The suspension is a good example of how dissonance works in music. In a suspension, two voices start out in consonance but then produce dissonance when one of the voices moves while the other does not. A resolution of the dissonance then follows. Schopenhauer writes: "[Suspension] is a dissonance delaying the final consonance that is with certainty awaited; in this way, the longing for it is strengthened, and its appearance affords greater satisfaction. This is clearly an analogue of the satisfaction of the will which is enhanced through delay" (Vol. 2, 455–6).

An even better instance of the connection between dissonance and will is the appoggiatura or leaning tone. This unprepared dissonance on a strong beat delays a tone of the melody and thereby heightens expectation. It is the perfect musical analogue of longing. An example occurs in Tamino's love song in Mozart's *Magic Flute* (the topic of a later chapter). Prince Tamino gazes on a picture of Pamina, his destined other, and falls in love with her. By singing in response to a picture, something seen, he moves from the world as Representation to the world as Will. His repeated leaning tones on the words "I feel it" ("*ich fühl es*") embody, from Schopenhauer's perspective, the universal truth of erotic love.

The word "analogue" is important here. The appoggiatura, like the suspension, is not the image or likeness of a specific desire that is eventually gratified but rather a tonal event that communicates, in a purely musical way, a universal truth about the will. When Schopenhauer says that music is the universal language, he is not being poetic. He means that although tones are not words, they function intuitively in the same way that words function conceptually—not as likenesses of the things they signify but as symbols, bearers of universal meaning. In the case of music, this meaning is directly perceived and felt rather than inferred. Listening to music is non-verbal symbol-recognition.

Music as force flourishes in the tradition of modern tonal harmony. This long and glorious tradition reaches from Bach and Handel, through Mozart, Haydn and Beethoven, up to Brahms and Wagner, and continues in our own century. Tonal music, as opposed to the mode-inspired music of the Middle Ages and Renaissance, exhibits the directed tension I mentioned earlier. There is a play of forces: tonal dynamism. This sort of music is friendly to the language of will, since will is tension, and force is will that has not yet attained self-consciousness.[29] The musicologist Heinrich Schenker applied this very term to music: *Tonwille*, the will of the tones.

In tonal harmony, tension is not confined to isolated events, like the suspension, but pervades the whole of a musical piece and constitutes its unity and arc. The term "tonal" refers to the rule of a single tone, the tonic or keynote, to which all the other tones in a tonal work point (or, as some theorists prefer to say, the centrality of the tonic triad, the 1-chord).[30] These tensions—Victor Zuckerkandl, a student of Schenker, calls them *dynamic qualities*—comprise the major scale and cause it to sound like a journey with clearly defined stages and a predetermined end: $\hat{1}$-$\hat{2}$-$\hat{3}$-$\hat{4}$-$\hat{5}$-$\hat{6}$-$\hat{7}$-$\hat{8}$ (*do, re, mi, fa, sol, la, ti, do*).[31] In the next chapter, we shall explore the deeper, metaphysical implications of dynamic qualities. Tension is especially urgent in degree $\hat{7}$, which strives toward $\hat{8}$, as desire craves its satisfaction. Degree $\hat{4}$ tends, less urgently, down to $\hat{3}$. Together, degrees $\hat{4}$ and $\hat{7}$ produce the dissonant interval of the tritone. This is the best example of directed tension in music, since the tritone, when combined with degree $\hat{5}$ in the bass, makes up the dominant seventh chord, which points to the tonic triad and so fixes the music in a key. Here is the V^7 chord resolving to the tonic in what is called a perfect cadence:

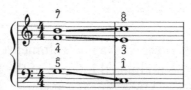

Thanks to their dynamic relations, which operate at many levels, tones and the triads they form generate musical wholes through the artful prolongation and eventual resolution of their will-like tension. We shall return to this tonal dynamism and its connection with nature and world in the next chapter.

I cannot leave the topic of musical tension and of tone as the symbol of desire without citing Wagner's *Tristan and Isolde*, which

Nietzsche famously called "the actual *opus metaphysicum* of all art."[32] In this work we hear extreme chromaticism, constant unresolved cadences, and the deceptive shifting of tonal centers. These phenomena form the tonal analogue of eros as infinite longing. The work pushes tonal harmony and musical tension to the absolute limit by extending the striving of tones over the course of several hours in what seems like one unbroken arc.[33] In a later chapter, we shall look more closely at the connection between Wagner's musical drama and Schopenhauer's book. Here I simply observe that the opening phrase of the Prelude, with its famous "Tristan chord" resolving to a dominant seventh chord, is perhaps the most powerful evocation of tension-as-desire in all of music.[34] Wagner's phrase sets up a cadence that is not completed until the very end of the work, when the crashing waves of the orchestra overwhelm the transfigured Isolde before settling into the blissful, post-climactic froth of B major. Richard Strauss made this ultimate resolution explicit in his ingenious stitching together of what he called "the beginning and end of all music":[35]

Excerpt from *Tristan und Isolde* (Wagner) connected and arranged by Richard Strauss

In Schopenhauer's terms, Wagner's immense prolongation of musical tension is the noumenal interior of the lovers' prolonged phenomenal eroticism. More cautiously stated, it is the analogical, symbolic representation of that interior. The universal, undying truth of the story is not in the death-bound characters but in the tones.[36]

The central teaching of Schopenhauer's metaphysics of music is that music is "a copy [*Abbild*] of the will itself," not of the Ideas of the will, as in tragedy (257). The notion of music as copy is problematic, since there can be no copy of something utterly indeterminate and therefore uncopiable. How can music, with all its intricate detail, be a picture or copy of the will, which Nietzsche rightly called "the unaesthetic in itself"?[37] But for now let us go with the flow of Schopenhauer's theory. To be sure, all the arts for Schopenhauer objectify the will, but the non-musical arts do so "only indirectly." They present universality through the medium of *things*. Music, by contrast, makes no such appeal and represents, imitates, the world's pure subjectivity. It does so through tones all by themselves.

We must bear in mind that by music Schopenhauer means "the sacred, mysterious, profound language of tones."[38] This includes tones' relation to *rhythm*, a relation that Schopenhauer discusses in Volume Two (454–55). The emphasis on tones and tonal motion signals the primacy of what Wagner called "absolute music" and what we now call instrumental music.[39] For Schopenhauer, music as the language of tones captures the Absolute through non-visual representations. It is the will "speaking to us" through the medium of composers, who are the will's symbolists, somnam-bulists, and high priests.[40] Because tones are meaningful all by themselves, Schopenhauer can make the astonishing claim that music, in passing over the Ideas and everything phenomenal, "to a certain extent, could still exist even if there were no world at all" (257). The reason is that music, while negating the world as thing, contains that world from the perspective of its deepest inte-rior, its immortal heart. Schopenhauer states this with maximum concision: "Music is the melody to which the world is the text."[41] In other words, tones all by themselves represent the indwell-ing, immortal spirit of the world. If we imagined the phenomenal world as a staged opera or a movie, then the orchestral parts and score would stand to it as inner to outer, essence to appearance, truth to seeming. As I observed in the case of Wagner's *Tristan*, the real drama, the world in its truth, would be taking place not in what we see but in what we hear. It would be a drama of tones.

But although music transcends the world as thing, it also has a profound connection with that world, by analogy. Schopenhauer is

fascinated by this analogism and speaks like an Archimedes who
has just made remarkable discoveries and cries "Eureka! I have
found it!" As I mentioned earlier, the major triad with its octave
captures in symbolic form the four natural grades of the will's
self-objectification and is a mirror of the Whole. The ground bass
mirrors inorganic nature. Each note of this bass functions as the
fundamental to the overtones that faintly sound above it (258).[42]
This mirrors what happens in the whole of nature, where higher
grades of being develop out of the lowest, and where organic
nature constantly depends on the inorganic, as the upper partials
depend on their fundamental. The tones between the bass notes
and the melody that floats above are the musical analogue of plant
and animal. These tones form the harmonic organism that binds
lower bass and higher melody. They mirror the way that plant and
animal life mediate between the inorganic realm and our higher,
human nature. This analogy exists within the scale itself, where
the hierarchy of tones mirrors "the whole gradation of the Ideas in
which the will objectifies itself" (258). To hear an ascending scale is
to hear the hierarchical order of the entire cosmos. Even the inevitable impurity of intervals that exists in all tuning or temperament is an analogue of phenomenal nature. An interval that is
slightly "off," say an equal-tempered major third, mirrors natural
idiosyncrasy, "the departure of the individual from the type of the
species" (258-9). The incompatibility of some intervals with others, the very problem that makes temperament necessary and that
Timaeus solved in Pythagorean fashion, is also an aspect of the
will: it is the musical analogue of the will's "inner contradiction,"
which is the whole concern of tragedy (266).[43]

Finally, there is melody as the musical analogue of phenomenal man: "in the *melody*, in the high singing, principal voice, leading the whole and progressing with unrestrained freedom, in the
uninterrupted significant connexion of *one* thought from beginning to end, and expressing a whole, I recognize the highest grade
of the will's objectification, the intellectual life and endeavour of

man" (259). Melody, the ultimate *mythos* and symbol of human life, "relates the story of the intellectually enlightened will, the copy or impression whereof in actual life is the series of its deeds." But melody, for Schopenhauer, "says more" because it goes beyond outward deeds and events. It also "relates *the most secret history* [my emphasis] of the intellectually enlightened will, portrays every agitation, every effort, every movement of the will, everything which the faculty of reason summarizes under the wide and negative concept of feeling, and which cannot be further taken up into the abstractions of reason" (259). Even death finds its symbolic correlate in the world of tones. It occurs in modulation, where a key-change "entirely abolishes the connection with what went before" (261).[44]

To sum up, there is nothing in the natural world or in the inner and outer life of man that does not find its counterpart in the all-embracing realm of tones. Music as symbol is the whole of all things. It is the world. That is why, as Schopenhauer says, "we could just as well call the world embodied music as embodied will" (262–3). Music, if it could speak, would be perfectly justified in proclaiming what Wagner's lovers say at a climactic moment of their impassioned duet in Act 2: "I myself am the world."

Coda: Another World of Longing

I end my musical-cosmological reflection with a composition that depicts the world as a kind of music: polyphony. It is Palestrina's four-part motet, *Sicut cervus*. Beloved by St. John's students on the Annapolis campus, the piece is a musical setting of the opening of Psalm 42 in the Vulgate: *Sicut cervus desiderat ad fontes aquarum, ita desiderat anima mea ad te, Deus*: "As the hart longs for flowing streams, so longs my soul for you, O God." The motet is a superb example of what Nietzsche called Palestrina's "ineffably sublime sacred music."[45]

Every musical composition is both a world unto itself and an image of the world in which we live. That is one of the central propositions of this book. The world of *Sicut cervus* is that of the Bible and the biblical God. Creation, here, is good. It produces beings, not images of intelligible originals or phantasms. The world is not confined to head and heart, to our subjectivity, but is "out there" and solidly real. The God of the Bible is not a crafts- man who leaves the world after having made it, or Aristotle's indif- ferent prime mover, but the God of promise and history, the God who cares for individuals and makes covenants with His people. He is someone to whom one can pray. Salvation comes not from dialectic, or astronomy, or art, or the death of care based on the gnosis of cosmic nothingness, but from faith in God.

Although the *words* of the motet express longing, the *tones* do not represent longing, at least not as stress and strain. The music is a continually graceful gesture that transmutes the pain of long- ing into a serene order of voices that seem always to know and love their place. *Sicut cervus* is composed in two senses of the word: it is well constructed, and it has an unperturbed disposition. Dur- ing the piece, motion goes on and time passes. But the overall "feel" of the music seems beyond time and change, like a musi- cal emanation of the *nunc stans*.[46] It is as if the waters of grace were already flowing, and the singers were experiencing, tasting, in the very midst of their yearning, prospective joy in the object for which they yearn. Aquinas cites three criteria of beauty: integ- rity or wholeness, proportion or consonance, and radiance (*clari- tas*).[47] *Sicut cervus* has these in abundance, especially radiance. The music seems to be suffused with warm light. It is full of feeling but also sounds intelligent, lucid, and self-possessed. The move- ment is a continuous flow, in imitation of the waters for which the hart thirsts. The tones seem to move not because they have to but because they want to, not out of compulsion but out of free- dom. The sound is a spontaneous unfolding. It is as if the four vocal parts were miraculously improvising their lines as they go along, only gradually discovering the perfectly coordinated whole they are in the process of forming. Dissonances occur to enhance consonance and beget motion, but they are not prominent, and the motet could not be described as a play of forces. *Sicut cervus*, although the prayer is all about desire, is music without will as Schopenhauer understands it.

This brings me to the most important respect in which Palestrina's motet is the image of a world. *Sicut cervus* is polyphony that lacks, because it does not need, the tonal-harmonic principles at work in the polyphony of Bach. Vertical relations are for the most part the result of simultaneous horizontal relations. The four voices that compose the piece enter one at a time in points of imitation. The voice that follows seems to be inspired to enter by the one that leads. The parts move in happy obedience to the rules of good voice leading. But they do more than exhibit formal correctness. They seem to delight in each other's company and to be naturally social. At times, they graciously step aside for each other, as if rejoicing in the being and individuality of other lines. In its non-urgent flow, *Sicut cervus* is a musical community that captures the sound and the being of friendship. And just as friends engage in all sorts of play, the vocal lines play off one another, often exhibiting contrary motion, that is, simultaneous movement in opposite directions. Thanks to this friendly contrariety, which keeps the parts audibly distinct, the voices celebrate, contrary to what Schopenhauer asserts, the reality and truth of the principle of individuation, as they conspire to form a perfect, natural-sounding republic of tones. The voices of *Sicut cervus*, in this respect, may be said to enact the contrapuntal play and gracious reciprocity that we find among souls in Dante's *Paradiso*.

With this anti-tragic image of the world, my study in contrast, with its biblical coda, reaches its end. These two philosophic works—Plato's *Timaeus* and Schopenhauer's *World as Will and Representation*—differ greatly in how they view being, becoming, and the human condition. But they also go together because, more than other discussions of music with which I am familiar, they invite us to consider that music is more important than even music lovers might think—that music, to quote Mann, is metaphysically significant and captures the whole of all things, not in concept but in intuition, symbol, and feeling. Are the cosmologies of Timaeus and Schopenhauer, separately or together, an adequate account of music? I think they are not. There are limits both to the hyper-rational Pythagorean approach to music and to Schopenhauer's romantic conception of music as representing feeling and irrational will. Both accounts are nevertheless inspired efforts that hit upon certain undeniable truths.

My closing note takes its cue from the philosopher Schopenhauer's personal love of music, which I share. Music, even the saddest music in the world—music that is worlds apart from *Sicut cervus* and may even be the sound of despair and crushing grief— is dear to us and makes us happy, if only for a while. Maybe this is because music, as a living bodily presence that comes to us, offers itself to us, assures us that we are not alone. It comes to tell us that there is something out there *in the world* that knows our hearts and may even help us know them better. Thanks to music, we experience what it means to be intimately connected to the whole of all things, even when life seems tragic; what it means to have a soul and not just a mind and a body; to have depth rather than mere rightness of feeling and being; and, above all, what it means to be open to ourselves and our world—through listening.

CHAPTER TWO

Victor Zuckerkandl
on Music and Nature

> I found then that their nature [the nature of
> substantial forms] consists in force, and that from
> this there follows something analogous to sensation
> and appetite, so that we must conceive of them
> on the model of the notion we have of *souls*.
>
> G. W. Leibniz, *A New System of Nature*

In the previous chapter, I introduced Zuckerkandl's dynamic qualities in the context of tonal harmony and its connection with Schopenhauer's cosmic will. The dynamic qualities of tones are the will-like forces at work in most of the music we are used to hearing. They will play a central role in the following two chapters, where I reflect on arias by Bach and Mozart. In the present chapter, I explore the metaphysical implications of dynamic quality and compare the musical-cosmological views of Zuckerkandl and Schopenhauer.

Zuckerkandl's account of music is contained in three highly original books: *The Sense of Music, Sound and Symbol: Music and the External World,* and *Man the Musician* (*Sound and Symbol*, Volume 2). The first is an introduction to music as a liberal art. It is part of the music program at St. John's College on the Annapolis campus, where Zuckerkandl taught from 1948 to 1964. The second, which reads like an Aristotle's *Physics* for music lovers, investigates the musical primitives: motion, time, and space. As its subtitle indicates, the book focuses on music in relation to the objective world, the world outside of the human listener. The third book, left unfinished, complements the second by turning to the musical subject. It deals with our musicality as human beings, musical hearing, and the musical thinking of great composers.

My chapter is on the first volume of *Sound and Symbol*. I plan not just to summarize the author's often-difficult ideas but also to interpret them and use them as provocations to further inquiry. In the Foreword, Zuckerkandl calls music "a window opening in the world of objects that closes in on us" (4).[1] Music, as many have said, transports us. But to where? To what does music give us access? For Zuckerkandl, the answer is not a supersensuous Beyond (to use Hegel's phrase) but nature's "internal transcendence" (147). My effort in this chapter is to determine what this claim means and whether it is true.

The goal of *Sound and Symbol* is stated retrospectively in the book's final chapter. It is to present "a musical concept of the external world" (363). The goal has a polemical side: to counteract the prevailing scientific-materialist accounts of nature that may be said to have originated with Democritus (146). In reaction to these scientific accounts, some have sought refuge in the better world to which music, with its consoling ideality, invites us—the *bessere Welt* of Schubert's *An die Musik*.[2] But this well-intentioned view, Zuckerkandl claims, is an error in the opposite direction: "The moment music becomes the voice of the 'other' world, musical experiences can no longer challenge our concept of reality: where there is no connection, there can be no conflict" (363–64). A musical concept of the external world is possible, Zuckerkandl says, only once it is demonstrated "that musical experiences are not experiences of 'another' world, of an 'unknown ideal life,' and that the audible and the visible belong to the same reality" (364). I mention all this now because it will be helpful, as we move forward, to follow the wisdom of Solon in Herodotus and "look to the end."

Tone

Zuckerkandl is always careful to stress that dynamic quality is not a theoretical entity that must be postulated but something we directly experience in listening to a melody. Invariably, he draws our attention to the end of a tune, where tension and resolution are most keenly perceived. In *Sound and Symbol*, his example is the well-known Ode to Joy from the Ninth Symphony (17):

The melody consists of four four-measure subsections or phrases. The first and second are very similar, the third is different, and the fourth repeats the second. Zuckerkandl directs our attention to what would happen if the fourth, concluding phrase repeated, not the second phrase, but the first (18):

Most listeners will agree that the melody now sounds unfinished. The reason lies in the heard difference between tones D and E. There is a palpable tension in the E, a will-like tendency to resolve to the D just below it. This tension is what Zuckerkandl calls *dynamic quality*.[3] We hear in the D "a state of disturbed equilibrium." The disturbance is directed. It is the tendency of $\hat{2}$ to resolve to $\hat{1}$, the melody's tonal center and place of maximum stability. The relation of $\hat{2}$ to $\hat{1}$ is a play of forces, like that exhibited between a needle and a magnet: "The activity of the one is a placing itself in a direction, a pointing toward and striving after a goal; the activity of the other is a dictating of direction, a drawing to itself" (20).[4]

These tonal tensions make the melody a coherent whole. Thanks to Beethoven's intelligent (and hard-won) arrangement of tonal forces, the sequence of tones is an articulated flow with a beginning, middle, and end.[5] We do not need to see a score or know any music theory to hear the symmetry of the four complementary phrases and the convincing close at the end. The ear gets it. With repeated listening, we can hear that each of the four phrases of the tune begins with the relatively stable $\hat{3}$ and teases us with the unstable $\hat{2}$ as an almost there, before letting $\hat{2}$ resolve to $\hat{1}$ at the very end.[6] The overall motion is $\hat{3}$-$\hat{2}$-$\hat{1}$. Zuckerkandl calls this dynamic structure the *meaning* of the melody. Meaning, here, is the directedness that the ear gets and intuitively grasps.

As we read in *The Sense of Music*, dynamic qualities, without being explicitly acknowledged and named, form the basis of our conventional ear training. They are in themselves nothing new. What is new is Zuckerkandl's claim that dynamic quality is not one among several properties of a tone but "*the* musical property of tones, the property that makes music possible."[7] Here in *Sound and Symbol*, Zuckerkandl adds an additional claim: "A tone is a phenomenon of the external world" (21). With this claim, the inquiry moves from the role of dynamic qualities in music to their mode of existence. The phenomenal basis for the claim that tones are part of the external world is that when we listen to music, the tones *come to us*.[8] That is how we experience them. But can this not be said of all sounds? How are tones different?

A possible answer is given by the phenomenologist Erwin Straus, whom Zuckerkandl occasionally quotes. Straus distinguishes between tone and noise: "The sound that detaches itself from the sound source can take on a pure and autonomous existence; but this possibility is fulfilled solely in the tones of music, while noise retains the character of indicating and pointing to."[9] The sound of a siren is not like the melody played by a violin. The former draws us to its material source, whereas the violinist produces sounds that seem to have a life of their own apart from the violin and are not properties of the instrument. The violinist, in playing, seems to cast a spell over space, to enchant space with tones. The tones reach us and spirit us away with them. Straus concludes: "There is no visual art that is analogous to music, and there can be none because color does not separate itself from the object as tone does. In music alone tone reaches a purely autonomous existence. Music is the complete realization of the essential possibilities of the acoustical."[10]

Tonal externality is evident in the difference between tone and pitch. The latter can be mathematically defined as a wave frequency (so many cycles per second) and visually represented with the aid of an oscilloscope. It can be treated as a quantity. Not so for the dynamic qualities that we hear in the Ode to Joy. The oscilloscope never fails to register what is there in the material sound of a vibrating body. But it is powerless to detect a tone's function in a musical context.[11] The directed tension of $\hat{2}$ in the phrase just discussed is beyond its technological genius. And yet, the tension is there, somehow *in* the material sound, the pitch, while not being reducible to it: "When we hear a melody, we hear things that have no counterpart in physical nature" (23). This is the first sign of the internal transcendence mentioned above.[12]

Zuckerkandl cites two theories devised to avoid the conclusion that there is something in nature that transcends the merely physical (24). One is the so-called "pulse theory." Masterfully set forth by Helmholtz, it explains the behavior of tones in physical-mathematical terms.[13] The other, "associationism," argues that the tensions in tones have nothing to do with anything external and are the result of subjective habit: we hear tensions because we have gotten used to hearing them. Zuckerkandl proceeds to discuss the first theory and returns to the second only after he has introduced all the dynamic qualities of the major scale.

As Zuckerkandl observes, the attempt to understand music in mathematical terms has been around ever since Pythagoras discovered the wondrous correspondence between musical inter-

vals and ratios of small whole numbers. This discovery is the basis
for the construction of the diatonic scale in the *Timaeus*. In modern times, these ratios are interpreted as frequencies of vibration.
The claim is that even if nothing in the physical vibration of a single tone causes the tone's musical quality, the relations between
tones are the underlying causes of tonal tensions. In hearing these
mathematically precise vibrations, some part of our ear vibrates in
this same way, sympathetically. Certain patterns of vibration produce equilibrium, others a disturbance that provokes a return to
equilibrium. The pulse theory elaborates Leibniz's view, quoted in
Chapter One (note 25), that listening to music is an unconscious
exercise in mathematical operations.

The pulse theory is easily refuted, since it accounts for disturbance of sound patterns but not direction of tones. It explains
consonant and dissonant intervals in terms of stable and unstable combinations of tones through the interference of various
rhythmic patterns or "beats." But it cannot explain a tone's pointing in a certain direction, for example the pointing of $\hat{2}$ to $\hat{1}$ in
the Beethoven melody. Moreover, it fails to explain why, in a musical phrase in which the same interval appears between different
degrees of the scale, that same interval is not heard in the same
way throughout but varies according to context. A good example is the subject of Bach's C-major fugue from Book 1 of the
Well-Tempered Clavier. It contains four appearances of the perfect
fourth, no two of which sound the same:

In the section "The System of Tones," Zuckerkandl expands his
account of dynamic quality to include all seven tones of the major

scale. This scale corresponds to a specific "cut" in the *diatonic pattern*, on which Western music is based:

The pattern is a fixed sequence of whole steps and half steps. It is the origin of the various modes mentioned in the last chapter: Dorian, Phrygian, Mixolydian, etc. The pattern can be seen in the order of white keys on a piano.[14] Each modal scale is defined by its unique sequence of whole and half steps and can be generated by starting on a specific tone-line in the pattern. The major mode (Ionian, as it was called) is given in the sequence "two whole steps, half, three whole steps, half." The starting tone is the $\hat{1}$ of each modal scale.

It is uniquely the Ionian mode, our major, in which dynamic qualities come into their own. It is the only scale that has the character of a tonal journey with well-defined waystations (*do, re, mi, fa, sol, la, ti, do*). The tones point directly or indirectly to the governing $\hat{1}$, which for this reason functions as a keynote.[15] The major scale is the source of all dynamism, chordal as well as tonal, and the minor scale is simply the Aeolian adjusted to give it the same dynamic structure as the major. Directed tensions are to a certain degree present in other modal scales, but they are far less determinate. It is precisely this non-urgency that gives the modal world of Gregorian chant its free-flowing otherworldly charm.

Major and minor scales present the full set of dynamic qualities, $\hat{1}$ through $\hat{7}$. Zuckerkandl argues that we hear these forces when we listen to a melody. In hearing the Ode to Joy, we are not (musically speaking) hearing F-sharp, G, A, etc., but rather $\hat{3}$, $\hat{4}$, $\hat{5}$, etc., in other words, directed forces. The claim is supported by the phenomenon of transposition or change of key. If we heard G,

A-flat, B-flat, etc., we would still recognize the Ode to Joy, now in the key of E-flat, where the pitch G, formerly $\hat{4}$, now plays the role of $\hat{3}$. It has gone from being an unstable, tense tone to being a relatively stable one. The dynamic qualities are like roles in a play, each pointing to $\hat{1}$ "in its particular, one might say, almost personal, way, with a gesture that is its own, a tonal gesture" (34–35).

Armed with all seven dynamic qualities, Zuckerkandl now turns to the second theory that denies nature's immanent transcendence: associationism. According to this view, the tensions we hear in music are exclusively *in us*. Listening to music is explained as a psychological event in which we hear tensions because we have become habituated to associating the behavior of tones with certain patterns. On this view, we do not *perceive* tension in dynamic quality $\hat{7}$ but rather *feel* it as a completely subjective contribution formed by habit.

Zuckerkandl admits that there is something plausible and attractive about this commonly held view: "it settles so many vexing questions and fits the refractory phenomenon of music so neatly into the current system of ideas" (44). But how did a given habit get started in the first place? How, for example, did we come to hear $\hat{2}$ to $\hat{1}$ (E to D) in the Beethoven tune as a standard concluding formula? One difficulty is that it is earlier, modal music that uses this move more exclusively as a concluding formula (46). The $\hat{2}$-$\hat{1}$ formula was not, therefore, the result of some natural selection that over time made the move continue to predominate as an ending. Moreover, there are plenty of instances in music in which the $\hat{2}$ to $\hat{1}$ move is not heard as a conclusion.

The strongest argument against associationism comes from the medieval Aeolian scale, which is represented by the white keys of the piano from an A to the A an octave higher (47–48). With the onset of tonal as opposed to modal music, the $\hat{7}$ of this scale (in this case, G) had to be raised to strengthen the sense of conclusion that is inherent in the Ionian, major scale. The move from lowered $\hat{7}$ to $\hat{8}$ in the Aeolian, so-called natural minor scale was recalcitrant to the desired effect and had to be changed. No one had been habituated to hear the "old" move as dynamically conclusive. On the contrary, it sounded as it sounded—pointing weakly, if at all, to $\hat{8}$—and had to be changed to give it a new power, a power grounded not in habit but in the inherently tense character of a raised $\hat{7}$.[16]

Zuckerkandl ends his critique of associationism with a brilliant reflection on "the most discussed measures in the entire literature of music." This is the resolution of the "Tristan chord" to a dominant seventh at the beginning of Wagner's *Tristan and Isolde*. I discussed this chord in Chapter One and shall revisit it in a later chapter. The dominant seventh chord, heard countless times before as tensing toward the tonic triad as its goal, here functions in the opposite way, as "the comparative relaxation of attaining a goal." It is only comparatively relaxed because there is still the need for the phrase to move on in this erotically tense opera. As Zuckerkandl observes, this famous cadence was not rejected by hearers as wrong because it failed to accord with prevalent habits (51). Nor did it start a new habit in which the V^7 chord ceased to be heard as the dominant of its tonic. On the contrary, the cadence was heard as the revelation of a potential that lay dormant until Wagner awakened it. The revelation shows more clearly than anything else what associationism can never explain: "the fact of creation" (52), the birth of the musically new, in this case, of an unprecedented function of a standard chord.

Zuckerkandl follows up his critique of associationism with an illuminating discussion of "the three components of sense perception" (53–63). The three components are objective material sound, subjective or psychic response, and dynamic quality. Zuckerkandl critiques the usual two-world scheme and lays the groundwork for the "third stage" on which tonal motion takes place (142). He begins with the observation that our experience supports a distinction between two worlds: the outer world of non-illusory perceptions and the inner world of subjective phenomena (thoughts, feelings, dreams, etc.). He reminds us that the outer world is the arena not only of bodies but also of forces (magnetic, electrical, gravitational, etc.), and that in musical tones we hear an action of forces "which not only does not coincide with its material consequences but with which no material phenomena can be correlated at all" (56). This recapitulates what we already know: that the oscilloscope is tone deaf.

All three components of sense perception—body, psyche, and tension—are in play when we listen to music. Tones sound in the outer realm of material bodies; they affect how we inwardly feel; and they are forces with a life of their own, a purely musical life. Zuckerkandl offers a helpful statement of how these three are connected: "What makes tone musical tone is so much the work *not* of the physical and *not* of the psychic components but of the third, a purely dynamic component, that, compared with the latter, the two others sink to the functions of trigger and aftereffect: a physical process sets off the dynamic phenomenon; the latter reverberates in a psychic process" (61).

Zuckerkandl ends this section with a daring speculation about all sensory perceptions. He quotes Gustav von Allesch, a perceptual psychologist who posits a dynamism of colors analogous to that of tones: "the essential element in the impression of color is dynamic in nature, based upon a movement toward a definite goal or movement away from a goal . . . In any case the apprehension of a color is an event in which a direction, a drive, a will, becomes perceptible" (62). Perhaps, Zuckerkandl speculates, what is true of music, that forces constitute the core of musical perception, is true of "all that is manifest to the senses" (63).

In the final section of his chapter on tone, "The Dynamic Symbol," Zuckerkandl reflects on what it means for a dynamic quality to be "in" a tone, as the power of $\hat{2}$ in the Beethoven melody is "in" the pitch E. He continues to clarify the meaning of meaning in tones in order to explain why someone not familiar with Western tonal music would not detect dynamic qualities (64). He appeals to the analogy between music and language, both of which make use of symbols: "Music and language ... have one thing in common—that tones, like words, have meaning and that the 'being in' of the meaning in the word, like that of the musical significance in the tone, is of a non-material nature" (67). But there the similarity ends, since "[t]he word and its meaning are independent things," whereas "[t]he tone and its meaning ... are connected in a far more intimate way." In fact, "[w]hat tones mean musically is completely one with them, can only be represented through them, exists only in them." Zuckerkandl implicitly rejects Schopenhauer's view that musical meaning lies in the representation of a mode of will as feeling or emotion. On the contrary, the meaning of a tone "lies not in what it points to but *in the pointing itself*; more precisely, in the different way, in the individual gesture, with which each tone points toward the same place [the governing î]" (68). Words, Zuckerkandl says, "lead away from themselves," whereas tones "lead into themselves."

A symbol is meaning that is present in some entity but not a property of that entity. A red light means "stop." This meaning is obviously not a property of the color red. The same is true for the symbolic character of dynamic quality, which is a meaning, a pointing, that is present in a physically heard pitch. This symbolic "being in," Zuckerkandl claims, is like the presence of the divine being in the religious symbol (69). To a believing Catholic, for instance, divine love is present symbolically in the crucifix. The difference, however, between the believer's experience of symbols and the musical listener's is that the latter does not depend on faith. But it does depend on something in the listener: an openness, a focusing of attention. All listeners, not just those from non-Western backgrounds, must be active listeners. Only through active listening and the focusing of attention do we begin to hear and enjoy tonal forces and to engage in the intuitive symbol recognition that is integral to musical listening. Hearing the directedness that is there sometimes requires continued listening—and effort.[17]

Motion

Zuckerkandl now turns to the central question of *Sound and Symbol*: What is tonal motion? Up to this point, tones have been treated as elements of musical contexts (75). These contexts are the vibrant wholes of which tones are parts. The question then arises: "What do I hear when I hear context? What do I call the thing that, interpenetrating the multitude of successive tones, connects them together?" Do tones move? Does something move through tones?[18]

Zuckerkandl approaches this perplexing phenomenon by citing the rousing opening of the *Marseillaise*:

Bypassing the technicalities of music theory and whatever emotions the tune stirs in us, Zuckerkandl focuses on what we hear in the tones themselves. What do we hear? An ascent, as it seems, in tonal space. When we consider motion in music, we tend to think of rhythm, which "seems to us to be the real kinetic element in music" (76). In fact, it might be argued, has been argued, that the temporal dimension of music, the musical ordering of time, is what is most fundamental in music. After all, there is no melody without rhythm, but there is rhythm without melody, as in the case of drums.[19]

Zuckerkandl, however, excludes rhythm as the kinetic aspect of tones. Rhythm, he claims, "is not a specifically musical phenomenon" (76). There is a rhythm to one's walk and speech, to a gymnastic exercise, to our heartbeat and breathing, to embryonic development, to the motions of the heavenly spheres. But these patterns are music only metaphorically (unless there is an audible "music of the spheres"). Music proper, for Zuckerkandl, requires tones, and it is in them that we must search for the truth about the motion we hear in the opening rise of the *Marseillaise*.[20] Moreover, as Zuckerkandl observes, what we mean by rhythm is not what rhythm meant in the music of earlier periods. In Gregorian chant, for instance, there is a purely tonal ebb and flow. It is the apotheosis of tonal motion unhindered by constraints of modern relative time values, bar lines, beats, and the syntax of rhythmic periods.[21]

Music is motion. But what sort of motion? We hear the approach and departure of the band playing the *Marseillaise*. But this is not the motion that concerns us, which is the melody's opening ascent (82). Motion seems to imply something that moves—a bird that flies by or a snowflake that falls to the ground. But what in the melody may be said to move? The answer is: "Nothing at all." No tone in the melody moves. If we approach the melody with the assumption that its tones are the bearers of motion, we reach the Zeno-like conclusion that melody is "nothing but stops, a stringing together of static tones, and, between tone and tone, *no* connection, *no* transition, *no* filling up of intervals, nothing. It is the exact opposite of motion" (83). This is the *paradox of tonal motion.* Zuckerkandl proceeds to drive the final nail into the coffin of moving tones: "if we attempt actually to connect tone with tone, to create transitions, to fill up the intervals completely, taking real [i.e., bodily] motion as our model, the result is the familiar screeching glissade of the siren, in which melody and music are destroyed" (83).[22]

And yet . . . and yet, we hear motion in the opening phrase of the *Marseillaise*, an ascent in tonal space. Whatever motion means here must have something to do with what distinguishes one tone from another. This is pitch: some tones are higher, we say, than others. But what does "higher" mean? Is one tone truly higher than another, and is there some real space in which tones move and have a location? Or are we perhaps under the spell of "a primitive verbal and emotional suggestion" (85)? Zuckerkandl will return to the question of space in his final chapter. For now, I simply observe that the phenomenon of tonal motion, once it is removed from the rhythmic determinations of *time*, is seen to depend on the need to clarify *space*.

Having generated the paradox of tonal motion, Zuckerkandl proceeds to the true motion of tones (88). In this context, he will move toward a definition of music as "motion in the dynamic field of tones" (95). This provocative borrowing of the field concept shows that Zuckerkandl owes a greater debt to modern physics than might be apparent. Like force, the dynamic field of tones is an immaterial principle that allows individual entities to act on each other reciprocally. This immaterial field lies at the heart of Zuckerkandl's understanding of music, since it allows him to account for tonal interaction and tonal flow. In the final section of his chapter on motion, he will speculate on the metaphysical implications of motion without a moveable and the deep connection between music and nature.

Let us return to the opening phrase of the *Marseillaise*. We notice that the first interval traversed is a *perfect fourth* from E to A. Zuckerkandl uses this simple observation to reinforce the fact that in listening to a tonal major-minor melody, we are not hearing pitches per se but tendencies to move in a certain direction. These tendencies are the proper object of musical perception. For the same reason, we do not experience melody as a sequence of horizontally traversed intervals or pitch distances. A melody that was a succession of intervals (perfect fourth, then major second, etc.) would bring about, just as would a mere succession of tones, the annihilation of tonal motion, of itself as melody. It is not intervals that bring about dynamic qualities but the other way around: "It is not the difference in pitch but the difference in dynamic quality which generates the interval as a musical [not merely acoustical] phenomenon" (92).[23] Dynamic qualities bring intervals to musical life.

So then, in the opening of the *Marseillaise*, we are hearing not only the traversed interval between E and A but also, and more importantly, the immaterial purely dynamic transition from $\hat{5}$ to $\hat{8}$, a pointing that achieves its goal, an *arrival*.[24] This fact leads to an insight that will be the key to understanding melodic continuity: "To be auditively *in* the tone now sounding [in this case, $\hat{5}$] means . . . always being *ahead of* it too, on the way to the next tone" (94). In short, tones are not static things (and certainly not bodies) but acts of directed beyond-ing and between-ing. They are moments of a motion. Tones share the dialectical nature of the arrow symbol, →, which in Hegelian fashion negates itself in pointing beyond itself. This self-beyonding inherent in dynamic quality will later be linked with another arrow—the arrow of time. Tone will be time's *image* (248).

Zuckerkandl now returns to the major scale, the simplest case of tonal motion (95). As I mentioned above, it is the only scale in which the dynamic qualities are in full force and that most manifests music as "motion in the dynamic field of tones" (95).[25] Here is the C-major scale:

On hearing this scale, we are immediately aware of the goal-directed journey mentioned earlier. Tone, not pitch, makes this possible, and the scale is musically understood, because heard, as a gradual progression of dynamic qualities, tendencies "toward" and "away from." The first part of the journey is an adventure. As we move away from $\hat{1}$, our tonal home, we move against the force of tonal gravity: *do, re, mi, fa, sol*. Relatively stable $\hat{5}$, *sol*, is a turning point.[26] We hear it as the end of the first phase of our journey and the beginning of the next. Beyond $\hat{5}$, the dynamic situation is inverted, as we detect the pull *upward* toward $\hat{8}$, the $\hat{1}$ in the other direction: *sol, la, ti, do*.[27] "Away from" becomes "toward," adventure becomes homecoming. The scale has revealed itself as not linear at all but circular, a return-to-origin that displays "the miracle of the octave" (102).

   Zuckerkandl gives us the following diagram of the scale conceived as an order of dynamic qualities:

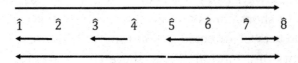

The uppermost arrow indicates the direction in which the scale
is sung or played. The middle arrows show the dynamic qualities
between adjacent tones. The arrows at the bottom show the dou-
ble role of $\hat{5}$, which can point down toward $\hat{1}$ or up toward $\hat{8}$. $\hat{6}$, too,
"plays a double role, since it can be heard either as a moment in the
succession $\hat{5}$-$\hat{6}$-$\hat{7}$-$\hat{8}$ or as bound to and pointing toward its comparatively stable adjacent tone" (97).
   Zuckerkandl puts forth various ways of picturing the configuration of the scale's tonal field, but we need not dwell on them.
The essential point is that the scale is the dynamic frame or background against which tonal music moves (95). Melodies are interesting to us because tones are free to obey or contradict their
inherent tendencies. The scale is the norm that inspires and
makes sense of departures from the norm. Thanks to the dynamic
qualities of the major scale (and by extension the minor), music
can generate heightened tension and artful forms of delayed gratification.
   Melody, however, is not the only form of musical motion. There
is also harmony as the movement of *chords*: "The most revealing
manifestation of tonal motion, however, is not found in melodic
processes; it is found in harmony, in the motion of chords" (104).[28]
Chords in tonal harmony are vertical stacks of tones, or rather of
thirds. They are named after and represented by their so-called
"roots." Like tones, chords have dynamic quality. In the previous
chapter, we saw this chordal dynamism in the perfect cadence,
where the V[7] chord points to the tonic triad of the key, the 1-chord,
to which it resolves:[29]

This harmonic move from V^7 to I is the chordal equivalent of the melodic move from $\hat{5}$ to $\hat{8}$ in the opening phrase of the *Marseillaise*. Both are instances of heard arrival. Chords, like tones, acquire their dynamic function only in context. The C-major triad (C-E-G), while remaining acoustically the same, is I in the key of C but V in the key of F. Also, chords, like tones, can be arranged in a scale, a scale of harmonic degrees, in which the basic "step" is the interval of a fifth: I-V-II-VI-III-VII-IV-I. Zuckerkandl explores this harmonic scale in greater detail in *The Sense of Music*.[30] In the harmonic force-field, there are moves toward and away from an established center of force, the I-chord or tonic triad. I→V is "away," V→I is "toward," and I→V→I is "away and then toward" (112).

What, then, is a chord? The C-major triad consists of C, E, and G. It is a whole that is more than the sum of its parts.[31] Even when a chord is heard out of context, we perceive a real unity, a structure in which the constituent tones, in coalescing, are audibly preserved. It is this wondrous One-in-Many that makes polyphony possible. Zuckerkandl calls the chord an "aura" that radiates from its tones (113). He makes the astonishing but nonetheless correct observation that "a chord can, strictly speaking, be neither played nor sung nor written" (107). All this we can do with the individual tones but not with the chord, which is conjured into being by its tonal parts. A chord is not an illusion. It is something that is heard as a One that functions in tonal harmony as an entity endowed with a distinctive power (V, IV, VII, etc.). If this were not so, harmony would be a mere sequence rather than a movement of chords. Tonal dynamism was the first step toward music's transcendence. The chord, which cannot even be said to be *in* a single material sound, is "one further step removed from materiality."[32] In *The Sense of Music*, Zuckerkandl calls the chord "an *idea*—an idea to be heard, an idea for the ear, an audible idea" (184).[33]

Earlier, I described dynamic quality as an act of beyond-ing and between-ing. To be audibly "in" a tone is already to be ahead of it, following the arrow that is the tone. Herein lies the continuity of tonal motion: "To be in motion does not mean to be first here, then there; it means to be on the way from here to there" (126).[34] In listening to a melody, we are never "at" a tone but always "*between* the tones, *on the way* from tone to tone" (137).[35] As we have seen, tones are not body-like bearers of motion in space. In music, because we are hearing (strictly speaking) not pitches but forces, we are hearing not a thing moving but *moving as such*, "the core of motion" (138). Contrary to the claim of some that musical motion is ideal and abstract, tonal motion turns out to be what motion most is. It is "the most real motion" (139). But if tonal motion is motion as such, pure passage apart from all movables, then music acquires an unprecedented cognitive potential. It provides, Zuckerkandl claims, a locus for the paradigmatic study of motion, including the motion of bodies (141).

The designation of music as the realm of motion as such, heard motion, brings us to what Zuckerkandl calls "the third stage" (142). This difficult, mystical-sounding section of the chapter gives an overview of Zuckerkandl's tonal cosmology, his musical view of the world. The account rests on the distinction between the inner world of the psyche and the outer world of bodies. Citing William James's stream of consciousness, Zuckerkandl reminds us that the word motion "is as native to the inner as to the outer world" (143). In what world, on what *stage*, does musical motion take place?

It would have been a good deal easier, if dishonest, Zuckerkandl claims, to treat music as an internal rather than external phenomenon, as simply psychological (144). That would accord with Hegel's connecting music with pure subjectivity and the claim that music "'echoes the motions of the inmost self'" (142–43).[36] Zuckerkandl, of course, rejects this subjective view of music. As the subtitle of his book indicates, the focus is on music and the *external* world: "[Music] is not felt, it is not imagined, it is not willed—it is perceived. It does not arise from our psyche; it comes to us from the world around us" (144). Zuckerkandl continues: "Tones move where birds fly and meteors fall" (144).

No one would deny that music is profoundly related to our inner life. But musical phenomena are not the creations of consciousness. In James Joyce's "The Dead," Gabriel catches sight of his wife Gretta, as she listens on the stairs to the tenor singing *The Lass of Aughrim*. The tones of the song strike a psychic chord. They summon within her the memory of the boy who loved her, died for her, and used to sing the same song. Gretta is held in the moment, inwardly moved. The poignancy of the scene depends on an event in which tones saturated with meaning come to her from the external world.[37]

But neither does music exist on the stage of body and bodily motion, as we have repeatedly seen. Dynamic quality, the essentially musical aspect of tones, slips through the net of acoustical determination and is "in" acoustical pitches only as the material precondition of real sounding. This leads Zuckerkandl to posit the existence of a third stage that is "neither the world of the psyche nor the world of bodies nor yet a mixture of both" (145). The metaphor of the stage is no doubt intended to reinforce the idea that the world in all its dimensions consists of events rather than objects. It is where things happen. The third stage is the primordial, universal realm of which bodily and psychical motions are offspring and special cases. As the world of motion as such, it may be spoken of as an inner realm that embodies "the core of every motion, even the motion of bodies" (145). In all forms of motion, then, "music lies hidden." The third stage may be regarded, in the case of external nature, as external inwardness, the indwelling essence and vitality of the external world—the world as force.[38]

The third stage reveals the internal transcendence mentioned at the beginning of our journey. It is the transcendence not only within music but within the no-longer-merely-material world, which music allows us to grasp, interpret, symbolically (147). In the musical view of the world, the entire universe, Zuckerkandl affirms, "would have the nature of a symbol," and "musical experience might be distinguished by the fact that in it the symbolic nature of the external world would be revealed in direct perception," that is, in hearing the hidden meaning and "core of the world" (147). In short, although music is, to be sure, "a source of knowledge of the inner world," "the deeper teaching of music concerns the nature not of 'psyche' but of 'cosmos.'"[39] Here, Zuckerkandl comes very close to positing, with Schopenhauer, a cosmic will.

Meaning, for Zuckerkandl, is not the world's pointing beyond itself. The world is not the symbol of a timeless Beyond, or God, or Divine Love, or universal suffering. It is symbolic in the sense that it is the realm of the sheer striving to be and the enduring through time that lie hidden within material being.[40] This vibrant cosmic interior is close to what Leibniz means by force (*vis viva*), if we remove force from its material actions and interactions. For Leibniz, force as the substance of things is thought rather than sensed. In music and its third stage, it is directly perceived and intuited.

To support the connection between music and cosmos, Zuckerkandl cites Sir Thomas Browne's striking claim that every melody is "an Hieroglyphical and shadowed lesson of the whole World and creatures of God" (147).[41] But the lion's share of praise goes to Schopenhauer, whose musical cosmology in many ways resembles Zuckerkandl's musical concept of the external world. Zuckerkandl quotes, with approval, a passage from *The World as Will and Representation*: "A correct, complete, and detailed explanation of music—that is, a full restatement, in terms of concepts, of what music expresses . . . would be a sufficient restatement and explanation of the world in terms of concepts, or completely in harmony with such a restatement and explanation, and hence the true philosophy" (147–48).[42]

The musical cosmologies of Schopenhauer and Zuckerkandl

are united by the centrality of force as will. Both thinkers regard the cosmos as a manifestation of modes of tension or striving. Both privilege music as giving us unique access to "the core of the world." They differ, however, in important respects. The most obvious is that Zuckerkandl does not, like Schopenhauer, regard the external world as an illusion. He is the tireless champion of real externality. Another difference is that music for Zuckerkandl is not the symbology of emotion, although it certainly arouses emotions. It is symbolic, as it is for Schopenhauer, but it is not the realm of archetypal emotional modes.[43] Finally, Zuckerkandl is not a gloomy existentialist. Music, for him, is not private momentary refuge from the wheel of Ixion, the suffering that is life. In its deepest origins, it is the frequently communal flourishing of our innately musical nature and a celebratory mode of being-in-the-world.[44]

Time

Not surprisingly, Zuckerkandl gives a dynamic account of musical time. Like tone, musical time is a force or tendency. It will even have a will (222).

Zuckerkandl begins by recalling the conclusion of the previous chapter: there can be motion without a moveable and therefore without bodies and their space (151). But motion, albeit disembodied and de-spaced, cannot dispense with time. Time is essential to music, because music is motion. Zuckerkandl draws a theological inference: "A God enthroned beyond time in timeless eternity would have to renounce music" (151). To preserve God's experience of music (how could we have such a wondrous thing and He not?), Zuckerkandl affirms the temporal existence of God: "to save music for Him, we shall hold, with the Greeks, that God cannot go beyond time. Otherwise what would He be doing with all the choiring angels?" By "the Greeks," Zuckerkandl must mean the Greek poets, since Aristotle's god (the divine intellect) is beyond place, time, and motion and therefore beyond music.[45]

Let us leave this musical-theological speculation, which Zuckerkandl does not develop, and turn to his account of musical time.
Just as the inquiry into tonal phenomena focused on tonal harmony (the musical language of Bach and Mozart), time in music
is most genuinely revealed for Zuckerkandl in *measured music*—
that is, music with bar lines, measures, and time-signatures (2/4,
3/4, 6/8, etc.). These limit the freedom music had enjoyed in the
absence of these modern constraints, as in Gregorian chant. But
"rhythm bound to the law of meter" is in fact a Hegelian *Aufhebung*: "Voluntary subjection to strict constraint has, in the course
of evolution, led to a victorious advance into a new freedom"
(160). What, then, is rhythm in the context of tonal harmony and
its concomitant temporal constraints? What is musical freedom
under law?

To answer this question, we turn to the *measure*. We see bar
lines and measures in a score. They are there on the page. But do
we hear and feel them? The fact is that we do. Hearing a waltz
makes us want to dance the waltz. We are, so to speak, invaded
by the beat and the underlying 3/4 pulse given visually in the
time-signature. We begin to sway with the rhythm that comes to
us: 1-2-3, 1-2-3, 1-2-3. The *Skaters' Waltz* is a good example of felt
bar lines and measures:

What is remarkable is that we can waltz to this sparse tune even
in the absence of the accompaniment that spells out the pulse. We
get it. We perceive and feel in the relative time values and tones the
underlying lilt of the dance. We move our bodies, not in accordance with the relative time-values, but with the *rhythmic field* they
have induced as their soul-like form, a form made visible in the bar

lines and measures of the score. And when a tone holds for a long
time, as in the third and seventh measures of the waltz, the dance
goes on, the beat goes on.

The dynamic quality of meter comes to light when we interpret the time-signature of a piece of music as a *wave* (169). Meter
as wave transforms a static sequence of beats into an ordered flow,
a continual "to and fro, an away and back." It is rhythmic continuity: "The machine runs metrically; man walks rhythmically" (170).
When learning to waltz, we follow a static sequence of steps. We
look like robots. But once we have learned the steps—why then,
we are dancing! We no longer count beats but connect them into a
seamless flow. We experience, intuit, meter as something alive and
ensouled. We are not so much making bodily movement happen
as moving with a force that is already there. We are experiencing,
celebrating, the dynamism of meter.

As an example of this dynamism, Zuckerkandl cites the opening two measures of Chopin's A-major Polonaise (171):

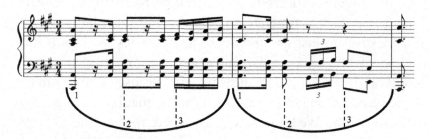

The diagram shows how the rhythmic life of this dance consists of two layers of rhythmic organization: "The tones fall upon
the wave that they themselves have generated . . . The wave is
the meter; rhythm arises from the different arrangement of the
tones on the wave (171–72)." This synthesis of law and freedom
defines the rhythmic life of tonal harmony. Just as tones are free
to obey or contradict their inherent dynamic qualities, so too relative time-values are free to obey, contradict, or artfully obscure

the underlying pulse. The opening theme of Wagner's *Parsifal* is a stunning example of this last case (165):

"Here tones sound," Zuckerkandl observes, "on only 4 of the 11 strong beats and, of the total 21 beats, 13 are marked by silence." These different ways in which tones may obey, subvert, or obscure the underlying meter are possible because, just as melody is motion in the dynamic field of tones, rhythm is motion in the dynamic field of meter (174).

Why does the time-wave work as a dynamic structure, a force? As Zuckerkandl observes at a later point, "[t]he wave is not an event *in* time but an event *of* time." He continues: "Time happens; time is an event" (184). The arrow of time works as a principle of rhythmic motion because the measure consists of beats of different dynamic qualities, upbeats and downbeats dynamically connected—troughs and crests of the self-perpetuating time-wave. The upbeat does not merely precede the downbeat but points to and "desires" it, just as $\hat{7}$ points to and "desires" $\hat{8}$. This is how we know when to begin dancing a waltz: not because of a stress accent on the first beat of a measure, but because we detect in the wave the beginning of a cycle, a beginning that has been pointed to by an upbeat. We know intuitively where the bar line goes. We detect and then move with time as a dynamic order that perpetuates itself, feeds on its own propulsive periodicity, and endures even in the waits and rests that often occur in music, moments when it seems that nothing is happening.

What I have called propulsive periodicity Zuckerkandl calls "polarity and intensification" (174). The time-wave of an individual measure, like the one in the Chopin Polonaise, has a beginning and an end. This is its *polarity* or periodicity: "The individual measure does not merely traverse a definite and definitely divided interval of time; in every measure a cycle begins and closes, a road

is traveled, a goal attained—in short, something is *accomplished*."
A wave begins and ends. But it also goes on, past the individual
measure. In this act of rhythmic procreation, subsequent measures are not mere repetitions but produce an "increase in accomplishment" (175). Like Rumor in the *Aeneid*, the time-wave gains
force with its going.[46] This is the wave's *intensification*. As examples of this accumulation of rhythmic pressure, Zuckerkandl cites
the opening of Bach's *St. Matthew Passion* (to which we shall return
in the next chapter) and the Gloria fugue from Beethoven's *Missa
solemnis* (174). The best example is Ravel's *Bolero*, which is based on
"the endless repetition of the same rhythmic formula" (176, note).

As Zuckerkandl observes, polarity and intensification are opposite potentials contained in the individual measure. They work
together alternately to bring about "the *forms* of music, the ever
astonishing, often overwhelming constructions of an architecture in time, serial structures ["arrows," like the fugue] and symmetrical structures ["circles," like sonata form] of the smallest and
largest dimensions, and structures in which the two principles
interact in the most various ways" (180).[47]

Time, then, is not empty, as philosophers like Kant and
Schopenhauer assert. It is not "a mere *form* of experience" (182).
Nor is it the motion of beats projected onto the tones by our physiological responses to external stimuli. Although we certainly
respond to external stimuli in hearing music, we cannot derive
the *ordering* of beats from these stimuli, as Zuckerkandl argues at
length (185–200). The perception of rhythm is, on the contrary, an
act of discovery: "My feeling of rhythm is a feeling of something,
of some *thing*, a genuine experience, a cognizing if you like" (199).
This fits our experience of dancing a waltz, which is not just bodily
motion but an encounter with a rhythm-ensouled external world.
Gretta hears a tune that comes to her, and she is moved. We hear
the waltz-wave that comes to us, and we move with it.

The general account of time is crystallized in the all-important
field concept. "A field," Zuckerkandl says, "is the region in which a

force is active—active, in accordance with a definite order, differently at every point of the field" (205). The temporal field reminds us that just as tonal motion (the ascending phrase of the *Marseillaise*) is not pitches moving in an imagined space, time is not the motion of a body but rather the action of forces experienced in the time-wave. It is, like tone, both external and immaterial, an internal transcendence. Like tone, it has something analogous to a will, a soul-like urge to perpetuate itself but always with freedom to vary: "The will of time that on one occasion is bent upon note-for-note repetition, on another occasion motivates variation from exact repetition" (222).

Zuckerkandl proceeds to his most astonishing statement about time musically understood: "Time knows nothing of transience" (223). This is the opposite of the destructive causality that many thinkers, including Schopenhauer, have ascribed to time: *khronos* as Kronos, the giant who devoured his children.

To demonstrate his provocative claim, Zuckerkandl returns to the wave-nature of meter. His example is 2/4 time. How do we experience this? The first thing to note is that one measure is not enough to hear the wave as a wave. The downbeat of the measure needs to be pointed to by a preceding upbeat if it is to be felt as a downbeat, just as $\hat{1}$ must be pointed to by other dynamic qualities if it is to be heard as $\hat{1}$. Let us assume that this has already taken place, that we are hearing what we know is a first beat followed by a second. Beat "two" follows beat "one." If "two" is present, "one" is past (224). Does "one" vanish for us in the experience of "two"? If it did, we would experience "two," not as "two," but as another "one." Zuckerkandl observes: "'Two' is not simply the beat that follows 'one'; it is . . . its symmetrical complement, completion and fulfillment." In beat "two," we hear the back-bound-ness of "two" to "one." In Hegelian terms, "one," in being negated, is preserved as a having-been in the arrival of "two." The dynamic relation of the two beats makes this necessary. Something similar happens in the other direction. As we move over the bar line, a new "one" follows

the "two" just heard. Just as "two" is heard in relation to the previous "one," the new "one" is heard in relation to the previous "two."
It is like the tonal $\hat{5}\rightarrow\hat{8}$ relation we saw earlier—an arrival.

Is this the work of memory and anticipation? Zuckerkandl
argues that this is impossible and that the psychological account
of musical time falsifies the facts. When we hear "two," we are
"entirely concentrated upon 'two,' on what is directly present"
(226–27). We do not remember "one": "if we tried, by remembering, to make 'one' present simultaneously with 'two,' all perception
of meter would instantly cease, to be replaced by something as
meaningless as a photographic double exposure" (227).[48] The same
chaos would follow if, while hearing beat "one," we reproduced in
anticipation an about-to-be-perceived "two." On the basis of this
phenomenological description, we reach the following conclusion:
"The present of musical meter, then, contains within it a past that
is not remembered and a future that is not foreknown—and not as
something to be supplied by thought but as a thing directly given
in experience itself" (227). This leads to an even more striking conclusion. In music, "[t]he past is not extinguished, but not because a
memory stores it; it is not extinguished because time itself stores
it, or better put, because the being of time is a storing of itself; the
future is not an impenetrable wall, but not because a foreknowing
or forefeeling anticipates itself; it is not impenetrable because time
always anticipates itself, because the being of time is an antic-
ipating itself" (228). Zuckerkandl states his QED with a rhetorical question and a culminating statement: "Where, in the frame
of this concept of time, is there a place for transience? It would
seem that things pass, not because of, but in spite of, their tempo-
rality" (228).

Zuckerkandl now returns to melody, this time considered as a
"temporal *Gestalt*" (228). The word *Gestalt*, made famous by Gestalt
psychology, comes from the verb *stellen*—to set, place, or arrange.
It is often translated as form or shape.[49] *Gestalten* are "totalities . . .
distinguished by the characteristic that in them the individual

part does not acquire its meaning from itself (or not exclusively from itself) but receives it from the whole" (229). The only *Gestalten* would seem to be spatial objects, since their parts make sense visually only in the context of the whole to which they belong. The question then arises: if a melody is a flow of parts that are never simultaneous but always successive, and the whole of the melody is consequently never given all at once, in what sense can a melody be a *Gestalt*, a whole? How is a *temporal Gestalt* possible (230)?[50]

Here Zuckerkandl combines his earlier account of tonal continuity with the dynamic account of meter and the experience of hearing a melody: "In the hearing of melodies, nothing is remembered and nothing anticipated" (230). He cites the following experiment: break off a melody you are singing and try to reproduce the tone or tones that immediately preceded it. I have tried this often and am always surprised by how difficult it can be, how unnatural it seems. It is jarring to go back when the impetus of the melody is to move forward. And if someone does succeed in recalling a previous tone, the experience is like remembering a fact that has no meaning: "*the instant he does so, he will have lost the thread of the melody*" (231). Zuckerkandl's fascinating conclusion is worth quoting in full:

> The hearing of a melody is a hearing *with* the melody, that is, in closest connection with the tone sounding at the moment. It is even a condition of hearing melody that the tone present should fill consciousness *entirely*, that *nothing* should be remembered, nothing except it or beside it be present in consciousness. The essence of the musical tone, its dynamic quality, lies precisely in its relation to something that itself *is not there*; any turning back of consciousness for the purpose of making past tones present immediately annuls the possibility of musical hearing. Not only, then, is the individual tone in a melody understood in itself, without the slightest regard for whether anything is remembered, it *cannot* be understood if something is remembered (231).

Zuckerkandl follows this up with a concise description of what it means to hear a melody: "hearing a melody is hearing, having heard, and being about to hear, all at once" (235).[51] The reason for this is the dynamic pointing and beyond-ing that have been with us from the start, the force that we do not infer but directly perceive. A melody is a *Gestalt*, a genuine whole of parts no less than a visual *Gestalt*, not because we remember previous tones that have been stored in consciousness, but because time "stores itself and anticipates itself" (235).

Zuckerkandl uses these insights into musical time to give an account of *form* in music. His example is the tripartite scheme known as "sonata form" (235). He argues that the sections of a large-scale movement of a piano sonata, string quartet, or symphony are not statically successive, as diagrams would suggest, but dynamically interrelated. We hear form not as something imposed from without but growing from within. Form in music is time shaping itself. Time, at this larger level of organization, is seen to "store itself" in an especially impressive way, as in Beethoven's symphonies. If architecture, as some have said, is frozen music, then music may rightly be called "flowing architecture" (241). If time indeed stores itself, then time is a constructive rather than destructive force, and a melody is a building in flux, a structured coming-to-be.

Does this accord with experience? It does. At the end of a musical work, we are gratified by the final cadence, not because the music has stopped but because a living motion has reached its fulfillment, its *telos*. The final cadence is no mere gimmick tacked on to bring motion to an end. It is rather the moment in which the musical edifice is perfected. It is like the end of a story, in which the final moments contain all that has happened and give the last sentence its specific weight. It is like the end of Joyce's "The Dead": "[Gabriel's] soul swooned slowly as he heard the snow falling faintly through the universe and faintly falling, like the descent of their last end, upon all the living and the dead." Why is it that at the end of tonal-harmonic pieces of music, the V-1 cadence we have heard countless times before never bores or fails to please? It is because the standard formula is an organic outgrowth of this piece and not another. The universal V-1 formula is therefore never heard in the same way twice. The rich past that it contains, the motion of which it is the *telos*, makes every final cadence new and distinctive, an event.

Musical time is amazing. But does it tell us anything about time outside the realm of music? Are there perhaps two times, one for music and one for nature? That is the question Zuckerkandl poses next (242). He enlists the aid of Henri Bergson, who gives an essentially musical description of time as a seamless flow, duration (*durée*) as opposed to the cinematographic snapshots of physics-time (143).[52] Zuckerkandl quotes Bergson's observation that melody captures a flow that comes close to coinciding with time as "the very fluidity of our inner life" (244). Bergson calls this *fundamental time*. But is this also *physical* time? Or does Bergson's fundamental time remain, as his critics argue, confined to the psyche? Whether or not the criticism is valid, Zuckerkandl's stance is clear: "the attempt to restrict the new time concept by shutting it up in the inner world, by subjectivizing it, collapses in the face of the testimony of music" (245). On the contrary, time, as the phenomena of music show, is "out there" in the external world. Musical time "cannot be 'in me,' it is not 'my' time. It is where music is; I find it where music is—that is, in the same direction in which I find the sun, the moon, and the stars."

Physics, as Zuckerkandl reminds us, is not the only science of the natural. There is also biology, which studies time as it appears in the wondrous timing of organisms—biological time. It is in biology that musical time and natural time meet or at least overlap. Both are real and out there, both are bound up with causality (as in embryonic development), and both manifest living rhythms. The time of physics does not need to be refuted, Zuckerkandl claims (247). It just needs to be placed within a larger context that allows for a gradation of time as force: "Physics and music stand to each other as realms of the minimum and maximum activity of time. Physical events are less the work of time [i.e., time as dynamism], musical works more the work of time, than events in any other realm." In any case, as the argument has shown, time is no mere formality but rather an active force.

The complex chapter on time ends with yet another remarkable claim: that tone is "the image of time" (248). Zuckerkandl approaches this idea by asking whether time in music is limited to meter and rhythm. Echoing Bergson's notion of *durée*, he locates an additional dynamic quality of musical time in the sheer duration of a tone, which we experience as a gradually increasing *pressure* (249). His example is the opening sound of Beethoven's *Coriolanus* Overture, where a lone C is held for two measures:

As we listen to this tone and submit to it, we hear, not self-sameness over the course of several seconds, but an intensification, a force in the absence of other dynamic qualities: "in the phenomenon of the first tone, we have in germ the same process which, in the case of the repeated tone, led to the metric wave" (250). Time, here, reveals itself not as something added to the held tone but in it. Tone makes it possible in this way to *hear time* as the propulsive self-replicating force of meter, dynamically defined as the time-wave.[53] In the opening C of the Overture, we hear "the germination of the first metric wave," the nascence of time's formative potential and the promise of things to come. It is "time become perceptible—one might almost say, become tangible, plastic" (250).

Tone as the manifestation of time becomes even more pronounced when dynamic qualities are in play and we go beyond an opening tone. To hear $\hat{2}$ (our old friend) is to hear a determinate beyond-ing, a self-negation. The demand of $\hat{2}$ "is not directed toward adding something to the datum, but toward *replacing* the datum—not only toward the appearance of something that is not yet, but at the same time toward the disappearance of what is now present" (252). Put dramatically, we are hearing the tone's will to die to itself so that something else might live, something that completes its desire. In Hegel's terms, $\hat{2}$ declares itself as a passing moment in a dialectical process and is experienced as an active, dialectically charged non-being.[54] This is precisely the being-on-the-way and pressing-forward that characterizes time: "To *hear* incompleteness [in the tone] is to hear time" (253).

Time's plasticity, the potential for metrical molding that we hear in the opening C discussed above, leads Zuckerkandl to conclude that tones are "time become audible matter, as corporeal things are space made visible and tangible matter" (254). Time as the time-wave is the dynamically organized *out-of-which* that will shape itself in various ways as the musical piece goes on. The dynamic plasticity of time leads to the designation of tone as the *image of time*. Image, here, is neither metaphor nor copy. It is helpful to think of the German word for image, *Bild*, which refers to something that is *gebildet*, that is, shaped or molded. To say that tone is the image of time means that tones are "time become audible matter; to form in tones is to form in the stuff of time; an image composed of tones is always at the same time a time image—not an image *in* time but an image *of* time" (258). In sum, tone is the perceptible being-there, the *Dasein*, of time. It is the audibility of time as impulse and tendency.

In the final pages of his chapter on time, Zuckerkandl reflects on the power of images and their importance for human life. He cites image-formation and thinking as "the two gifts that distinguish human existence from animal existence" (259). Images, he says, "conquer strangeness; create the first intimacy between man and his surroundings." They support and orient. Through image-formation, "man reaches beyond himself." Images and symbols are the guardians of traditions: "it is community of images more than community of thought that binds and delimits human societies." As we shape images of all kinds, we are shaped by them. For the most part, such images are visual: a flag, a crescent moon, a star of David.

Now in a historically triumphal vein, Zuckerkandl claims that with the birth of "our music" (262), the music of tonal harmony, "for the first time since the beginning of human thought, the bond between image and eye, between image and space, is broken" (260). The reason is that tonal harmony succeeded in generating temporal *Gestalten* and tonal images of time. Human beings can now find in these audible images a "new freedom" (260), a new meaning, a new way of being. What is musically new? The simple answer is *instrumental music* or, as Wagner dubbed it, absolute music. This is music that is nothing but tones: "in the music of earlier times, tones were not free; they were bound to words, as in song, or to actions that call for regular bodily movement, as in dance, work, ceremonial. Thus the world of things, the spatial world, forced itself into the tonal world, mingled with it, and was able to prevent an insight into the very essence of music" (260). Once freed from the confines of spatial thingliness, tones can again be linked with words and actions, in song and drama. But now they "bring a new dimension to view in them." This new dimension is not the dreamy supersensuous Beyond of the Romanticists. It is rather "*time*, and everything for which the word stands: flowing, becoming, change, motion." Time, through tonal music, becomes the new medium for image-formation, the medium in which human beings can now find a paradigmatic meaning that is more faithful to the dynamic, forward-moving world in which they live and to the ever-developing freedom of the human spirit.

The time-images of tonal harmony break the spell of our former bondage to space. They liberate us, Zuckerkandl claims, from the space-prejudiced view of philosophers of old (Plato comes to mind) who prefer rest to motion, being to becoming, self-sameness to the self-otherness of change: "The old prejudice in favor of being, rest, changelessness, which had the whole weight of our symbols on its side, is discredited [by the time revelations of tonal harmonic music] (262)."[55] Zuckerkandl does not say why this Bergsonian liberation from spatial images would be better for human beings, or how a time-image of the world might serve as a guiding norm for human life. He seems to rely on a Hegelian supposition of historical progress and what he calls in another work "the culminating phase" of music.[56] His point is that after three centuries of great tonal music, "[w]e have begun to think temporally, in the image of time" (263), which is to say, musically. A sign of this paradigm shift from space to time, Zuckerkandl asserts, is the employment of musical formulations and concepts in modern biology and physics.

Space

The musical concept of the external world is completed with the musical nature of space. As with tone, motion, and time, the nature of space will be revealed as consisting in force. As we know, Zuckerkandl is at pains to stress the real externality of musical phenomena. But only now does he directly address what this externality is and the meaning of the book's subtitle: *Music and the External World.*

Zuckerkandl begins by reminding us that in the previous inquiry, "tones have freed themselves from every connection with things and the spatial" (267). And yet, the persistent claim has been that music "does not arise in me; it encounters me," that music is external and out there. But what is the meaning of terms like "outside" and "from outside"? What is the difference between "inner" and "outer," if I am not allowed to think of space (268)? The *chord*, which we discussed earlier, now enters in a way that seems to make space a musical necessity. In the major triad, as we saw, three tones coalesce but do not vanish as individuals. How could they be separately sounding if space did not keep them apart? How could *polyphony*, many voices at once, be possible without a space in which the many voices pursued their distinguishable linear careers? Then there is the powerful moment in Bach's *St. Matthew Passion* when male and female voices sing, in octaves, "*Ich bin Gottes Sohn*" (269). What, if not space, allows us to hear the tones of these octaves as distant, far apart from one another, in their very closeness?

Zuckerkandl anticipates the answer. Contrary to Schopenhauer's claim that music is perceived solely in and through time, to the complete exclusion of space, the experience of music is also an experience of space, "and indeed a particular experience of space" (270). Tones, as we shall see, "are not transcendent in respect to space as such but to *the* space in which bodies and objects have locations."

"Is space audible?" This is the question Zuckerkandl takes up next (271). To approach it, he asks another: "How can music take place *where* bodies move, and at the same time be transcendent in respect to the space in which bodies move?" He cites (and eventually adopts) Heidegger's definition of space as "*that whence something encounters me.*" Tones presuppose space as a "whence" because they come to me, encounter me. I am their destination and addressee. In hearing tones, I hear the "whence" as the origin that tones bring with them and in which they live. This happens with eye and hand (272). Seeing a color and touching hardness bring with these sensations the spatiality of their objects. But there are also things that are immune to space, like the thought or idea that comes to me from what someone says or what I read in a book. The non-spatial thought comes to me, encounters me, but not from space. Is a tone-encounter like a thought-encounter—utterly non-spatial?

The answer is "no." I can encounter a thought that comes to me from reading a book, but I need not. I can summon it later from within. In any case, a thought is not in space: "The distinction 'within-without' is not applicable to thought" (274). Tones, by contrast, always come to me from without. Their without-ness is essential to our experience of them: "Hearing a tone includes a sensation of 'without'; it is not a wholly nonspatial experience. The listener is aware of space." This fits our experience of hearing music. Tones comes to us from the external world, and we are transported, like Gretta on the stairs as she listens to *The Lass of Aughrim*.

Zuckerkandl notes that resistance to the idea of audible space is rooted for the most part in assumptions about space that apply to bodies but not tones. To the eye, objects have a bounded place in space as the place of all places. This is a space that can be divided into parts and measured. But tonal space is no such thing. A tone does not sound *here* rather than *there*. It sounds everywhere, all around me. To the ear, space is "an undivided whole . . . The space we hear is a space without places" (276).

The peculiar spatiality of tones is perfectly captured by Erwin Straus, whom I quoted earlier: "Of color we must say that it always appears as confronting us, confined to a locality, organizing and delimiting space into parts; of tone, on the contrary, we must say that it comes toward us, reaches us and seizes us, passes by, occupies and integrates space" (276).[57] Géza Révész, a psychologist whom Zuckerkandl often quotes, adds a further touch to our musical experience of space. When we hear a tone or a tonal complex, Révész writes, "it seems to us as if the space around us were suddenly filled with life" (277).[58] Perhaps this is more than mere seeming. Zuckerkandl proceeds to draw an analogy between the present account of space and the earlier account of time: "Not tone that occurs in space, but space that becomes an *occurrence* [my emphasis] through tone." Tone-space is not body-space. It is experienced as charged, ensouled, and "in a sort of motion." Borrowing an idea from the physicist Melchior Palágyi, Zuckerkandl calls it *"flowing space"* (278).[59] Zuckerkandl returns to this novel idea in the next section of his chapter.

According to Révész, auditory space lacks the three-dimensionality of optical space (285). Is this true? More precisely, is it true that heard space lacks the dimension of depth? By hearing, we certainly distinguish sound sources that are nearer to or farther from us. We can localize sounds. But hearing music, as Straus observes in his comments on tonal autonomy, is not about hearing where sound sources are located and where they are coming from. Tones are neither signals nor properties of the instruments that produce them. Zuckerkandl's dynamic approach to music helps to clarify how, in the absence of a spatial coordinate system, we nevertheless experience space as a form of depth: "in tone, space itself . . . is in a unique way directed toward the hearer; is experienced as motion toward him. In this sensation—'directed from . . . toward'—spatial depth is revealed to the hearer" (289). In sum, "Depth in auditory space is only another expression for this 'coming from . . .'." It is the *whence* of musical encounters.

For Palágyi (as for Minkowski), space and time are inseparable and constitute a space-time continuum: "to the continuing series of moments in time there does not correspond one space, one static datum, but an equally continuous series of spaces, whose totality must be designated as flowing space" (289). Zuckerkandl notes that recent physics treats space as "itself entangled in physical event. Space that is less and less distinguished from the dynamic field that fills it; space that curves; space that expands" (290). Music has in this way once more shown itself to be a window to nature. Indeed, music discloses a more genuine and certainly more immediate mode of access to the externality of the external world. The reason is the peculiar nature of tonal space: "The depth that I hear is not a being-at-a-distance; it is a coming-from-a-distance" (291). In listening to music, I experience tones as coming to me, bridging the gap between me and the external world: "The space experience of the eye is a disjunctive experience; the space experience of the ear is a participative experience." Far from being a purely temporal art, music reveals itself as an art of space no less than of time. In music, we experience space as not empty but full. It is space that is alive (292).

Tonal space, as we have seen, has no determinable places. There is no Cartesian coordinate system. But it does have an order. The clearest proof is polyphony, which flourished uniquely in the West, and of which Palestrina's *Sicut cervus* is a prime example. In this part of his discussion, Zuckerkandl explores the conditions for the possibility of such music: "The spatial nature of this order may remain veiled so long as music does not advance to polyphony, so long as tones are given only in succession—for space discloses itself in simultaneity of data. But in the polyphonic music of the West this very thing, order in the simultaneously audible, auditory-spatial order, is most magnificently revealed" (294).

The foundation of polyphony is the chord or triad, the simultaneous sounding of individual tones. The triad, as we have seen, is a whole in which this individuality is audibly preserved. Like the number "three," it is a real unity, an order that contains and preserves the units of which it is composed. These units, which are not in space, can be spatially represented as the vertices of a triangle. But three tones do not make a triangle in any sense of the term. Why is that the case? Why, in Ernst Mach's formulation, "do three tones form a triad and not a triangle" (297)? As Zuckerkandl reminds us, each of the tones in a triad fills all of space. If we assemble the C-major triad tone by tone, the C, in sounding, "spreads through space" (299). When the E sounds, it does the same, as does the G that follows. The tones overlap but do not "cover" each other. They are, so to speak, mutually transparent. Like nature and grace in Leibniz's cosmology, tones interpenetrate without disturbing each other. The corresponding juxtaposition in the case of colors would yield a very different result: they would not form a "color chord."

Tonal transparency is made possible by the dynamic quality, the directed tension, of tones: "Tones relate to one another. The chord is the fruit not of the simultaneous existence of tones but of their tonal relations" (301). Tones, in sounding, "encounter not only me but one another." This encounter, this being-toward-other, is the result of dynamic qualities. In other words, the answer to Mach's question is that tones are not in different places in space but designate "three particular states in space (or, shall we say, *of* space?)" (303). Zuckerkandl at one point refers to the triad as consisting of the states "$\hat{1}$, $\hat{3}$, and $\hat{5}$" (311). He does not mention, though it is true, that tonal transparency and being-toward-other is present even when the chord is not in a musical context. The reason is that it already *is* a musical context, a little musical world. To hear a triad all by itself is to hear a dynamic structure, in which two of the tones, $\hat{3}$ and $\hat{5}$, point to the third, $\hat{1}$, as their center. The chord is named after the root because it acts harmonically in a way that privileges the root. In that sense, the root is a $\hat{1}$, not perhaps the key of a harmonic composition but the chord's center of action. In the context of the C-major triad, E and G are heard as always in a dynamic relation to C, even when C is not at the bottom of the triad (i.e., when the triad is inverted and therefore not in root position). The ear intuitively knows the root.

To make the novel idea of a non-local space vivid, Zuckerkandl appeals to Faraday's speculations on the magnet, which generates a field to which iron filings or other magnets respond. To be sure, the field is in Cartesian space, but the magnet, as Faraday understands it, acts in a way that defies spatial boundaries.[60] Where is the magnet? If the magnet *is* where the magnet *acts* and exerts an influence, then the magnet, through its force-field, is everywhere: "the dynamic field of a magnet is the thing 'magnet' no less than is the horseshoe-shaped piece of metal at the center of it" (304).

Zuckerkandl now indulges in some highly imaginative thought-experiments. He proposes that we think of the magnet as a creature endowed with consciousness. The creature is sensitive over its whole body only to magnetic influences. Its magnetic sense would then be "telesthetic" (305). That is, it would be capable of feeling not just itself but "something coming from without, from a distance." Since it cannot see or touch, it has no awareness of determinable external places. It senses only tensions, perhaps in the way that a spider feels disturbances of its web-field. In any case, if another magnet (an ordinary one) were to approach our magnet-creature, it would not be sensed as "an object in space," but as "a state of space." If we surround our Faradayan creature with such magnets, it would sense all of them as "in the same place, 'without,' everywhere." It would distinguish them by tension, not by distance. In other words, Magnet Creature would have something analogous to a musical experience of the world.

Still in science-fiction mode, Zuckerkandl goes on to imagine the depths of the sea as endowed with consciousness. Sea Creature is sensitive only to gravitational influence, to gravity as the force it directly intuits. For it, "earth *is* the influence because of which it forever revolves in a circle; sun *is* the influence because of which it forever traces an ellipse; moon *is* the influence to which it responds by a constant rise and fall" (306). Sea Creature experiences, cognizes, not three bodies but three gravities, three separate dynamic states extending throughout physical space. This interpenetration of forces constitutes, for the creature, "a chord of gravity—simultaneous existence that is more like a triad than a triangle" (306).

So much for the non-spatial perception of states of the tonal field. What happens when the field *moves*, as it does in the electrical field in the generation of a current? The scale, the simplest example of tonal motion, offers the clue.

The major scale, as we saw earlier, is the only scale that conveys the sense of a journey with waystations: *do, re, mi, fa, sol, la, ti, do.* The *do* at the end is heard as an arrival, the completion of a journey. It is a perfect example of an ordering of the auditory space in which motion occurs. What does "motion" mean here? Zuckerkandl rules out the account given by Helmholtz, for whom "space is equivalent to physico-geometrical space" (311). For Helmholtz, tones move exactly like bodies in space.[61] The claim is easily refuted, since the space of bodies remains unaffected by bodily motions, whereas "the space in which a tone sounds is affected as a whole." The spider detects the presence of prey in its web, not because it sees the location but because it senses, in the phrase from *Star Wars*, a disturbance in the force, a change of tension in the configuration of the web-field. Two apples fall and "take no notice of each other" (to be precise, their mutual gravitational attractions are virtually nil). But simultaneously sounding tones or chords cannot help but affect each other. As we saw in the case of the C-major triad, E and G are heard as pointing to C, which is heard as governing them, drawing them to itself as their center of gravity.

Zuckerkandl reminds us that the major scale is different in kind from all other tonal series: "it, and it alone, is heard as motion" (315). To move from tone to tone is therefore properly understood as moving from *step* to *step*, from 1̂, for example, to 2̂. And the diagram of the scale, which we saw earlier, gives us in its vector-like arrows the overall "away-from-and-back-to" configuration of the field in which tonal-harmonic music moves. To hear the major scale, then, is to hear not a body moving in static space but the paradigmatic arrangement of dynamic states that constitute tonal motion—the dynamically structured *Urmelodie*, where all the tonal tensions are, so to speak, in their natural state.[62]

Zuckerkandl acknowledges at this point that there exist all sorts of scales, and that our diatonic scale, with its curious mix of whole steps and half steps, is only one among many. He cites in addition the then-recent "resolute experiments" in twelve-tone music by Schoenberg and his students. (This music will be the topic of a later chapter.) But whatever "kinetic meaning" might be found in such post-diatonicism, it is only in the major that a dynamic field is evident. Twelve-tone music eliminates the dynamic qualities that are the foundation of music from Bach to Strauss, the generators and guardians of "away-from-and-back-to." Motion in "the new music" (as Anton Webern called it), would be the motion of tones as acoustical pitches, *sonic* as opposed to *tonal* motion. In this new setting, rhythm emerges as a primary moving force and organizer.

Zuckerkandl continues his exploration of audible space as the paradigm of non-Cartesian order with some fascinating reflections on music and biology. He cites Jakob von Uexküll (1864–1944), who, in his *Theoretical Biology* (1920), puts forth an essentially musical account of the organism, using scale and melody as his models.[63] He posits an ordering principle that is not materially spatial but dynamic in the sense of directional, just like tonal dynamic quality. This principle is *Planmäßigkeit*, conformity to plan. It functions as a "super-mechanical law" that infuses into mechanical causality a "sense" and "purpose."[64] *Planmäßigkeit*, for Timaeus, takes the form of divine *pronoia*, forethought. For his modern counterpart Leibniz, it is Grace as final cause, which suffuses and guides Nature as efficient cause.[65]

We need not pursue the details of von Uexküll's vitalism, as it is called.[66] The important thing is that here music is clearly not confined to aesthetic beauty but enters the realm of cognition and truth. Von Uexküll's theory recapitulates Schopenhauer's view of nature as the realm of musical analogues and symbols, the view that nature as will incarnate *is* music. Music, as a human endeavor, is not just a fine art. Like philosophy, it is a mode of openness to the whole of all things, a cognitive attunement to the way things are, not conceptual but intuitive. When Joyce's Gretta hears the song, she is focused not on its aesthetic beauty but its personal truth.

Zuckerkandl loves talking about the octave, to which he now returns to throw further light on the order of auditory space (321). Octave, here, refers not to the static interval but to the endpoints of the scale as motion. The miracle of the octave, we read, "lies not so much in the sameness of different things; it lies, rather, in the way in which this sameness reveals itself in the course of motion" (322–23). Zuckerkandl regularly rejects appeals to a Helmholtz acoustics-approach to musical experience. The treatment of tones as frequencies fails to explain the sameness that we hear in the octave. For one thing, we do not hear frequencies but tones. For another, the 2:1 ratio that defines the octave as an interval in no way explains the heard sameness. Such a correspondence would be "hardly less miraculous than the phenomenon it is meant to explain" (323). No, the answer lies instead in the *ordered motion* of the major scale and the sense of arrival that is present when we go from $\hat{1}$ to $\hat{8}$ and hear $\hat{8}$ as an arrival, a return to $\hat{1}$. It is this sense of arrival through motion, in which $\hat{1}$ and $\hat{8}$ are heard as dynamically identical, that reveals "what is perhaps the most remarkable aspect of the order of auditory space" (321). The order is not linear but *circular*, and every adventurous move in this space is a move toward homecoming. Audible space is inescapably periodic and may therefore be characterized as "*rhythmically* organized space" (329).

The peculiar space of tones has profound consequences for music, especially, as we have seen, with the discovery of polyphony, many voices at once. The vocal ensemble regularly heard in opera is a case in point. Zuckerkandl cites the quartet from Verdi's *Otello* (331). In this quartet, two conversations are sung at once: that between Othello and Desdemona and that between Iago and Emilia. The order of auditory space, the living space of tones, makes this possible. It overcomes the chaos that would have ensued if the four characters had spoken rather than sung their words (332). Tones can do this because, as directed tensions in auditory space, they encounter one another, relate to one another in determinate ways. As a result, simultaneous vocal lines preserve their independence precisely because they are perceived as continuous lines, dynamically ordered coursings that interpenetrate without disturbing each other's tonal careers. The words ride, as it were, on the coattails of tones. Thanks to tonal relations, simultaneous *verbal* relations are thereby secured. The possibility of such a thing never ceases to amaze.

As we have seen often, Zuckerkandl seeks to make music special among human experiences, different in point of cognition from other experiences, like that of ocular proof. But he doesn't want to leave it at that. Just as musical time does not exist in some other world, the same is true of space. Recalling the inquiries of

Gestalt psychology, Zuckerkandl affirms the ability of the eye to see, not only material objects in bodily space but also forces: "colors appear to possess dynamic qualities" (344). Zuckerkandl goes on to cite revolutions in the concept of space in modern physics, in which "the line between space and dynamic field becomes blurred like that between matter and energy" (346). The dynamic character of the visual field, first revealed by Gestalt psychology, "could also be applied to the space of modern physics."

The conclusion is clear: there is "*one* space, the space that encounters ear and eye as place and force" (346–47). Despite this oneness, however, music remains primary because it is more primordial: "the space of our hearing, space as force, would be *more primordial* in comparison with the space of our seeing, space as place—and not only in the temporal sense but also in the ontological sense: that of being closer to origins, more in correspondence with the primal nature of the real" (343).

The final problem that Zuckerkandl addresses in *Sound and Symbol* turns out to be quite thorny. It is the problem of pitch or range. In listening to a movement from one of Bach's cello suites, we are hearing more than dynamic qualities and rhythms. It matters to our musical experience that we are hearing a cello rather than a French horn, and that the cello at a particular moment is in its high, low, or middle register. Tone color and register matter, as does volume.[67] Zuckerkandl focuses on pitch because of its problematic relation to auditory space. If there are no places in this space, how are we to understand the meaning of terms like "high" and "low," "upward" and "downward"?

Zuckerkandl approaches the problem by distinguishing between relative and absolute "above" and "below." If I am inside my house, the roof is above me. If I stand on the roof, it is below. This is the nature of geometric space. But there is also the designation of "above" as a metaphysical region or realm that befits a being of a certain kind, a qualitative "above." He cites a line from Hölderlin: "Ye move above in the light . . . ye blessed Geniuses!" (356)[68] The "above," here, cannot be transformed by a shift of perspective into a "below." I cannot, from any perspective, look down on it. It is not quantitatively but qualitatively above. It is this qualitative difference in auditory space that for Zuckerkandl defines high and low tones.

It is obvious that in listening to the stratospheric tones of Mozart's Queen of the Night, we are not responding to high frequencies, except accidentally. We are hearing the high-pitched *quality* of her tones. The high bird-like pitches are integral to the spell she is using to dazzle the defenseless Tamino. The Queen is "above," in her haughty region. Zuckerkandl observes that there is no contradiction between excluding from music differences in spatial location while affirming a tonal "above" and "below" (358). A location in geometric space (determinable by means of three coordinates) is not the same as a qualitative region or realm of tonal space: "The place of the high tone is 'above,' that of the low tone 'below,' in the same sense that 'above' is the place of light, 'below' the place of dark" (358). The appeal to this qualitative spatiality in no way undercuts what we already know about a tone: that it sounds everywhere and is not confined to a place. The high-sounding Queen of the Night and low-sounding Sarastro sing in one and the same auditory space but in differently modified regions. To explain this admittedly difficult notion, Zuckerkandl recalls the earlier comment by Révész that musical space is "the space that becomes alive through sound" (359). He suggests that musical space "is *differently alive* in high and low tones . . . In the simultaneous sounding of all registers, then, space would encounter us in the totality of all possible modes of aliveness" (360).

Zuckerkandl warns against treating high and low in music as unambiguous symbols of a moral better and worse. The Queen, who is hardly good, sings in a very high, one might say celestial, register; and the good Sarastro sings way down low, one might say in the *inferni*.

The inquiry into musical space ends with a historical addendum on tonal direction. Zuckerkandl reminds us that direction upward is the normal direction of our music. He cites the way in which we sing the scale and give letter names to its degrees. Similarly, in the case of intervals, if no further specification is given, a fifth means a fifth *up*. For the Greeks, the situation was the reverse. Their scales were written and sung from the top down, and our fifth (C up to G) was for them a fourth (C down to G). The shift has an important bearing on how one understands a first principle, that is, an *arkhê* or source. For the Greeks, the "region" of the *arkhê* is above in Hölderlin's sense of the word. As we saw in the previous chapter, generation in the *Timaeus* proceeds, like a scale, from the highest down to the lowest things. For us, the *arkhê* is in the "region" below. It is something one builds on in order to ascend. One cannot help but think of a Gothic structure like the Cathédrale Notre-Dame de Chartres, whose arches and proportions draw eye and mind ever upward—a dynamic quality made of stone.

Summary and Prospect

In the culminating chapter of *Sound and Symbol*, Zuckerkandl sums up his goal, which I cited at the very beginning of our journey: to give, in outline, "a musical concept of the external world" (363). This concept is at odds with a modern view of the world that tends to reduce reality and human life to mechanics and technology. Music, however, is not aesthetic liberation. It does not give us access to a romantically conceived "better world." Music, for Zuckerkandl, is not the voice of another world but rather a mode of access to the world in which we live. It is a cognitive mode of being in touch with what is real, indeed most real. Because music is not physics, it challenges and calls into question the concepts and assumptions of the modern, physics-grounded view of the world. This is the clash with modernity that Zuckerkandl wishes to bring about (364).

Throughout our journey, we have seen that the concept of force is central to the understanding of music as a phenomenon. Force as directed tension is the prime *aisthêton* of music, the proper object of musical perception. A musical work is most accurately described as a play of forces, in which tones are not objects but states of a dynamic field (364). Tonal forces act, to be sure, through bodies (materially sounding pitches) but not upon them: "the physical event is here only the conveyor of the action; it is not itself the action" (365).

Music as a play of forces opens up a new way of experiencing the world and of understanding the three primitives that bind music and nature—motion, time, and space—now, all dynamically conceived. Motion in music is motion as such, pure moving with no moveable. It belongs neither to the inner world of the psyche nor to the materially existing world but to "the third stage." This third stage is not a Beyond. It is rather the stage on which we experience the external world's internal transcendence. Body and tone belong to one and the same world, in which we find "two equally real, interpenetrating modes of existence" (366). Tones are superior to bodies in this respect: they "open a view that bodies obstruct" (367).

Music obliges us to broaden our view of nature. No longer confined to the Cartesian, mathematically governed realm defined by Heidegger as "the closed kinetic context of mass points in space and time relations,"[69] nature is seen to have through music an inner life, a kind of soul that animates and enchants the external world. Zuckerkandl sums this up in a simple way: *Music, too, is nature*" (367).

Zuckerkandl now turns to the subject-object relation in music. Inner and outer world, he reminds us, "meet in melodies." But they do more than meet: they "penetrate each other" (368). As I mentioned in my previous chapter, whereas the act of seeing posits distance, that of hearing posits intimacy, the overcoming of distance: "Tone penetrates into me, overflows the barrier, makes me conscious not of distance but of communication, even of participation" (368). This is the work of the third stage, which breaks the wall between listening subject and tonal object. Hearing tones is not a listening toward but a being with, even an identifying with. In listening to music, I am the music. The third stage, however, does not obliterate the distinction of subject and object (369). It is not the annihilating intimacy that Wagner's Tristan and Isolde seek. The encounter between inner and outer must be conceived dynamically, as a reciprocal flow between the poles of subject and object.

The curious encounter of listener and tone, subject and object, has important consequences for self-consciousness, my aware-ness of myself as self. In listening to music, tones come into their own by reaching me, partaking of my subjectivity. Correlatively, through tones I experience my inner world as object, as some-thing external and therefore real. It is the dynamic of a mutual gifting: "music brings to expression the mode of existence of the world that is the same nature as my 'within,' my psyche . . . in our encounter with tones, we are conscious of our self as immaterial living being" (370). To translate this thought into the language of Plato and Aristotle, music gives me direct experiential proof that I have a soul.

Music, for this same reason, has world-disclosing significance. Just as instrumental music, "nothing but tones," is the realm of pure motion, it is also the realm of pure meaning (371), where "meaning" means, not a particular meaning or meanings, but meaningfulness—what Roger Scruton calls "pure aboutness."[70] Through the power of tones, the external world "gives up its secret and manifests itself, immediately, as *symbol*." In other words, the external world is revealed as the material host and home of imma-terial tending. This is perhaps most simply understood as active persistence in space and time—the universal *conatus* or striving of all things to be and to become. In tones, saying and meaning escape the man-made-ness, the convention, of words and exist "*by nature*." They reveal the inner life—what might be called the *soul*—of the external world: "Because they are audibly meaningful by nature, tones hold up for our perception, as real, a dimension of the world that transcends all individual distinctions of things and therefore all verbal language" (372).

Zuckerkandl notes in passing that force in music is not a mere operational concept, as it might be regarded in physics. Whereas natural phenomena could conceivably be explained without reference to the concept of force (which, in physics, is theoretically postulated), "in music there would be hardly anything left to describe if force had to be excluded from the discussion. Force is as real as music itself" (372). It is curious, Zuckerkandl observes, that force can be doubted by physics but is "certain beyond any doubt" in the world of tones.[71]

But does this animism, this apparent attribution of spirit and soul to external nature, not represent a relapse into prescientific modes of thought? Zuckerkandl admits that his view of music and nature "much more nearly resembles the magical and mythical ideas of primitive or prehistoric peoples than it does the scientific conceptions of modern man" (374). He insists, however, that his path leads forward, not backward, and that "the goal remains knowledge, understanding." The goal is not primitivism but the raising of music "to the dignity of a problem for the questioning mind."[72]

Finally, Zuckerkandl returns to the question of God. He reminds us that the musical view of the universe differs from the religious view in not being based on faith, and that the immaterial element of nature is not God (374). He leaves open, however, the possibility that music might provide "a bridge between the scientific and the religious views." What that bridge might consist in, he does not say. Nor does he clarify what he thinks is or might be the nature of God. He rejects pantheism ("nature as the visible incarnation of the invisible Deity"), on the grounds that "the invisible is no more divine than the visible" (375). This, of course, excludes the idea of a transcendent God. The exclusion fits Zuckerkandl's claim that God, in order to experience music, must be in time (151). In any case, Zuckerkandl immediately backs away from theology, as if in fear of transgressing the boundaries of the natural. He retreats to the sense in which the universe embodies the immaterial, not as God but as the *meaning* we find in tonal dynamism—meaning as tending and striving to be. This is a "pansymbolic rather than pantheistic" view of the universe (375).

In his final remarks, Zuckerkandl reminds us that his focus has been, not great works of music, but the conditions for the possibility of music—any kind of music, even "rubbish." The focus has been music and nature. But what of music as an art capable of producing Bach's preludes and fugues, Mozart's operas, and Beethoven's late quartets? Do these tonal masterworks have a superadded cognitive value, a higher relation to truth?

Zuckerkandl answers this question with a bold claim about art in general: "Art does not aim at beauty; it *uses* beauty—occasionally; on other occasions it uses ugliness. Art—no less than philosophy or science or religion—aims ultimately at knowledge, truth" (376). On this point, he appeals to Heidegger, who calls art the "working-itself-out of truth."[73] The composer, Zuckerkandl claims, thinks in tones (377). This thinking is a path to truth. But what kind of truth? What can truth mean in a non-representational, non-verbal medium, in which tones point only to other tones? And how are we to distinguish truth from untruth "in tones"? Who are *we* who seek meaning and truth in music? With these questions, Zuckerkandl reaches an end that is also a new beginning. *Sound and Symbol* becomes a dynamic quality that points beyond itself to a set of tasks to be taken up in the second volume. Its title is *Man the Musician*.

Closing Thoughts: Music and Nature Revisited

As an epigraph to *Sound and Symbol*, Zuckerkandl cites Friedrich Schelling on the goal of explanation: "First and above all, an explanation must do justice to the thing that is to be explained, must not devalue it, interpret it away, belittle it, or garble it, in order to

make it easier to understand." In his discussion of musical primitives—motion, time, and space—Zuckerkandl aims at precisely
this goal. He offers an account of music that is faithful to music
as we experience it. He poses questions few would think to ask
and pursues them with insight and imagination. And he persua-
sively grounds the meaning and connectedness of tonal music in
directed tension. To listen to tonal music is to perceive a play of
forces. It is to hear and enjoy expectancy, digression, surprise, and
eventual gratification—the ingredients of a story and an adventure. All this is made possible by the directedness, the *sense*, of
tones as dynamic qualities.

As we have seen, *in Sound and Symbol* Zuckerkandl aims to
do more than explain tonal music. His goal is a musical cosmology, a musical concept of nature and of the external world. With a
few major modifications, his view is that of Leibniz and Schopenhauer. Nature at its deepest level is force. For Leibniz, force is an
object of the understanding and scientific study; for Zuckerkandl,
it is directly intuited in music. For Schopenhauer, force is ultimately the noumenal will; for Zuckerkandl, it is simply will-like.

In my closing remarks I wish to recall the *Timaeus*, which I
discussed in the previous chapter. Its musical-mathematical cosmology will help us determine some important limitations of
Zuckerkandl's dynamic view of music and nature.

Whereas Zuckerkandl identifies nature with force, Pythagorean Timaeus grounds nature and cosmos in number (*arithmos*) as
an assemblage of units. Number, for Timaeus, is the principle of
the ratios that form the scale of the world-soul and of the regular
solids that form the elements of the world-body.[74] It is the ground
of cosmic intelligibility and beauty. Number mediates between the
purely intelligible Ideas and the sensed realm of body. Through
number, change partakes of what is changeless and most divine.

Time, on this view, is a principle of stability and self-sameness. It is not a force but a pattern, the order of recurring motions
beheld in the heavens. Time is the cosmic clock: the measure of

motion and the moving image of eternally self-same Being. This conception of time belongs to what Zuckerkandl dismisses as "the old preference of philosophers for what is at rest, for what is removed beyond change" (261).

The basis of Timaeus's musical cosmology is the Pythagorean discovery that connects the most basic musical intervals with ratios of the smallest whole numbers. For the Pythagoreans, intervals are sensed ratios, and the music of the spheres and of nature in general is firmly grounded in mathematics and the inherent goodness of intellect. The mathematical bond between music and nature gains further support from the modern discovery of the overtone series. Every vibrating body that produces a tone also gives rise to an infinite series of overtones, each produced by a vibrating part of the sounding whole. These ghost tones are made prominent when harmonics are played on a guitar. The overtone series recapitulates the Pythagorean ratios. It also points to the primacy of the major mode, since the first and strongest tones in the series outline the major triad.

Of course, Zuckerkandl knows about all this and explains it lucidly in *The Sense of Music* (67–72). But the Pythagorean view of nature and its modern counterpart in the overtone series play no role in his theory of music. They dwell for him in the pre-musical, material region of mere pitches. It might seem strange that Zuckerkandl does not appeal to the overtone series as providing a natural basis for the major scale, the scale that highlights dynamic qualities.[75] Yet because Zuckerkandl rejects all scientific explanations of music as he understands it, his aversion to ratios and overtones makes sense. To be sure, Zuckerkandl acknowledges the mathematics of material sounding as the precondition for music. But he consigns this to the realm of what Timaeus would call Necessity.[76] It reveals nothing about music as music, since it deals with pitches rather than tones in the strict sense. Nor does it reach the inner truth of nature. For Timaeus, this inner truth consists in the beautiful mathematical structure of the cosmic soul and body.

For Zuckerkandl, it resides in force as tension. Whereas Timaeus affirms the bond between truth and Being, Zuckerkandl (in agreement with Bergson) identifies reality with Becoming and flux.

Now Zuckerkandl is right to the extent that intervals and their corresponding ratios cannot account for the directed tensions and the resulting motion we perceive in tonal music. But an interval nevertheless has a distinctive character that is independent of context. A perfect fifth sounds resonant and stable, and a third sounds either bright or dark, depending on whether it is major or minor. Resonant fifth and bright third combine to form the major triad. Intervals as such are musically meaningful, not just in tonal harmony but in all music. They form the basis of the rules of counterpoint or voice leading. These rules, which govern the succession of intervals, are the conditions for smooth, natural sounding movement. Moreover, they ensure that two or more simultaneously sounding parts not only fit together or harmonize but also maintain their individuality. To these ends, the rules prohibit parallel fifths and encourage contrary motion (parts moving in opposite directions).[77] Such rules are beautifully at work in the pre-tonal world of *Sicut cervus*. Intervals, no less than dynamic qualities, exhibit Zuckerkandl's internal transcendence. Their sound is a form, a relating, that cannot be reduced to the frequencies of two different pitches. The oscilloscope is deaf to dynamic quality. But it is also deaf to the distinctive musical sound of an interval.

To sum up, the *Timaeus*, in its marvelously mythic way, reminds us that a musical concept of nature cannot dispense with the natural grounding of music in the Pythagorean ratios and their later extension in the overtone series. Number is a bond between music and nature, and a cause of the world's beautiful order.

As we have seen, the dynamic qualities of tonal music are not theoretical entities but objects of direct perception. A raised $\hat{7}$ *feels* tense because it *is* tense. Are these forces there in the external world? It seems they are, regardless of whether we agree with Zuckerkandl that they give us access to the core of the world. As

I observed at the end of the previous chapter, listening to music of all kinds, not just tonal harmonic music, is an openness to the world and to ourselves as listeners. Tones come to us and address us. They penetrate and invade us, sometimes against our will (as in elevator music). In tones, the world speaks to us. It sings of a this-world that is nevertheless beyond bodily being, a world that is like us: inward, alive, striving. In tonal harmonic music, the world sings a song of *vis viva*, living force.

//////////////

As Zuckerkandl reminds us, once tones are liberated from words and actions, they can be joined to them once more in a new and potent way. In the following two chapters, I explore the marriage of words and tones in two arias, one by Bach and one by Mozart. Both are musical reflections on love: divine love and human romantic love, respectively.

CHAPTER THREE

The Power of Song in
Bach's *St. Matthew Passion*

> This week I attended three performances of the *St. Matthew
> Passion* by the divine Bach, with the same feeling each time
> of immense wonder. For someone who has totally given
> it up, Christianity here truly does sound like a gospel.
>
> The young Nietzsche, letter to a friend (1870),
> from *Nietzsche and Music* by Georges Liébert

My theme in this chapter is the power of song in Bach's "great Passion," as the *St. Matthew Passion* was called by members of the Bach family.[1] I shall focus on an aria that appears at an advanced stage of the drama: *"Aus Liebe will mein Heiland sterben,"* "Out of love is my Savior willing to die" (#58).[2] It is sung by a soprano and is in the key of A minor. My goal is to reflect on how the power of this aria can be made to appear through attention to its simplest elements. More broadly, it is to reflect on the world as seen, or rather heard, from the perspective of Bach's Christian faith made into music.[3]

The arias of Bach's *St. Matthew Passion* are the most stunning evocations of passion in the work. In moving us powerfully, they provoke our wonder. What is music that it can move us so? What is the relation here between words and tones? What role do our passions play in *the* Passion as depicted by Bach? What does Bach's music contribute to our understanding of Christ's suffering and death? Before turning to the aria and to these difficult questions,

81

I shall attempt a brief introduction to Bach's "great Passion" as a whole.

The *St. Matthew Passion* is astounding, even by Bach's standards. It is a several-hours-long musical drama that depicts, expands, and comments on two chapters from Matthew's Gospel (26 and 27), starting with Jesus's foretelling of the crucifixion and ending with Pilate's placement of guards at the tomb. The original version of the work was first performed in 1727 on Good Friday in Leipzig's St. Thomas Church, where Bach was organist. The revised version that we know today was first performed in 1736. The work consists of various kinds of music: large-scale choruses, chorales (harmonized Lutheran hymn tunes), elaborate arias often preceded by a recitativo, and narrative sections in which the Evangelist and the characters in the drama sing the words of Matthew's text in German. The Evangelist is a tenor, and Jesus a bass.

Supporting this vast web of vocal music is the orchestra. Bach uses a double orchestra consisting of two choruses (as they are called). Sometimes he brings all the instruments together, as in the opening number, to create a whole cosmos of sound. At other times, notably in the arias, a lone instrument—now the flute, now the violin, now the oboe—steps forward like a wordless singer, whose tones intertwine with those of the soloist. This fusion of voices and instruments invites us to enter the Passion as told by Matthew in order to experience it in a new way—a way opened by the power of tones in time.[4]

The opening Chorus of the *Passion* comes at us in waves. Its massive undulation sweeps us up in a stately lament in 12/8 time. Bach uses a double chorus, which makes the piece sound epic and stereophonic. The first chorus represents the Daughters of Zion, who in turn represent Jerusalem; the second represents the Community of the Faithful, in other words, the contemporary congregation. The Daughters of Zion exhort the Community to join them in their sorrow, to become one of them. "Come, you Daughters," they sing, "Help me lament!"[5]

The Chorus is in the key of E minor. We hear an extended orchestral opening, in which the entire universe seems to pulse in passi onate recognition of Jesus as Bridegroom and sacrificial Lamb. It features an extended pedal point on E, which, combined with the relentless dotted rhythm, has the sound of a cosmic heartbeat:

There follows a chorus that sings with a sad vigor in four-part counterpoint, as each part goes its own way in imitation of a confused crowd. Then we hear a dialogue between the Daughters of Zion and the Community of the Faithful, as the first group points to Jesus and the second asks questions: "Behold!" "Whom?" "The

Bridegroom. See him." "How?" "Like a Lamb." Then a third choir enters, unexpectedly—a boys' choir. The pure voices of children float on high, as if from the heavens, down upon the surging tide of all the adult complexity and confusion. The boys sing a hymn tune known to the congregation and in G major, the relative major of E minor. Our ears are grateful for this dawning of familiar simplicity and light upon the scene of so much dark turbulence.[6] The straightforward, unharmonized hymn tune reminds the congregation that what they are hearing is designed not just to impress and please, but to reach the hearts of the faithful and to make them participants in the drama.

This music is relentless in its surge and complexity. It is the sound of a depth that continually rises to the heavens. The opening melodic gesture of the adult chorus is a grand upward sweep, as the sopranos scale the ladder of the E minor triad, spelling out, as it were, the elements of grief. To recall a distinction made by Simone Weil, the opening chorus combines gravity and grace. The listener is pulled, sometimes simultaneously, in opposite directions, as Bach combines dark and bright, complex and simple, exotic and familiar, somber and joyous, bitter and sweet.[7]

Paradox is at work in the very rhythm of the opening Chorus. Like many numbers in the *St. Matthew Passion*, it is a dance: a siciliano. This is a dignified, swaying dance in compound meter. Closely related to the pastorale, the siciliano probably originated in the wedding celebrations of Italian peasants. This opening siciliano is in 12/8 time. Each measure contains four principal beats, each consisting of three sub-beats. The result is a rocking rhythm that goes like this: **1**-2-3, **2**-2-3, **3**-2-3, **4**-2-3; **1**-2-3, **2**-2-3, **3**-2-3, **4**-2-3. The rhythm works curiously on our souls. At the very beginning of the chorus, the underlying bass pulses deep down, somewhere at the bottom of the cosmos. It is the heartbeat of a world in lament. But at the same time, we are carried along gracefully, as we sway to a robust lullaby in 12/8 time. Even as we lament and are made awake to grief, we are lulled and soothed. As the two choruses begin their dialogue about the Bridegroom (mm. 34–35), the siciliano is magically transformed into what seems like a waltz. In the chorus with which Bach begins his *St. Matthew Passion*, in its gravity and grace, we experience an event that is both wedding and funeral. The union of opposites is perfectly suited to the Bridegroom who died for our sins.

∕∕∕∕∕∕∕∕∕∕∕

Whereas the text of Bach's *St. John Passion* has for its backbone the Gospel narrative, here in the *St. Matthew Passion* that role is played by the madrigal poems that provided Bach with the text for his arias.[8] These poems were written by Bach's librettist, who went by the name of Picander.[9] The two men worked together closely on integrating them into the ambitious whole that Bach envisaged.[10]

Before turning to *"Aus Liebe,"* let us enter the drama. Bach presents Matthew's Passion story as divided into scenes. These are living pictures, *tableaux vivants*, which may be compared to the Stations of the Cross. The arias are musical meditations on these sacred tableaus. They are musical perspectives in which a solitary singer, who is not part of Matthew's story, connects with the story in a way that is personally intimate and representative of all faithful listeners. The arias, as I observed earlier, are expressions of passion. But as musical meditations they are also a means by which the events in Matthew's story become objects of thought.

In the tableau on which *"Aus Liebe"* meditates, Jesus, having been arrested, stands before Pilate, who asks the crowd which of these two men he should release, Barabbas or Jesus. Bach's music raises our hopes with the prospect of a glorious cadence in D major—the triumphant key of the *Magnificat*, the *Easter Oratorio*, and the *"Et resurrexit"* from the *Mass in B Minor*. It is the cadence that would have been appropriate if the crowd had shouted "Jesus!" But the bright glory of D major fails to arrive. Instead, Bach assaults us with a shocking musical deception, as the crowd yells *"Barrabam!"* with an alarmingly dissonant diminished seventh chord, which is composed of two interlocking tritones (D-sharp and A, C and F-sharp):

Then Pilate asks: "What shall I do with Jesus?" The crowd responds: "Let him be crucified!" They sing a demonic, evil-sounding fugue in A minor, the key of our upcoming aria. The fugue, we must note for later reference, features the flute. The crucifixion fugue derives its power from a conspiracy of rhythm and interval. The fugue subject is a violent upward thrust that mimics the hoisting of Jesus upon the Cross and uses the dark, disjointed-sounding interval of the diminished fourth on the first syllable of "crucify." This fourth, which occurs between G-sharp (the raised $\hat{7}$ of A minor) and C, is followed by a tritone (a diminished fifth between D-sharp and A) and then another (less prominent) diminished fourth between F-sharp and B-flat:

In this demonic sound, with its wrenching syncopation on the first syllable of the word for "crucify," we hear more than the act of crucifixion. There is also the hideous pleasure that the crowd takes in the imagining of the act and that the music compels us to share. The fugue will return, to our horror, after the soprano has sung her quiet song of love.

After the first appearance of this fugue, the mood changes abruptly, as the chorus, representing the congregation, contemplates what they have just witnessed. They do so with a familiar hymn tune that has appeared twice before in the drama (#3 and #25). The opening of this chorale has one of the most tension-filled harmonizations in all the chorales in the *St. Matthew Passion*. It is a Bachic transformation of the familiar into the otherworldly. The chorus sings not of grief, or shock, or remorse, or indignation, but of wonder at the mystery that confronts them: "*Wie wunderbarlich ist doch diese Strafe*," "How wondrous indeed is this sentence [that has been passed on Jesus]!"[11] They sing of Jesus as the Good Shepherd, who suffers for his sheep. As we return, very briefly, to the narrative, Pilate asks, "But what evil has he done?" The question hovers, as a soprano steps forward to offer her musical answer.

The recitative, with its limping accompaniment played by oboes, strikes a pastoral note.[12] Echoing the preceding chorale, it puts us in the presence of Jesus as shepherd. The soprano sings about all the *good* that Jesus has done, how he has ministered to the blind, the lame, the possessed, the afflicted, the sinful. "Apart from this," the soprano sings, "he has done nothing," *nichts*.[13] The recitative begins in E minor, the key in which the *Passion* begins. In its orchestration and slow limping rhythm, it foreshadows the bizarre Golgotha music that we hear later (#69). The soprano ends her recitative with a gentle cadence in C major. She then sings the most hauntingly contemplative aria in the whole work. It is in A minor: the key in which Jesus dies (#71).[14]

The text of "*Aus Liebe*" consists of a single sentence. In translation, it reads as follows:

> Out of love is my Savior willing to die
> Though of any sin he knows nothing,
> So that eternal damnation
> And the sentence of judgment
> May not rest upon my soul.[15]

The aria is in the usual ABA form. In the first A section, we hear the opening of the sentence, the part about love as the wellspring of the sacrifice, and about the absolute innocence of Jesus.

Then, in the middle or B section, we hear about the purpose of the sacrifice: saving sinful man from judgment. The opening of the sentence then returns in the second A section. In this circular arrangement of the text, God's love for man and the innocence of Jesus frame the central part about saving man from a just retribution. Here, then, is the sequence of clauses in the aria:

> Out of love is my Savior willing to die,
> Though of any sin he knows nothing,
> So that eternal damnation
> And the sentence of judgment
> May not rest upon my soul.
> Out of love is my Savior willing to die,
> Though of any sin he knows nothing.

Thanks to this circular ABA form, the aria ends where it began, with an emphasis on Jesus's profound innocence, in which we see reflected our profound guilt. The last word of the aria is *nichts*, nothing. The word brings us back to Pilate's question, "But what evil has he done?" and to the spectacle of the unjustly condemned Savior.

How far removed the music of this aria is from the grand sweep of the opening chorus, or the consoling warmth of the chorales, or the high drama of parts of the narrative! The soprano, here, sounds lonely and bereft. Indeed, her song is the musical embodiment of bereftness. As the flute sings its plaintive song and sets the tone for the aria, we are transported to a sparse musical universe. The lushness of strings is withheld. Even more striking is the absence of the usual continuo part played by the organ or harpsichord and cello (or viola da gamba). In place of this continuo, Bach substitutes the spare duet of oboes.[16] The music seems to have no foundation, no ground, deeper than itself. In sharp contrast with the surging depths of the opening Chorus, the music floats like a pure spirit in the upper regions of sound. The suggestion may be that the love of which the soprano sings rests on nothing but itself and has no bottom.

In what follows, I shall point out and interpret various technical aspects of the aria. I shall try to keep the technical language to a minimum and to clarify musical terms as I go along. As I mentioned at the beginning, my goal is to explore how the power of the soprano's meditation derives from the simplest, most accessible musical elements.

The aria is in moderately slow 3/4 time. For the most part, the oboes in the accompaniment mark off the principal beats of the measure and play intervals of thirds and sixths. The aria is also on a small scale. All we hear at first is the sound of a flute accompanied by the two oboes (the oboes here being the equivalent of our modern English horns). Once the soprano enters, there will be a total of only four voices: a duet between soprano and flute, accompanied by a duet of oboes. The aria, in short, is all breath and nothing more—*pneuma*, which in Greek is both breath and spirit. The musical expenditure of breath has a withheld quality, as though it were constantly being taken in rather than let out, or rather as though it were being rationed. This is most evident in the halting staccato accompaniment of the oboes, which only occasionally distinguish themselves with more flowing, dotted rhythms.[17] Bereftness and desolation are conveyed in the bare key signature of A minor, which has no sharps or flats. Finally, perhaps what is most significant, the aria is not a dance.

It is worth dwelling on this point. There are sixteen arias in the *St. Matthew Passion* (counting the duet between Soprano 1 and Alto 1). All of them, with the sole exception of "*Aus Liebe*," either are dances or else are animated by marked rhythms that suggest a body in motion. Sometimes the rhythms are smooth and flowing, in imitation of the many fluids that course through the text: precious ointment, water, tears, blood, wine. Sometimes they are jagged, dotted rhythms, with which the singer seems to take up the

Cross (#65). At the Last Supper, as Jesus moves from the bread that is his body to the wine that is his blood, he sings a song that is also a dance—his only aria in the work. The song is like wine. It exudes warmth and majesty, as it flows to the flexible rhythms of a courante in 6/4 time. This is a courtly French dance, whose very name means running or flowing. In response to this majestic song and dance, the very same soprano who sings *"Aus Liebe"* here regales us with the lightest, swiftest, most beguiling dance-aria in the entire work (#19). The vertiginous gaiety of her song, whose 6/8 rhythm both mirrors and quickens Jesus's 6/4, makes her sound tipsy, as though she has gotten drunk on the French wine of which Jesus sang.[18]

In *"Aus Liebe"* we hear none of this. Dance rhythm is suspended, as the soprano sings the purest aria in the *Passion*, a song that is purely song. To be sure, there is rhythmic life and an underlying 3/4 pulse. But these are in the service of something sung rather than danced. One effect is a greater concentration on the words, which are both adorned and laid bare by the tones. Another is that we are not so much moved forward as held in a seemingly timeless moment.

The opening song of the flute is haunting. It is like music from another world. The sound somehow captures a warmth and a chill. The flute steps out of the silence with a lone quarter note, a relatively long time-value given the numerous sixteenth-notes in the piece. We feel anchored, stabilized by this upbeat that ascends a perfect fifth from tone $\hat{1}$ to tone $\hat{5}$ in the scale of A minor. Soon we begin to flow, as sixteenth-note scales, occasionally adorned with chromatic tones, cast a spell that is at once exotic and restrained, passionate and chaste. The opening phrase is especially beautiful, with its eloquent upward leap of a minor sixth from E to C, and appoggiaturas or leaning tones on either side. Tension mounts, as Bach takes us through a carefully controlled sequence of melodic phrases and underlying chords starting in the fifth measure.[19]

In the eleventh measure, there is a striking rhetorical gesture.

The music builds to a climax but then pauses at the fermata on an unresolved diminished triad, the VII of A minor. The pulse is suspended, breath held, and the listener is left hanging. A brief, limping cadenza brings us back to the marking of time, at which point the flute sings an impassioned flourish of thirty-second and sixteenth notes. After this burst of passion, the flute regains composure and returns to its former restraint. The spare trio of flute and oboes reaches its cadence in the home key of A minor. The built-up tension is at last released, only to build up again as the soprano enters and sings her song.

In "*Aus Liebe*," these fermatas, or interruptions of measured time, are not like the fermatas we find in other arias. Elsewhere in the *Passion*, fermatas are no more than markers that signal the transition from one section of music to the next. Here, in "*Aus Liebe*," they are internal to the musical phrases and are integral to the song's haunting beauty.[20] They recur throughout the aria (notably, at the end of the word *sterben*, "die), always at points where tension has built up and we are left suspended in a not-yet-finished cadence. It is as though, having taken in a long slow breath, we are then made to hold it before being allowed to let it out. The sparse, halting accompaniment, with its emphasis on the principal beats of the 3/4 measure, enhances this continual sense of breath withheld and time suspended.[21]

Bach's arias often feature a solo instrument that plays an obbligato part, that is, a solo part that cannot be omitted. Here, that part is entrusted to the flute, the breathiest of instruments. Through kinship with the pipes of Pan and the god Dionysus, the flute has associations with the erotic, the intoxicated, the ecstatic. What Bach does with this instrument in the *St. Matthew Passion* takes our breath away. The flute appears at key moments of the drama: when the high priests plot to arrest Jesus (#5); when the disciples chide the woman at Bethany (#7); when the crowd sings its crucifixion fugue (#54, #59). In these moments, Bach takes full advantage of the flute's power to summon the shrill demons of frenzy and mindlessness. But flutes are present in other contexts as well: when the alto, in the first aria of the work, sings of repentance and remorse (#10); when the soprano sings of the bleeding heart (#12); when the soprano and alto sing their duet in response to the arrest and binding of Jesus (#33). And at the final moment of unsettling consummation, as we reach the end of the *St. Matthew Passion*, we hear the flute. On the strong beat of the last measure, on the word *Ruh* ("rest"), the flute leaps upward and pierces the orchestra with a shocking dissonance—a B-natural that eventually resolves to the root of the C-minor triad with which the drama ends (#78). In this crowning appoggiatura or leaning tone, Bach sums up the whole Passion: the suffering of divine love as the ultimate expenditure of breath. The flute's dissonant lean is also a symbol of our longing for the resolution that only the Passion can accomplish: the removal of our guilt and the final rest of a tormented conscience. Never was so ordinary a musical device invested with such profound meaning.[22]

In *"Aus Liebe,"* the counter-song of the flute is like a ghost that haunts the musical space in which the soprano dwells. The flute's wordless song establishes a mood of sublime desolation. It transports the listener to a musical wasteland where some unbelievably exotic flower is in bloom. The pure but breathy tones of the flute make clear to us that the song we are about to hear is a love song. Eros, we might say, is summoned in order to be purified, purged of his self-seeking carnality.[23] The unearthly sound of the flute, with its breathy intimations of the erotic, and the soprano's song of love, are powerful reminders of the image with which the *St. Matthew Passion* began, that of Jesus as Bridegroom and beloved.

The singer is not part of the story. She must nevertheless be imagined as within the time of the drama she beholds. As Jesus suffers, so does she, reflectively. The falsely accused Bridegroom stands before her, as Pilate asks his question: "But what evil has he done?" After answering that question in her recitative, the soprano proceeds to sing of the love that is the source of everything that has happened, and will happen, in the Passion. "Out of love," her song begins, "*Aus Liebe*," as she reiterates the flute's quarter-note upbeat. Her melody resembles that of the flute but is less florid and more restrained.

Restraint is in her very words. Other arias in the *Passion* are either prayers or strong personal affirmations. These are often marked by an emphatic *ich will*, "I will," where *will* (from *wollen*) is not the future tense but an expression of resolve and willingness. In these arias, the singer is personally part of what the song is about. In the "tipsy" aria I mentioned earlier, the soprano sings to Jesus, "I will give you my heart as a gift" and "I will immerse myself in you" (#19); the tenor, in response to Jesus in Gethsemane sings, "I will stand watch by my Jesus" (#26); and in the very last aria the bass sings, "I will myself bury Jesus" (#75). In "*Aus Liebe*," the soprano refers to "my Savior" and "my soul." But beyond these fleeting if important moments of self-reference, the song is not about the subjective state, the resolve or willingness, of the singer. Neither prayer nor personal affirmation, it is the direct statement of a fact, the most wondrous fact the world has ever known, that Jesus, as the incarnation of divine love, submitted to a grossly unjust sentence (he "stood in" for man) so that the just sentence of eternal damnation would not fall upon us.[24] The song is not about the will of the singer but about the loving will of God. In this respect, too, "*Aus Liebe*" is remarkable for its purity.

Another element of restraint is the absence of metaphor. Picander's madrigal poems are sometimes wildly metaphoric. Tears are transformed into an adornment for the Savior (#10); a child nourished by Jesus becomes a treacherous serpent (#12); sins fall asleep (#26); the Lamb is caught in a tiger's claws (#36); false tongues wound (#41); the heart weeps (#47); sinful humanity is a group of forsaken chicks (#70); and the cold grave becomes the loving heart in which Jesus is laid to rest (#75). In "*Aus Liebe*," there are no metaphors. Even the image of the Good Shepherd, which appeared in the preceding chorale, is present only in the pastoral sound of the speechless oboes. What the soprano has to say here she says directly, without images. She gives passionate utterance to a theological doctrine.

It should be noted that the aria is not much of a melody. It is not a catchy tune that sticks in the mind. Its enchantment lies elsewhere. Many of the other arias in the *Passion* are very catchy indeed, in large part due to their dance-like rhythms. Not so with *"Aus Liebe,"* which has a rhapsodic, free-floating sound that reminds us of the formal recitativos that often precede an aria. The soprano begins by imitating the quarter-note upbeat with which the flute began the piece. But instead of going up a perfect fifth from A to E, she starts on the E and holds this single note for a very long time. This is followed by a somber melisma or vocalizing on the first syllable of the word *Liebe*, love. The held opening note conveys constancy, in imitation of the constancy of divine love. The melisma seems to float and wander, like a torn garment blowing in the wind, and yet in some curious way also to stand still. The soprano's melody line is in fact not easy to recall or reproduce. The comfy cushion of tunefulness has been removed in yet another instance of bereftness. The melody makes the soprano sound exposed. This is a manifest identification with Jesus, who has just been exposed to judgment. And, as I suggested earlier, this quiet imitation of lonely exposure is expository in another sense: by dampening musical elements that are prominent elsewhere, Bach deputizes the soprano to reveal the doctrinal core of Jesus's sacrifice. Jesus came to suffer and die, not merely because a debt had to be paid and only God could pay it, but because God loves man and desires to save him from the fate he deserves. That God alone can save fallen man is heard and felt in the soprano's lonely sound.

Word, tone, and rhythm are all carefully coordinated. The soprano sings her opening phrase: "Out of love is my Savior willing to die." She holds the word *Liebe*, love, for a long time, an entire measure, as the counter-song of the flute keeps the rhythm fluid.

She sings the phrase "out of love" three times: "Out of love, out of love, *out of love* is my Savior willing to die." No mere repetition, it serves to intensify the meaning of the words:

Bach gives the word *sterben*, die, a special rhetorical emphasis. The soprano stretches out the first syllable of the word, just as she had stretched out the first syllable of the word *Liebe*. (See the score at the top of the next page.) In the middle of the first syllable of *sterben* and on the last beat of the measure (m. 22), she sinks chromatically from a C-sharp to a C-natural. This chromatic going down on "die" adds a sad poignancy to the word. Having leaped up to an F-sharp, the tritone above C, the soprano outlines the falling degrees of a diminished seventh chord on D-sharp, recalling the dissonances in the *Passion* that are associated with the Cross. The chord is a so-called *secondary dominant* (symbolized as "vii of V"). It adds considerable tension to the upcoming half cadence (the musical equivalent of a question). As the soprano approaches the end of the word *sterben* with this sinking and falling, she pauses on one of the literally breathtaking fermatas that occur through-

out the piece. The note on which she pauses is G-sharp, the raised $\hat{7}$ of A minor and the note of the scale that has maximum tension. Harmonically, too, we are in suspense, since this G-sharp is part of a not-yet-resolved dominant seventh chord—the chord that points most strongly to the tonic chord, in this case the A-minor triad. Time is arrested, and in that moment of suspense we feel the weight of what has just been said. We feel an emptiness that offers a foretaste of the word *nichts*, nothing, in the very next phrase. What does this beautiful nothing signify?

To begin with, Jesus himself is at this moment bereft. There is no one to save him from what he has willingly taken on. The sentence of crucifixion has just fallen like a hammer from the lips of the crowd, or rather has risen like a hook. Pilate washes his hands and Jesus' fate is sealed. The true agony of the Passion is now about to begin. Throughout the *Passion* we are made to feel a deep personal relation to Jesus, who is very often referred to as "my Jesus." This intimacy is most present in the arias. Here in Aria 58 the bare, lonely sound captures the terrifying vulnerability of Jesus. It also captures the profound awareness of this vulnerability by the singer, who speaks and feels for all. The nothingness or bereftness we hear is no mere expression of emotion. It is that but also much more. The lonely sound is the singer's effort to identify with Jesus, to be one with the act of divine love, which empties itself of all self-withholding,[25] all guardedness, all celestial safety. The aria is the sound of love as self-divestment, love as sacrifice.[26] The loneliness we hear is an emptiness that is filled with this love. It is the sound of Love incarnate.

The sound of self-divestment, self-emptying, is highlighted by the word for nothing, *nichts*, which sounds like the spending of breath. The soprano repeats this word with a strong rhetorical gesture as she goes from a B-natural up to an F-natural, that is, through the dissonance of a tritone. Jesus has done nothing, *nothing*, to merit what is happening to him. We are in mid-sentence at this point, just as we reach the soprano's first full cadence. That cadence is in C major, the relative key of A minor and the key that was prepared by the previous tritone. Here we reach the serene and lucid center of the aria, as the words take us from Jesus's willingness to suffer an unjust death sentence to the purpose for which he did this: "So that eternal damnation / And the sentence of judgment / May not rest upon my soul." The sound of C major momentarily transforms the desolate A minor music of the opening into something serene and pastoral. It is like the gentle smile of divine love that emerges from within all the abandonment and accusation Jesus has suffered. It is as though Jesus, the Good Shepherd on whom the death sentence has just fallen, turns to the soprano at this point and gently smiles at her as the representative of fallen Man. The pastoral smile of C major seems to say: "This is why I have done what I have done: for you, my beloved."

The soprano now makes a new beginning. Her opening rhythm emphasizes two quarter-note upbeats. These quarter notes give her line even more a sense of standing in place rather than moving on. The sense of a firm stand is also conveyed by the two quarter notes that repeat the same tone (G), and by the two German words that sound identical: *daß das*. She holds the first syllable of *ewige*, eternal, for slightly more than an entire measure, in candid enactment of the meaning of this word. It echoes the other opening word that was drawn out for rhetorical emphasis: *Liebe*, love. The suggestion is that nothing less than an eternal love was necessary if we were to be saved from eternal damnation. After holding her G, the soprano completes her word by rising through the degrees of a so-called half-diminished seventh chord: E, G, B-flat, D.[27] The upward arpeggio seems to be the very act of lifting us above the fate we deserve. The soprano picks up the key of C major, but not for long. F major is hinted at but never established, as the harmony, now shifting and fluid, returns to the dark realm of the minor: to G minor, and then D minor, keys closely related on the circle of fifths.

With the advent of D minor, the soprano returns to the first part of her song. Her melody, however, is noticeably different from its earlier appearance. On the opening words, "*Aus Liebe*," she ascends through a dark minor sixth. Her melody now has far fewer sixteenth-notes. And whereas in the first part of her song, the soprano had uttered the phrase "out of love" three times, here she utters it only twice, as if time were running out. This return to the opening melody is more intense, more impassioned than what was heard at the beginning. The aria now has more momentum and dramatic tension. The word *sterben*, die, is more prolonged and insistent, as if the singer, in an act of identifying with Jesus, was now feeling death itself as more impending and inexorable. And when the soprano returns (m. 59) to the breathy word *nichts*, nothing, she gives it even more dramatic emphasis than before with an upward leap of a minor seventh.

Bach cunningly manipulates the harmony so that having begun this return in the "wrong key" of D minor and with dramatic variations on the initial melody, the soprano soon returns to the home key of A minor. This complete return happens in measure 53, at one of those breathtaking fermata moments. Here Bach gives us a tense, dark chord that points to A minor—a diminished seventh chord based on G-sharp, the $\hat{7}$ of A minor. This is soon followed by yet another fermata moment, where Bach gives us the *dominant* seventh of A minor, which further solidifies the home key. Such are the glories of that astounding musical language Bach inherited and advanced—the language of tonal harmony. The singer finishes her song and returns to the silence whence she came. We hear again the unearthly tones of the flute's opening music as we come full circle.[28] After a final flurry of notes played by the flute, the three instruments reach a gentle cadence in A minor, as the aria reaches its end. The spell of meditative tranquility is then broken by the tenor-Evangelist, who dramatically sings, "But [the crowd] cried out yet again and said . . ." His alarming musical gesture—an octave leap upward—paves the way for a return of the crucifixion fugue, now made even more horrifying by contrast with the aria that has preceded it.[29]

Earlier, I noted the curiously halting rhythm of the aria and its sense of stability or standing still. I also noted the terrifying directness of the soprano's words, which state, without metaphor, the objective truth of divine love unmixed with the will of the singer. The stark standing-there of the tones recalls the stark standing-there of Jesus in his exposure to judgment. This is intimately related to the remarkable directness of the text, which captures in a few words the central teaching of Matthew's story of the Passion. We encountered this rest-in-motion, this standing-there of moving tones, in the stabilizing quarter-note upbeats with which flute and soprano begin their melodies. In the standing-there of "*Aus Liebe,*" we experience the quiet unmoving pivot and meditative center around which the entire *St. Matthew Passion* turns.[30] Through the power of tones in time, tones that both express a passion and release the spirit of words, the listener is put into direct contact with a felt symbol of that eternal love around which human history turns. We are arrested by the sound of Bach. We hear and feel something haunting and mysterious but also precise and orderly. Through the power of music—the music of tonal harmony—we are made to experience, with our whole soul, what Good Friday is all about.

Closing Thoughts

Having examined *"Aus Liebe"* in some detail, I turn to the broader theme of this chapter: the power of song. In the phenomenon of song, tones bring singer and listener into immediate contact with what the words of the song mean. Through the power of tones in time, we do not just register meaning but experience it.[31] In Bach's *St. Matthew Passion*, this power can sometimes be unsettling, as in the crucifixion fugue that frames *"Aus Liebe."* It is the prerogative of tones to do with words what words cannot do for themselves. Tones take us beyond words and at the same time more deeply into them. Words that are sung take on new life. They become winged, in Homer's phrase, as tones transport us from the letter of the word to its indwelling spirit. Music strikes us. And when words and tones are wedded, words strike us, come home to us, in a most intimate and powerful way.

The power of tones has an important bearing on human learning. Often our failure to comprehend something fully is due to a failure of feeling. We hear or read words and register their conceptual meaning, but we fail to feel, and therefore properly to grasp, their weight and power. In failing to be struck, we fail to live up to the demands of the meaning that is intended. It is like reading a poem only in order to decode its "message." The phenomenon is nicely captured by the twentieth-century physicist Niels Bohr, who was reported to have said in a conversation with Heisenberg: "Anyone who is not shocked by quantum theory has not understood it."

So too, in order to be fully awake to faith, we must be struck, perhaps even shocked, by the objects of faith. Great sacred music is in this way faith's faithful ally. The music of Bach's *St. Matthew Passion* stirs feeling. In doing so, it can strengthen faith by bring-

ing about a renewed, vigorous, and more reflective relation to that
faith. This power to renew, invigorate, and summon thought is
most pronounced in the arias, which, as musicalized reflections,
depict in tones the various ways in which a contemporary individual may be imagined as responding to the sacred tableaux in
Matthew's story. As we have seen, emotion is no simple thing here,
since Bach's music sometimes stirs contrary emotions at one and
the same time. Paradox is everywhere heard and felt. By evoking
the paradoxical unity of contrary feelings and ideas, the fusion of
gravity and grace, Bach captures a truth in its wholeness. He puts
our souls, as I noted earlier, into direct contact with the bitter-
sweet meaning of Good Friday.

"*Aus Liebe*" pierces us with its beauty. It does so by means of
the musical elements I have pointed out in my analysis. These elements are describable and learnable to an astonishing degree. In
being pierced by these elements in their precisely defined relations, we are made to reflect on the meaning of Christ's sacrifice as
rooted in God's love for man. The tones of the singer beautify the
words. But they also interpret them. In the *Passion* Bach, as theologian and teacher, inflects aspects of the story in order to stress
themes close to the heart of the fervent Lutheran: the tormented
conscience, the profound innocence of Jesus, the human passions
of Jesus, the believer's passionate and personal relation to Jesus as
Bridegroom, the frailty and folly of our good intentions, and the
treachery of the human heart.[32] God is in the detail. In the beautifully precise details of the *St. Matthew Passion*, Bach gives us something to ponder as well as experience. Perhaps most amazing of
all, Bach's music offers the listener food for thought. He does so
through the listener's faculty for delight. What the French poet
Paul Valéry says of lyric poetry applies to the music of Bach:

Thought is hidden in verse like the nutritive virtue in fruit.
A fruit is nourishment but it seems to be nothing but pure
delight. One perceives only pleasure but one receives a sub-

stance. Enchantment veils this imperceptible nourishment it brings with it.[33]

Could it be, precisely because its fruit is so delicious—passion fruit—that Bach's *St. Matthew Passion* is for the nonbeliever as well as the believer, not just for his delectation, but also for his redemption?

The question raises the possibility that the beauty of all great sacred music, not just that of Bach, is invested with a conversionary power, a power to bring the not-yet-believing soul, if not to faith, then at least to the threshold of faith. It is not difficult to imagine that music, like Dante's Beatrice, is one of the ways in which grace operates through beauty—that music, like Beatrice, is a mediator. Bach's *Passion* is unique in this regard. The music is seductive, even voluptuous. One can only imagine what St. Augustine, who agonized over the sensuous appeal of chant, would make of it![34] In the *St. Matthew Passion*, Bach indulges his gypsy soul. It is as though Bach, in his broad and deep humanity, his capacity for feeling all kinds and degrees of sorrow and joy, were reaching out to all his fellow human beings, believers and nonbelievers alike, and impressing upon them what was for him the potent truth of Christian faith. All the exotic chromaticism, the dance rhythms, the tender passions of the arias are so many ways in which Bach puts carnality and sensuousness, the earthy passions we all feel, in the service of transcending carnality and sensuousness.

"How wondrous indeed is this sentence that has been passed on Jesus!" On this note of wonder I bring my reflections to a close. Music does not merely sound; it enchants. To listen to music is to give our souls to its power. We do not merely hear and feel but are held and possessed. In the musical meditation that is *"Aus Liebe,"* Bach evokes a twofold wonder at a twofold mystery: wonder at the sacrifice that is at the center of Christian faith and at the power of music that can bring about a more intimate union with that faith.

CHAPTER FOUR

The Musical Universe and Mozart's *Magic Flute*

> For the singer, words acquire a very special plenitude
> and depth of meaning. Something that remains silent
> in words merely spoken begins to flow, to vibrate;
> the words open and the singer opens to them.
>
> Victor Zuckerkandl, "Words and
> Tones in Song," from *Man the Musician*

We now go from Bach's musicalized world of divine love to the love between man and woman and the secular religion of Mozart's *Magic Flute*. I shall attempt the musical equivalent of a close reading of a text, the aria *"Dies Bildnis ist bezaubernd schön"* ("This image is enchantingly beautiful"). One of the most beautiful love songs ever written, it occurs early in the opera and is sung by Prince Tamino, as he gazes upon a likeness of Pamina, daughter of the Queen of the Night and Tamino's destined Other. The aria will give us a further opportunity to reflect on the power of song.[1]

The *Magic Flute* has been called Mozart's Masonic opera, and so it is. Mozart was a serious Freemason. So was his librettist, Emanuel Schikaneder, at whose Viennese theatre the work was first produced and who was the first to play the birdman Papageno. The opera (or rather Singspiel, "play with songs") is filled with Masonic ideals, symbols, terms, rituals, and numerology.[2] The Mystic Three is prominent: three flats in the opera's key

(E-flat), Three Ladies, Three Boys, Three Temples (of Wisdom, Reason, and Nature), and three tones in the major triad, which Mozart highlights, indeed celebrates, in various ways throughout the opera, notably in the middle section of the Overture. I say all this now because the Masonic influence, though pervasive, will not be my concern. I wish to focus instead on the beauty and precision of Mozart's music.

We love music because of how it makes us feel. We listen to some works more than others because we sense a kinship with them and want to experience the feelings they stir in us. But feeling is not primary in music. Nor is it always the reason why we listen. Most of the time, we listen to a piece of music simply because we want to hear it; we take pleasure in the hearing. But the pleasure is not in the feeling of pleasure, as though music were a drug used to produce a rush. It is in what we are hearing, in the distinctive *aisthêton* or object of musical perception. Sometimes we listen to a musical work because we wish to hear a quality or perfection that is present in it: a well-constructed melody, a beautiful or perhaps enigmatic chord progression, a distinctive rhythm, the interplay of voices in a polyphonic composition. The list goes on. We listen for the sake of an active contemplation that allows us to participate in, be one with, the life and shape of the musical object. To be sure, feelings are aroused, but these are grounded in and prompted by what we perceive in the tones, in what is there in the phenomenon we call music. We might say that in responding to music we perceive feelingly and feel perceptively. Perception, however, is primary. We do not, except incidentally, hear musical sounds and associate them with various feelings, images, and experiences. On the contrary, we perceive what is there and take on the condition that rhythms and tones communicate to us.[3]

There is a wonderful passage by Paul Valéry on "the musical universe," the phrase that inspired the title of this chapter. It occurs in his lecture, "Poetry and Abstract Thought." The passage makes clear the primacy of musical perception:

> The musician is . . . in possession of a perfect system of well-defined means which exactly match sensations with acts. From this it results that music has formed a domain absolutely its own. The world of the art of music, a world of sounds, is distinct from the world of noises. Whereas a *noise* merely rouses in us some isolated event—a dog, a door, a motor car—*a sound evokes, of itself, the musical universe.* If, in this hall, where I am speaking to you and where you hear the noise of my voice, a tuning fork or a well-tempered instrument began to vibrate, you would at once, as soon as you were affected by this pure and exceptional noise that cannot be confused with others, have the sensation of a beginning, the beginning of a world; a quite different atmosphere would immediately be created, a new order would arise, and you yourselves would unconsciously *organize* yourselves to receive it.[4]

The entities that populate the musical universe are, for Valéry, tones pure and simple. If words are to gain entrance to this world, they do so by the grace, as it were, of tones. The tones are primary. This is crucial in the essay in which the passage quoted above occurs, since Valéry wishes to stress the poet's problem by contrasting the musical universe with the poetic universe. The former is an autonomous realm whose objects, tones, are perfectly suited to the art of music, whereas the poetic universe, Valéry observes, is forced "to borrow language—the voice of the public, that collection of traditional and irrational terms and rules, oddly created and transformed, oddly codified, and very variedly understood and pronounced."

Let us now enter the musical universe of Tamino's aria. It is a universe that unites words and tones. The aria is inspired, as I mentioned earlier, by an image of Pamina. The portrait is given to Tamino by the Three Ladies, servants of the Queen of the Night. As we discover, the Queen means to use Tamino's love for Pamina to seduce the hero into saving Pamina from Sarastro, the supposed villain who has abducted Pamina. Given the young hero's fervent devotional response to what he sees, we might call this image an icon. It is said to be magical, but surely it needs no magic beyond Pamina's likeness to enchant the young prince, who sings as if caught up in a dream. The words to his song, in translation, are as follows:

> This image is enchantingly beautiful,
> such as no eye has ever seen!
> I feel it, I feel it, how this divine portrait
> fills my heart with new emotions.
> I cannot name this,
> yet I feel it here burning like fire;
> could the feeling be love?
> Yes, yes, it is love alone, love, it is love alone!
> O, if only I could find her!
> O, if she were already standing before me!
> I would, would, warm and pure . . . what would I?
> Enraptured I would press her to this burning breast,
> and forever would she then be mine.

The fire-filled words trace a progression in three stages. Tamino begins by marvelling at a divine image. Then he asks whether the feeling it inspires in him, and which he cannot name, is love but then affirms that it must be love. Finally, he wonders what he would do if the beloved were standing before him, concluding that he would press her to his breast, and she would be his forever.

Tamino is doing more in this song than expressing his feelings: he beholds his inner state and makes it an object of reflection. He marvels at the power of the magical object that he perceives and at his passionate response to it. He does not immediately identify his emotion with love (how could he, since he is experiencing love for the first time?) but rather reaches that conclusion through inner dialogue and questioning. As we shall see, Mozart's music perfectly captures the stages of Tamino's awakening, the meaning of his words, and the motions of his soul.

I begin with the observation that the aria is a precisely formed, perfectly balanced whole. Tamino is agitated and confused, but his music, though passionate, is restrained, stately, and inward sounding. It embodies, as I noted earlier, not merely his feeling but his awareness. The music critic and writer of tales E. T. A. Hoffmann once said that Haydn, Mozart, and Beethoven all had the musical virtue of *Besonnenheit*.[5] The word means something like rational awareness, sensibleness, being in one's right mind. Tamino's passionate aria, in its concision and restraint, is a superb example of this virtue.

The song is in E-flat major—the solemn, heroic key of the opera—and has a moderately slow two-beat measure. It is scored for strings, clarinets, bassoons, and French horns (no flutes or oboes). Their sound is like a warm glow emanating from Tamino's heart, or rather like the sound of the new world, now enchanted, in which Tamino finds himself. The aria is in a truncated version of sonata form and follows the usual tripartite structure: exposition, development, and recapitulation. Its key-area plan goes from tonic (I) to dominant (V) and then back to the tonic, but there is no repeat of the opening theme, as is customary in the sonata. This allows for maximum concision and dramatic urgency.

The aria opens with a tender statement of the E-flat major triad—the sound of an awakening—spelled out in dotted rhythms and played by the strings, which give Tamino his cue. Clearly, the singer we are about to hear, unlike Papageno, with his bouncy bird-catcher song, is noble. Tamino's first utterance is an upward leap on the words "*Dies Bildnis*," "This image"—a rising major sixth from $\hat{5}$ in the E-flat major scale up to $\hat{3}$ (B-flat to G). The leap is an event in Tamino's soul, the sudden wonder inspired by Pamina's likeness. When his sentence is spoken in German, the accent is on "*schön*," "beautiful." But the tonal ascent to the high G puts the stress on the word "*Bildnis*," "image," leaving no doubt that for

Tamino the focus is on the visible image that is the occasion and cause of his surging passion.

After the inspired leap from $\hat{5}$ to $\hat{3}$, which sounds like an enchantment of space and world, the melody gently descends by steps, pausing on degree $\hat{4}$ (A-flat), an unstable degree that tends downward toward $\hat{3}$. The musical phrase corresponds to the first phrase of the sentence: "This image is enchantingly beautiful." As Tamino moves to the second part of his sentence—"as no eye has ever seen"—he sings a second rising sixth, from $\hat{4}$ up to $\hat{2}$, A-flat to F. He then descends by steps to $\hat{3}$, the tone to which his earlier $\hat{4}$ was pointing. Whereas the first phrase landed on a tone that was unstable and "wanted" to move, the second complements the first and brings it to rest:

Dies Bild – nis ist be-zaubernd schön,   wie noch kein Au-ge je ge - sehn!

Thanks to the postponement of the move from $\hat{4}$ to $\hat{3}$, the two phrases form a single phrase, not two sets of tones but one coherent *movement* composed of two *sub-movements*. The entire phrase is bounded by an octave that extends from the high $\hat{3}$, to which Tamino leaps, to the low $\hat{3}$, to which he descends by step. This $\hat{3}$, this G, will play a major role in understanding the arc of the musical whole.

Mozart's musical language is that of tonal harmony. This refers to music that is grounded in a tonal center (the tone to which all the other tones point) and has an underpinning in the movement of what we call "chords." We sometimes call this underpinning or harmony an accompaniment, but it is more precisely the *structured movement* that interprets the melody and reveals its depth. Harmony in this sense is present in the two-part phrase we have just examined, as the chordal movement goes from the I chord or tonic to the V^7 chord or dominant seventh and back again to the tonic:

This works because the V^7 chord, thanks to the tritone formed by degrees $\hat{4}$ (A-flat) and $\hat{7}$ (D) and $\hat{5}$ in the bass, points in a precise direction: to the 1 chord, here the E-flat major triad. The opening phrase of Tamino's song is in this way the cooperation of two kinds of tension that beget movement: the melodic tension of individual tones and the harmonic tension of chords. For Victor Zuckerkandl, as we saw in Chapter 2, these directed tensions and their various relations to one another are the primary object of musical perception. To listen to music in the tradition of tonal harmony is to perceive not mere pitches but forces within the tonal field—*dynamic qualities* that manifest themselves in and through pitches and hold the piece together. Chords, in this context, are most precisely understood as dynamic qualities or tensions raised to a higher power.

After the opening phrase, which goes, as we have seen, from 1 to V^7 and back again, the tones open up and move forward. This is due largely to the harmony, which, having so far confined itself to the 1-V^7-1 oscillation, now moves briefly to the IV or subdominant chord over a continued E-flat in the bass and then returns to 1.[6] The IV chord, here the A-flat major triad, signals the "away move" in a harmonic journey and produces a lessening of harmonic tension. Tamino here moves from the picture to his inner state: "I feel it, I feel it, how this divine portrait fills my heart with new emotions." As he says, "I feel it, I feel it," he sings appoggiaturas on "feel"—B-natural to C, then A-natural to B-flat. Appoggiaturas are leaning tones, unstable tones on strong beats, which briefly delay the arrival of a main tone in the melody. The leaning tone is an affect perfectly suited to the word "feel." The accompaniment echoes this affect. As Tamino leans into his feeling, the strings lean in sympathy with him.

Right after his leaning tones, Tamino speaks of his heart and the new emotions that Pamina's image has aroused in it. His outburst on "*Götterbild*," "divine portrait," occurs at the exact center of his opening 13-measure period. Tamino here sings his second dramatic leap, from B-flat up to A-flat, the highest tone of his song. The interval, a minor seventh, is an even bigger leap than his opening sixth, and signals a sudden flaring up of the passion that the "divine portrait" inspires. The melody on "*Götterbild*" outlines part of the V^7 or dominant seventh chord. The music does not resolve this tense chord, which points to E-flat, but rather stresses it and lingers on it.

When the tonic chord does arrive, it is not the end of the previous phrase but the beginning of a new one. Now past the flareup on "*Götterbild*," Tamino retreats to a more inwardly focused mood as he completes his sentence: "fills my heart with new emotions." The accompaniment is measured and lovely, like the gentle strumming of a guitar: bass note, chord / bass note, chord. The harmony takes us on a little musical journey, as the melody begins and ends on an E-flat or degree $\hat{1}$. The sequence of chords arouses the expectation that the tense V^7 chord will resolve on the tonic, which would fit the E-flat or $\hat{1}$ in the melody. But this does not happen. When Tamino sings his $\hat{1}$ on "*füllt*," "fills" (which in German closely resembles "*fühlt*," "feels"), the harmony subverts the expected closure and assimilates Tamino's E-flat into a dissonant diminished seventh chord based on A-natural (A-natural, C, E-flat, and G-flat). This tense passionate chord, which consists of two interlocking tritones (A-natural and E-flat, C and G-flat), appears four times in the aria. On each occasion, it functions as an audible "heat element" that captures a surge of the love-embers burning within Tamino's breast.

With the sudden appearance of the diminished seventh chord in place of the expected tonic, the tones seem to have gone off course. We have here a *deceptive cadence*: the cadence formula leads us to expect an end, but the harmony takes a detour at the last minute and puts instability—in this case, extreme instability—in place of stability. This produces tension and the need for continued movement:

The diminished seventh chord here functions as an applied dominant (or secondary dominant). This is a chord that tenses toward a chord other than the tonic, in this case, to the V^7 of E-flat: a B-flat dominant seventh chord. It is called "the seven of five." To sum up, three kinds of musical tension unite in a single chord on the word "fills": deceptive cadence, applied dominant, diminished seventh chord. Tamino's unassuming E-flat in the melody (dynamic quality $\hat{1}$) fails to reveal the full meaning of the word he sings or the heat it embodies. This revelation falls to harmony, which interprets Tamino's E-flat by releasing in it an unexpected potential. The deceptive diminished chord is the harmonic interior— the soul—of Tamino's melodic tone. The inner, soul-like aspect of harmony recalls what Wagner once perceptively said, that harmony is "the first thing that fully persuades the feeling as to the emotional content of [the] melody, which otherwise would leave to it something undetermined."[7]

Right after the deceptive cadence, the first violins, as if inspired by Tamino, sing rising phrases that form a gentle two-part wave: up and down, up and down. Their tones outline the degrees of the B-flat dominant seventh chord, to which the diminished seventh chord was pointing. With this move, the tones regain their direction.

The dominant seventh chord spelled out by the first violins gently leads Tamino to repeat his sentence, this time with musical closure. Again, he sings his rising sixth from B-flat to G on the words "*mein Herz*," "my heart," and then goes even higher—to his A-flat. He ends his phrase with a smooth $\hat{3} \rightarrow \hat{2} \rightarrow \hat{1}$. The harmony here traverses a complete period or cycle, at the end aligning itself, this time non-deceptively, with Tamino's E-flat. A gentle rhythmic emphasis on the E-flat triad marks the end of Tamino's opening 13-measure period.

Tamino then pauses, as clarinets in gentle thirds take us into a new section of the exposition. Here, the music changes key from E-flat to B-flat, from I to V.[8] The circle of fifths makes this standard move for a sonata-form piece in a major key perfectly natural. But observe how easily E-flat is dislodged and B-flat established as the new tonic. The upper clarinet goes from G to F, $\hat{3}$ to $\hat{2}$ in E-flat, and then repeats the F. Had it gone from G to F and on to E-flat, the former key would have been maintained: $\hat{3} \rightarrow \hat{2} \rightarrow \hat{1}$. It is the emphasis on $\hat{2}$ that subtly begins to move the tonal center from $\hat{1}$ to $\hat{5}$. It blocks the move to E-flat as scale degree $\hat{1}$ and begins to set up F as degree $\hat{5}$ of our new key, B-flat. The appearance of A-natural, degree $\hat{7}$ in the B-flat scale, solidifies this move.

Earlier, Tamino sang his leaning tones, and the orchestra followed. Now the reverse happens. The upper clarinet introduces a new musical strain, which Tamino follows, as if inspired by it. "I cannot name this," he sings, "yet I feel it here burning like fire" ("*Dies Etwas kann ich zwar nicht nennen; doch fühl ich's hier wie Feuer brennen*"). In imitation of the clarinet, Tamino begins on his high G (now degree 6) and descends stepwise. His gently undulating phrase ends with a leaning tone (C-sharp to D) on "*nennen*," "name." He then repeats the phrase, with a slight variation: "yet I feel it here burning like fire." The chordal movement is a simple oscillation between the new tonic (B-flat) and its dominant (F).

A brief transition in dotted rhythms played by clarinets and bassoons takes us to Tamino's first question, which he stresses by singing it twice: "Could the feeling be love?" ("*Soll die Empfindung Liebe sein?*") Both phrases end on tense chords: the first on an applied dominant (the V^7 of V), the second on the dominant of B-flat (an F-major triad). This harmonic tension—this upward interrogative gesture—is reflected in the melody. Tamino's first utterance of his question outlines the B-flat triad and ends on an E-natural, a tone foreign to B-flat. This E-natural is highlighted by the preceding F, which serves as a leaning tone. Tamino's second utterance begins with a downward leap from G to B-flat (the reverse, we should note, of his opening sixth) and ends on the unstable degree, $\hat{2}$. The E-natural with which Tamino ends the first utterance of his question is especially beautiful: "Could this feeling *be love* ("*Liebe sein*")?" The chromatic E-natural on "love," the applied dominant of which it is a part (C^7), and the florid notes of the first violin all sound as though a light was beginning to dawn, as if the question "Could this be love?" was more than just a question. The anticipation of the answer is heightened by the brief interlude played by the clarinets, whose rising phrases in dotted rhythms gently nudge Tamino and give him his cue. His "*Ja, ja!*" completes the sequence of upward melodic gestures.

Tamino answers his question: "Yes, yes, it is love alone, love, it is love alone." He sings the word "*Liebe*," "love," four times in all, three times with an expressive leaning tone and once with a climactic flourish called a "turn." On the first "*die Liebe*," Tamino sings a G down to a B-flat—the major sixth with which he began his song, now in the opposite direction. At the end of his first phrase (right after "*Ja, ja!*"), he sings a straightforward $\hat{3} \to \hat{2} \to \hat{1}$ (D→C→B-flat) on the word "*allein*," "alone" or "only." But the harmony once more undercuts the stability of his melodic $\hat{1}$ with a deceptive cadence. Instead of harmonic V→I, we get V→VI, where VI is a minor chord. Musically, this is a subtle way of extending the phrase and producing the need to move on. The minor chord adds warmth to the word *"allein."* This fits the ardor that Tamino is feeling. But the deceptive cadence also subtly undercuts the certainty Tamino would like to have.

As Tamino repeats his sentence ("It is love alone"), he *dwells* on "Liebe" and makes it into its own musical phrase in three parts: first a leap that gently descends by a step, then this same phrase repeated, and finally an embellished ascent to a high G. The chord on this G is a dramatic diminished seventh chord that points to the F major triad, the V of B-flat. Both melody and harmony are at this point up in the air, begging for resolution. The eighth-note rest that follows heightens the suspense. After the rest, tension is released, as Tamino completes his sentence. He drops more than an octave to an F and proceeds by step to B-flat, our new Î, this time supported rather than undercut by the accompanying harmony. The cadence, embellished by a turn played by the first violins, brings the section to a close. It completes the musical thought that the preceding deceptive cadence had postponed.

We now enter the middle section of the aria, the so-called development section. Although not much time has passed, much has happened. That the tones are embarking on a new large section of the piece is signalled by two whole measures in which the orchestra shifts to quicker rhythms that give the song more forward momentum. It is as if the embers in Tamino's soul flame up with greater intensity. Something is *happening.* The strings play sixteenth and thirty-second notes, as the winds enter with a recurring pattern of syncopations or offbeat rhythms. The first violins surge upward in thirty-second notes grouped in quick pairs, then play a rapid succession of appoggiaturas, as the second violins play a lovely countermelody in contrary motion. The appoggiaturas then take over and become the first violins' principal theme. They are little flutters of the heart born of heightened expectation. They may also represent Tamino's soul in the act of racing after his beloved. Beneath this dense rhythmic complex, the bass viols provide support with a persistent B-flat in six-

teenth notes—the quickened pulse and heartbeat of this part of
Tamino's music. All these rhythms together form a complex musical image of the passion that leads Tamino to his second question:
"O, if only I could find her! O, if she were already standing before
me! I would, would, warm and pure . . . *what would I?*"

Tamino's melody on these words begins as a passionate stepwise swell on his two exclamations. The ascent begins on B-flat or
1̂ and reaches its peak on the high A-flat. At the end of each phrase
(on "*könnte*" and "*stände*"), Tamino sings the same tones he sang
earlier on the word "*Götterbild*"—A-flat, F, and D, which are part
of the dominant chord that points to E-flat. But the harmony does
not go there. The tones seem to be caught in a region of harmonic
indeterminacy. As Tamino now moves beyond his two exclamations, he breaks the pattern and sings a calm perfect fourth from
C up to F on "*ich würde*" ("I would"), then another perfect fourth
a whole step down, from B-flat up to E-flat on "*würde*" repeated.
The repetition suggests that Tamino is suspended in mid-thought
by the indeterminacy of his feelings and intentions; he does not
know how to complete his sentence. The sense of indeterminacy is evident in the accompaniment, which plays mysterious,
dusky-sounding measures with a flurry of chromatic appoggiaturas. When Tamino sings "warm and pure," he uses a warm-sounding G-flat, as the little heart flutters played by the first violins
outline the same diminished seventh chord on A-natural that
we heard in the exposition. This chord points to the B-flat major
triad that immediately follows. The tones seem to have found
their direction, their tonal center or 1̂. But as Tamino utters his
second question ("*what* would I?"), he ends his phrase by falling a
major sixth from F down to the A-flat an octave below the A-flat
we heard earlier. The gesture is an anti-climax, coming as it does
after Tamino's three dramatic ascents: two to A-flat and one to
G-flat. The "fall" in the melody sounds like a momentary deflation—rising confidence that is suddenly at a loss. The low A-flat
blocks the reassertion of B-flat as key. It is part of the dominant

seventh chord in E-flat major, the home key of the aria. Tamino's "What would I?"—a deflating fall from F to A-flat—finds a fitting harmonic correlate in the unresolved V^7 chord that leaves this passionate middle section and interior of the aria hanging.

The intense anticipation that has built up during this middle section of the aria, and which seems to stall on the V^7 chord, is emphasized by the full measure of *rest* that follows. This is the longest, most dramatic pause in a song full of pauses and withheld resolutions. The soundless measure prolongs and heightens the tension of the preceding V^7 chord—the harmonic image of Tamino's erotic aporia, his being at a loss for what to do with his feeling. The measure of rest is a dynamic, charged silence. It is a superb example of how silence is part of the musical universe, how silence in music is not void but order, a form. No doubt we are to imagine that during this measure Tamino's soul is gathering itself for a further revelation, an answer to the question "What would I?" Indeed, he finds an answer, but not through words and questioning. The answer, or rather the inner experience that leads to the answer, wells up in him wordlessly during the silence. He is listening for the promptings of his heart and the music of his soul. These promptings will show him the way and will soon become articulate in song.

The music continues, not *after* the measure of silence but *from* it. Silence has become a source. The strings re-establish momentum with an oscillating, so-called Alberti bass played by the violas and persistent sixteenth notes on a low E-flat played by the bass viols. They combine the quickened pace of Tamino's newfound resolve with the tenderness that characterizes the whole aria. The oscillation played by the violas is a straightforward I-V^7-I in E-flat major. This confirms that we have returned to the home key and that the recapitulation has begun. In this final section of his song, Tamino, with rising self-confidence, answers his second question: "I would press her to this burning breast, and forever would she then be mine."

Tamino takes his cue from the first violins, which play a gently rising phrase that becomes a countermelody, as singer and strings engage in a musical conversation. The melody is straightforward: a little melodic wave that starts on a B-flat and rises to E-flat through an appoggiatura on F ("I would *her*"), then the same melodic phrase repeated ("enraptured"). The next phrase, which begins similarly, introduces a pattern of skips and ends on a warm-sounding chromatic D-flat ("press to this burning or heated breast"). The phrasing exploits German word order in a gradual revelation of meaning: "I would her," "enraptured," "to this burning breast," and finally the crucial infinitive "*drücken*," "press," which completes the earlier sentence Tamino could not finish. The E-flat to D-flat on "*drücken*" captures the very act of pressing. This chromatic tone tenses forward and conspires with the tones in the accompaniment to form a I^7 chord—the E-flat major triad with the D-flat as a de-stabilizing seventh. The I^7, which interprets and deepens Tamino's D-flat, is an applied or passing dominant that pushes into the final phrase of the song: "and forever would she then be mine." In her upcoming aria, the Queen will echo these words to bedazzle and seduce the unwitting now-in-love Tamino: "And if I come to see you as victor [by saving Pamina], then she is yours forever." Her mind-numbing tone-witchery occurs, significantly, on the tantalizing word "then," "*dann*."

Tamino repeats the phrase "*und ewig wäre sie dann mein*," "and forever would she then be mine," five times in all, three times with the upbeat "*und*" ("and") and twice without. The phrases without the "*und*" have greater urgency and are allowed to begin on the crucial word "*ewig*," "forever." The I^7 chord on "*drücken*" tends toward an A-flat triad, the IV chord or subdominant in E-flat major. But as Tamino moves to his first "and forever would she be mine," Mozart substitutes the ii6 chord: the first inversion of the F minor triad. This chord plays the same role as IV in the harmonic cycle—the moment of stepping away and preparing for the dominant. Why the substitution? No doubt because the ii chord,

being minor, has greater warmth. On this ii6 chord, which lasts
an entire measure, Tamino sings a smooth measured ascent to his
high A-flat. He then drops to D, degree $\hat{7}$ in E-flat, by way of a leaning tone. The first violins join him in this gently ascending phrase.
The D is part of the chord played by the strings: the V^7 of E-flat.
The music pauses on this tense dominant chord.

Then, as Tamino sings "and forever would she then be mine,"
we hear the calm measured phrase from the exposition, where
Tamino sang "fills my heart with new emotions." The first appearance of that phrase ended, we recall, with a deceptive cadence on
a diminished seventh chord. Mozart repeats that cadence here.
But whereas in the exposition Tamino ended his second phrase
serenely on scale degree $\hat{1}$, here, at the corresponding moment,
he bypasses the E-flat and leaps to his high G on *"mein."* In this
measure, phrases with *"und"* switch to phrases without it—a shift
that quickens the song's momentum. It also produces a happy elision on the tones G, E-flat, and C that allows Tamino to combine
"mine" and "forever" in one phrase to form the unit "mine forever."

Tamino goes on to stress the degrees of the E-flat major triad
in a smoothly flowing phrase that seems destined to land on a low
E-flat or $\hat{1}$. But at the last minute, he leaps from low F (scale degree
$\hat{2}$) to the G *a ninth above* on the word *"mein,"* and then overtops the
G with an A-flat on *"ewig."* This is the most dramatic moment in
the aria, as Tamino intensifies his previous elision—his musicalized, heat-filled dream of eternally possessing the beloved. Tamino
sounds very heroic and confident here. He sings his signature G a
lot, as though this single tone, scale degree $\hat{3}$, embodied the whole
of his passion. When he gets to the last utterance of his phrase, his
melody again emphasizes the tones of the E-flat major triad. He
leaps, one last time, to his signature G—this time, significantly, on
the word *"sie,"* "her." This G, however, is not a stable degree of a
chord but an appoggiatura tending toward F, $\hat{2}$. Tamino, in other
words, does not merely stress the pronoun that refers to Pamina
with a high note; he puts his whole heart into the word and leans

heroically toward the beloved. Having reached high G, the tones now descend to E-flat, scale degree $\hat{1}$, by step, with the assistance of D, scale degree $\hat{7}$: $\hat{3} \rightarrow \hat{2} \rightarrow \hat{1} \rightarrow \hat{7} \rightarrow \hat{1}$ ("*sie dann mein*"). A straightforward cadence affirms closure.

The full orchestra ends the piece with a brief coda consisting of two complementary phrases. The phrases capture the two complementary sides of Tamino's nature: the first heroic and *forte*, the second tender and *piano*, a recollection of the fervent E-flat chords with which the song began. The song ends in a hush. What Tamino ultimately desires is not continued arousal or heroism for its own sake, but rest—the blissful repose and heart's ease that comes from lasting union with the beloved.[9]

So ends our journey through Tamino's aria. I have tried to be faithful in speech to what is there in the tones. I have not, of course, captured all that is there. No one could. Mozart's music, like all great music, is inexhaustible, and every act of listening brings new discoveries. I have tried to present the aria as a tonal time-structure that comes to us as a gift from the musical universe and is welcomed by our musically receptive souls. The time-structure "speaks to" our passion and our perception, just as the divine portrait, a visual or spatial form, "speaks to" and inspires the soul of Tamino. And just as his world is transformed by what he experiences, so too is ours by the magic of Mozart's incomparable music.

I have placed special emphasis on directed tension as the ground of coherence in tonal music. This wholeness through tension is evident in the song's overall form. The first section is an ordered accumulation of tension. The second heightens that tension. It is, as we have seen, Tamino's point of maximum anticipation and perplexity. The third reaffirms E-flat as key, recalls part of the music from the exposition, and brings the whole time-structure to perfect balance and resolution. It does all this by accumulating ordered tensions of its own, with which the tones move swiftly to a satisfying close.

To listen perceptively to the aria, to hear what is there, is demanding. It takes effort and study. Following the thought of Heinrich Schenker, I would like to suggest that behind all the complexities, a simple scheme prevails. The melody, as we know, begins with a rising sixth to a G, the $\hat{3}$ of E-flat major. The entire piece may be heard, and certainly most simply conceived, as the attempt by $\hat{3}$ to reach $\hat{1}$ through the extended intermediation of $\hat{2}$: G→F→E-flat.[10] Recall that the first key change came about because the first clarinet played $\hat{3}$→$\hat{2}$→$\hat{2}$ rather than $\hat{3}$→$\hat{2}$→$\hat{1}$. This facilitated the transformation of degree $\hat{2}$ in E-flat into degree $\hat{5}$ in B-flat. The rest of the piece—key changes and all— exploits and further develops this move to $\hat{2}$. In other words, $\hat{2}$ (F) is not just an *element* of the E-flat major scale; it is also a *principle* of the unfolding time-structure. To be persuaded of this fact, one has only to observe the crucial role that $\hat{2}$ plays throughout the piece. The completion of the move $\hat{3}$→$\hat{2}$→$\hat{1}$ in the overarching scheme takes place only at the end, only after the recapitulation has affirmed E-flat, not merely as the key of the final section but as the governing tone of the entire piece. Only at the end of the journey do we really have, and know, the beginning.[11]

My account of Tamino's aria would be incomplete if I did not say something about Pamina, the enchanting object of Tamino's love. Pamina is the focal point of the opera. Of all the virtuous characters, she endures the greatest and most prolonged sufferings: her mother's absence, the stern tutelage of Sarastro, the violent advances and blackmail of Monostatos, and the revelation of the mother she loves as a demon bent on a murder Pamina herself is ordered to commit. Finally, she suffers despair over what she thinks is lost love and is almost driven to suicide. She sings of her despair in what Joseph Kerman does not hesitate to call "Mozart's greatest aria."[12]

Pamina is an exalted figure in the opera. It is she who most embodies what is new about the previously all-male Order, which now, through the "noble pair," as Tamino and Pamina are called, will overcome the opera's primordial opposition between Male and Female. It is Pamina, a virtuous woman, who gives the lie to all the negative things said about women in the opera. It is she who, at a crucial moment of the drama, reveals the strange origin of the flute made by her magus-father. In the Finale of Act One, Sarastro tells Pamina that a man must guide her heart. That is true: Tamino gives Pamina's heart its proper object and bearing. But in the last two trials that Tamino must undergo, it is Pamina who guides Tamino, as love guides her: "*ich selbsten führe dich; die Liebe leite mich.*" Finally, it is Pamina who reveals that the magical vocation of music is not to gain power over others, or to court, or merely to amuse oneself, but to ward off the fear of death.

When Pamina joins Tamino for the final trials near the end of the opera, the two lovers face each other in more than the obvious sense. They now see each other clearly for the first time; there is mutual recognition. This recognition is evident in the complementary phrases the lovers use to sing each other's names: "*Tamino mein! O welch ein Glück!*" "*Pamina mein! O welch ein Glück!*" "Tamino mine! O what a stroke of good fortune!" "Pamina mine! O what a stroke of good fortune!"[13]

The phrases they sing are two halves of a little musical circle in F major. They constitute a wedding ceremony in tones. When Pamina sings Tamino's name, she does so with a rising major sixth (C to A), the same interval with which Tamino's soul rose up in response to Pamina's divine image.[14] But the phrase is no mere repetition. Tamino's sixth was the sound of passion that aspired to noble heights but did not know itself. It had shadow and heat. Pamina's sixth is very different. It is pure, luminous, and rationally aware. It has *Besonnenheit* to a superlative degree, and in more than the strictly musical sense. Pamina's sixth is the moral perfection of Tamino's. It is the sublime moment in which passion, now perceptive, finds its purpose.

When Tamino first responded to the magic that was Pamina, his love was mediated by an image. He asked himself what he would do if the beloved were standing in front of him. That moment has arrived, for here stands Pamina, not as a two-dimensional image but as solid reality. Tamino's first rush of love was itself a kind of image and dream. It was the first step in his journey from erotic confusion and heroic aspiration, through painful disillusionment and trials, to the moment of enlightenment, when images are seen for what they are and when the lover, having transcended mere feeling, now grasps love as *act*. Pamina is the Other, in and through whom Tamino can know himself as the man who loves Pamina, not as an eternal possession but as a partner in the trials of life. He can see who he is in the eyes of the beloved because the sound of her rising sixth, as she sings his name, shows him how. Her sixth, her love in musical form, is his unfailing guide. Pamina is more than Tamino's beloved, more than a symbol of virtuous womanhood (her mother in redeemed form), more even than the first woman to gain priestly status within the sacred Order. Beautifully conceived and realized, she is Tamino's wisdom and the true magic of Mozart's *Magic Flute*.[15]

Having treated the two lovers in some detail, I return by way of conclusion to the larger world to which they belong. It is a world that celebrates—in word and tone, action and symbol—various forms of marriage.

There is of course the literal marriage of Tamino and Pamina. But there is also the symbolic marriage of Man and Woman that now perfects the once male-only Order. It is the marriage of marriage and politics, private and public, love and rule. Then there is the marriage of high and low stations. This appears in the friendship of Tamino and Papageno. It is most delightfully present in the lilting ode to marriage shared by regal Pamina and rustic Papageno. In the sweet intertwining of their tones and musical making way for one another, the two friends enact the happy life of which they wistfully sing. Another marriage—that of heaven and earth, grace and nature—is the topic of this same duet. In the natural union of *Mann und Weib* (Man and Woman/Husband and Wife), human nature, in its earthy goodness of heart, "touches unto divinity." At the most universal level of the opera, there is the marriage of mind and heart, reason and sentiment, sense and sensibility. It is a union to which the magic of music as *felt order* is uniquely suited. All these marriages, as I have called them, celebrate the overcoming and reconciliation of elemental oppositions. The musical universe of *The Magic Flute* is the sounding soul of that reconciliation.[16]

CHAPTER FIVE

Schopenhauer's Will and Wagner's Eros

They who were two and divided
now became one and united.

Gottfried von Strassburg,
Tristan and Isolde

In the previous two chapters, I explored the musicalized perspectives of two worlds. These were the world of divine love in Bach's *St. Matthew Passion* and that of idealized human love in Mozart's *Magic Flute*. Both may be characterized as religious worlds: the former the world of Christian sacrifice, the latter that of a secular, enlightened Order consecrated to the reconciliation of primordial opposites.

I turn now to the musical universe of Wagner's *Tristan and Isolde*. This world, too, may be characterized as religious, insofar as it consecrates a love that combines the human and the divine—not in Christ as Mediator or in marriage and a perfected social order, but in eros and its bond with death as a sacred consummation. In its dark and dreadful way, the opera embodies Wagner's religion of Love. I plan to explore this world with the help of Schopenhauer, whose cosmic pessimism, depiction of erotic love, and metaphysics of music I discussed in the opening chapter.

It is well known that in the middle of working on his epic *Ring* cycle, Wagner read *The World as Will and Representation* at the urging of a friend (the poet, Georg Herwegh) and was enthralled. The

composer saw in Schopenhauer's cosmic gloom the perfect conceptual articulation of what he, Wagner, was feeling at the time
and what he thought was the ultimate truth about life and the
world.[1] The musical genius had found his philosophic muse, and
the pessimistic Schopenhauer, whom Wagner called "a gift from
heaven to my loneliness," replaced the utopian Feuerbach as Wagner's intellectual hero.[2] The offspring of this ideological turn was
Tristan and Isolde.

Schopenhauer, as it turns out, had no use—and no ear—
for Wagner's chromatic harmonies. Wagner sent him a beautifully bound copy of the *Ring* with the inscription, "out of respect
and gratitude." The Sage of Frankfurt was not impressed. He
instructed the Swiss journalist, Franz Wille, to convey a message
to his friend Wagner: "tell him that he should stop writing music.
His genius is greater as a poet. I, Schopenhauer, remain faithful to Rossini and Mozart."[3] The rude response was not surpris-
ing, since Schopenhauer, who played the flute (not, like Nietzsche,
the piano), was a lover of catchy diatonic tunes. My concern, however, is not with personal stories but with the philosophic teaching
of the one man and the *Tristan* music of the other. Where do the
teachings of will and the music of eros meet, and where do they
part company? What light can Schopenhauer and Wagner cast on
music, a phenomenon at once familiar and mysterious? And how
might music and eros reveal each other's elusive depths?

Eros Unbound

The story of Tristan and Isolde goes back to the twelfth century.
Among the several versions that survive, the best known is that of
Gottfried von Strassburg, whose poem Wagner used as the basis
of his opera.[4] In his far-ranging book, *Love in the Western World*,
Denis de Rougemont asserts that Wagner completed the Tristan
myth by transposing it into its proper domain—music. "Music
alone," Rougemont writes, "could utter the unutterable, and music
forced the final secret of *Tristan*."[5] The secret, which up to now

had been concealed by medieval courtliness and diverting adventures, is that Eros is a terrible, not-be-sentimentalized god (or in this case goddess, Frau Minne) who inflicts horrible suffering, the pain of separation, and, above all, a longing for death.[6]

Wagner's Prelude tends to support Rougemont's view. In his program notes to the concert version of *Tristan*, which paired the Prelude and Finale, Wagner left no doubt that the Prelude, which he called *Liebestod*, was meant to capture the endless torment of Love: "longing, longing unquenchable, desire forever renewing itself, craving and languishing; one sole redemption: death, surcease of being, the sleep that knows no waking."[7] But there is also the Transfiguration music of the Finale, which depicts, in Wagner's phrase, Love's "blessed fulfilment." This fulfilment is not for Tristan, who is love's tormented victim and who dies ecstatically but without, so to speak, a moment of grace. That moment is reserved for Isolde, who dies in a state of bliss.

As Joseph Kerman observes, Wagner never intended his opera, with its unified poles of suffering and bliss, to be a tragic love story. It is most precisely understood, according to Kerman, as a religious drama that depicts, inexorably, the progressive yielding of the lovers to a vision and experience of reality itself, here understood as the cosmic surge that lies beneath the realm of finite, determinate *things*.[8] This is the infinite, eternal surge that Schopenhauer calls the will, the thing-in-itself that lies beneath all finite appearances. It is the dynamic source of all feeling, desire, and emotion. What the force of cosmic Eros does to the lover-acolytes, Wagner does to his listeners through tones. The music seizes us violently, tyrannically, like love itself, and does not let go—not, that is, until the final serene chord, which Richard Strauss called "the most beautifully orchestrated B-major chord in the history of music."[9]

The musical world of *Tristan and Isolde* begins with a moan, a hushed woe-filled rising minor sixth played by the cellos. The phrase to which it belongs is sometimes called the *Liebestrank* or love potion motif. In his first complete sketch of the Prelude's opening seventeen-measure unit, Wagner used, rather than the now-familiar sixth from A to F, a tritone from B to F.[10] The tritone certainly conveys the extreme tension of the erotic will. But it lacks the moodiness of the minor sixth and mutes to some extent the shock of the Tristan chord, which contains this same tritone. Wagner must have realized early on that the sixth was better suited to Schopenhauerian gloom and to what the opening of his opera musically and dramatically required. The haunted sound of this sixth is love's dark longing rising out of the depths of the soul. It is the felt onset and intimation of what Isolde calls the *böse Ferne* or "evil distance" that separates the lovers. But the sixth also has a cosmological meaning, like everything else in the opera. In mythic terms, it is the infinitely sad emergence of the phenomenal world out of the depths of the Will. At the very moment that the cellos complete their phrase on a G-sharp (the raised $\hat{7}$ of A minor), bassoons, clarinets, English horns, and oboes join the cellos to form the famous "Tristan chord."[11] Here is the opening phrase to which it belongs:

Sounded mostly by wind instruments, the chord is the first breath of the newborn world of *things*, the burst of the World Spirit into Baudelaire's *brumeuse existence*. World and Woe come on the scene together. In a letter to Mathilde Wesendonck, Wagner states this very connection between the opening of *Tristan* and the Buddhist story of creation as the primordial clouding of "the clear expanse of heaven."[12] As noted in Chapter 2, the Tristan chord is followed by a dominant seventh chord (the V^7 of A minor), which in this context is heard, amazingly, not as an unstable chord tending to the tonic triad but as itself the moment of resolution.

Wagner's notion of a love-death stands in sharp opposition to Schopenhauer's metaphysics of sexual love, according to which love is the will to *life*. Being in love, for Schopenhauer, is no more than a ruse that the noumenal will employs to propagate the species: ". . . nature can attain her end only by implanting in the individual a certain *delusion*, and by virtue of this, that which in truth is merely a good thing for the species seems to him to be a good thing for himself, so that he serves the species, whereas he is under the delusion that he is serving himself."[13] By rejecting this cynical reduction of sexual love to the physiological, Wagner saves the phenomenon and experience of Eros as a relation of spirits rather than mere bodies. In mythic terms, he preserves the eternal bond between Eros and Psyche.

Wagner pared down Gottfried's story to its bare essentials, all the better to focus on the inner drama of the lovers' emotions and metaphysical flights. He writes the following about the composition of *Tristan*: "Here, in perfect trustfulness, I plunged into the inner depths of soul events and from out this inmost center of the world I fearlessly built up its outer form."[14] Wagner's devotion to interiority and the wordless music of Eros is no doubt why he chose to call his opera not a music drama but more simply a *Handlung* or action, thereby distinguishing it from his more spectacular works that depict outward deeds and epic events. The fierce focus on inner movement—the raw subjectivity of feeling—lifts the story of the lovers out of its medieval setting and puts it beyond time and place in the realm of eternal universal truth, the realm of Schopenhauer's archetypal Ideas.

Wagner brilliantly divides the drama into three acts. Rougemont calls them, respectively, "initiation, passion, fatal fulfilment."[15] We are plunged *in medias res*, as Tristan, King Mark's most trusted knight, is conveying Isolde from her native Ireland to Cornwall as Mark's bride-to-be. Other elements of the story—the death of Morold, Isolde's betrothed, at the hands of Tristan, her nursing the wounded Tristan back to health when he comes to her disguised as

Tantris, and the fatal "glance" that begets Love—are not dramatized but recollected by the lovers. Knight and Lady drink the potion and proceed to express in passionate death-devoted terms the love that was already burning within them. Back in Cornwall, while Mark and his knights are on a hunting party, the lovers meet, in defiance of the urgent warnings of Brangäne, Isolde's lady in waiting. The lovers indulge in a long, Dionysian outpouring of their love-death passion but are discovered by Mark, who has been informed of the affair by the jealous Melot. Tristan provokes Melot to fight and practically throws himself on Melot's sword, whereupon the wounded Tristan, accompanied by his servant-friend Kurvenal, flees to his native Kareol in Brittany, where he suffers from his physical wound, which is the symbol of the wound of erotic longing in the absence of the beloved. Upon news of Isolde's approaching ship, Tristan, in a fit of delirious excitement, rips the bandage from his wound and eventually dies in Isolde's arms. When Mark and Melot come on the scene, Kurvenal attacks and kills Melot but is in turn killed by Mark's defenders. Brangäne informs Isolde that Mark now knows about the potion and has come to forgive all and to give Isolde to Tristan in marriage. But Isolde is beyond all this. As she gazes in rapture on Tristan's face, she follows her lover to Hamlet's undiscovered country. Isolde does not merely die but is transfigured, made radiant, as she sinks on Tristan's body and breathes her final breath, having experienced the world, mystically, as music:

> In the billowing surge
> In the ringing sound [*in dem tönenden Schall*],
> In the World Spirit's fluttering All—
> To drown,
> To sink—
> Unconscious—
> Highest bliss!

Isolde's concluding rhyme between *Unbewußt* and *höchste Lust* may be said to capture the teaching of the whole opera: bliss is the state of unconsciousness achieved when love as Eros is pushed to its extreme point. The uncomprehending (indeed deluded) King Mark blesses the dead during the final soothing chords of the opera. Metaphysically, he is the lovers' exact opposite and is to them as the Day of consciousness is to the Night of unconsciousness.

In Wagner's version of the story, as opposed to Gottfried's, the lovers never physically consummate their love-passion. They are chaste, like the Night that protects them in Act 2. When a "climax" occurs for each of the lovers, it is in the absence of the other and takes place not so much in the bodily world as in the act of ecstatically leaving it.[16] Wagner's lovers forego the trivial transitory pleasures of sex for the final rush of self-immolation and metaphysical union. This, death, is what their love-passion seeks, since death is the ultimate union—union of the lovers with one another through union with the World Spirit, in which all distinctions are overcome and dissolved. By preventing the lovers from engaging in sex, Wagner preserves Eros as infinite striving with only one release. The absence of physical completion also points to the radical purity that the lovers are religiously seeking. This purity, this catharsis or purification, is freedom from bodily, worldly taint and from the principle and prison of individuation.[17]

Wagner's drama is framed, significantly, by two sea voyages, two transitions or transports involving Isolde. Throughout his writings, Wagner uses the image of the sea to describe harmony as the movement of chords. As I noted in the previous chapter, harmony, for Wagner, interprets and completes melody by giving it emotional depth: "The sounding out of the harmony to a melody is the first thing that fully persuades the feeling as to the emotional content of that melody, which otherwise would leave to it something undetermined."[18] Harmony, Wagner's musical strong point, is the realm of feeling, the primordial undercurrent and ocean of the Unconscious.

Flow and fluids are central to the drama and are always connected with transition and transformation. Even the leitmotifs here are handled more fluidly, organically, than in Wagner's other operas and cannot as a rule be confined to a single meaning, since meaning here is itself not fixed but fluid. The crucial fluid is of course the potion, which neither causes the love (as Mark mistakenly thinks at the end of the opera) nor causes the lovers to realize that they are in love (they know that already).[19] The potion, in addition to being the sacred symbol of Love, simply allows Tristan and Isolde, who think they are drinking a death potion, to confess their love openly—to let love flow in what seems like a sacramental event, the first stage of Wagner's religious drama.[20] There is also the flow of Tristan's blood in Act 3. Another crucial flow is the lovers' desire to destroy their identities and cancel the principle of individuation—the *und* that separates them—so that they might flow into each other and die in each other. There is, finally, the passage from being to non-being. This is the Great Crossing—from life, day, and memory to death, night, and oblivion—a crossing over that Isolde interprets as a return to origin. Her metaphysical homecoming is prophesied by the song of the young sailor at the very beginning of the drama: *Frisch weht der Wind / der Heimat zu* ("The wind blows fresh toward land of home."). All these instances of flux have as their metaphysical wellspring the perpetual transmutations of eros or Schopenhaurian will—the cosmic force that none can resist.

In a well-known letter to Mathilde Wesendonck, the composer boasted of having perfected in the love duet of Act 2 his "most delicate and profound art"—the "art of transition [*Kunst des Übergangs*]."[21] Wagner achieved this effect largely through enharmonic modulation, where, for example, a D-flat mutates into a C-sharp, thereby smoothly, magically, changing the harmonic landscape, or rather seascape. These beautifully managed enharmonic transitions are the continual "death" of one harmonic region and simultaneous "birth" of another. What is harmonically distant becomes intimately close, in fact identical, in imitation of the ineluctable call to union that the lovers are experiencing. Other devices

include extensive use of non-diatonic or chromatic tones, unresolved cadences, and the deceptive cadence, which is employed
to great effect in the heart-melting "glance" motif first heard in
the Prelude (mm. 16–17). Wagner's art of transition, of which he
rightly boasted, is more than a compositional technique. The elusive harmonic flow that Wagner miraculously achieved is a metaphysical analogue and symbol meant to produce in the listener the
very experience and act—the *Handlung*—of eros as infinite striving, or, as Schopenhauer calls it, Will.

In the words of Ernest Newman, "if ever there was an opera
born of the spirit of music itself it is *Tristan and Isolde*."[22] In this
work, it seems that music, through the combined efforts of Dionysus and Apollo, has taken form as a determinate story in word
and image that constantly points beyond itself to its transcendent ground and origin—to what is always already there—just as
Schopenhauer's noumenal will objectifies itself in the realm of
determinate phenomena. There is no need to infer this transcendence. It is explicated relentlessly by Wagner's lovers, who constantly provide sung metaphysical commentary on the wordless
text that is their love. It is not so much they who sing but Love
that sings through them. The tone-obsessed character of *Tristan*
has led some to speculate that Wagner's drama is in fact a gigan-
tic symphonic work with words attached.[23] Nietzsche, who spoke
of "the shivery and sweet infinity of *Tristan*,"[24] wondered whether
a human being "would be able to perceive the third act of *Tristan
and Isolde*, without any aid of word and image, purely as a tremendous symphonic movement, without expiring in a spasmodic
unharnessing of all the wings of the soul."[25]

Images and words are nevertheless vital to Wagner's purpose and cannot be dispensed with, not just because they shield
us from the destructive power of orgiastic tones but more essentially because we need the images and words, especially the words,
to provide an intelligible context for the awe-inspiring unintelli-
gibility of Eros. Put simply, the Beyond, represented by tones all

by themselves, must reveal itself as the Beyond of something. The most illuminating example of the need for words occurs precisely at a moment when words fail. In Act 2, at the very end of his long gloomy reflection, Mark asks Tristan to make clear to the world "the inscrutable, deep and mysterious ground" of his betrayal. Tristan confesses that he cannot. But before he speaks, and in direct answer to Mark's question, the potion motif, sounded only by winds, wells up darkly, as if from a tomb. The "answer" to Mark's question is in the irrational realm of tones, in the wordless uncanny reality and music of love. But we wouldn't recognize this purely tonal response as the absolute "answer," unless someone (in this case, Mark) had asked the question in words and someone else (Tristan) had said, in effect, "It is beyond words."

Nietzsche's comment about the devastating emotional effect of Wagner's *Tristan* music corrects a major problem in Schopenhauer's metaphysics of music. For Schopenhauer, music, like all art, is a form of detached aesthetic contemplation.[26] But it is undeniable that music moves us, sometimes overwhelmingly. The phenomenon of being moved by music was in fact the basis of Socrates's moral-political critique of music in the *Republic*. It may seem paradoxical that Schopenhauer, the philosopher of feeling and will, would short-change, of all things, feeling. But his emphasis on detached aesthetic contemplation and the corresponding exclusion of feeling in musical experience become understandable given what music was for this Eros-tormented philosopher: solace and momentary release from what Schopenhauer calls "Ixion's wheel," that is, "the miserable pressure of the will."[27] For Wagner, the metaphysical situation is quite different. Music, for him, is the realm of feeling rather than detached contemplation. We should note, however, that despite their difference on this point, Wagner and Schopenhauer agree that music is to be regarded as a form of cognition. As Wagner puts it, the goal of drama, which he considered "the most perfect artwork," is "the *emotionalizing of the intellect*": "in the drama we must become *knowers* through *the feeling*."[28]

And harmony, the musical language of the Unconscious, surpasses Schopenhauer's beloved melody, the symbol of the rational will, because harmony is the ground of feeling in music and the source of music's emotive truth.

The sharp metaphysical difference between the philosopher and the composer regarding the role of feeling in musical experience helps us to understand Wagner's intention of writing to Schopenhauer in an effort to urge him to correct his metaphysics of sexual love by allowing for the possibility of redemption precisely *through feeling*—through love's rapture, which Wagner believed was the ultimate pacifier of the will.[29] One can only imagine what Schopenhauer's response would have been to this well-intentioned advice. I would suggest, however, in Schopenhauer's defence, that Wagner, as a Romantic, in both his music and his theoretical writings tends to overdo the role of feeling in music to the detriment of aesthetic contemplation, the act in which we take pleasure in the perceptive and rational aspects of musical works. These features are stunningly present in the arias of Mozart and the polyphonic works of Bach.[30] Indeed, Wagner's own music, in its very emotionality, gives the listener much to perceive and contemplate. Witness the opening phrase of the Prelude, with its carefully structured voice-leading and orchestration. In music, passion and perception always work together. We are moved because we have perceived something, some intelligently conceived structure that is there to be heard and contemplated—whether a tonal phrase in a melody, the interplay of voices in polyphony, or a chord progression—and what we perceive moves us. If Schopenhauer is right (and on this point I think he is), then in music we are hearing tonal analogues, symbols, of that of which we ourselves are made. Music is therefore an occasion for insight and self-knowledge. But, on Wagner's side, this knowledge comes with, if not through, an emotional impact. It was this impact that Wagner, in his music dramas, was able to generate on an unprecedented scale.

This brings us to the most important respect in which Wagner and Schopenhauer part company, and to the apparent doctrinal tension within Wagner's *Tristan*. Wagner's lovers obviously do not renounce love, as Schopenhauer would have them do. They do not go quietly into the night of asceticism but hurl themselves headlong into love's abyss—Tristan by tearing off his bandage to expose his wound, and Isolde by rising to an orgiastic pitch before gently descending on Tristan's body, in effect closing the wound he had opened for her, the wound that was his agonizing Love. Isolde, Wagner's Irish Bacchant, throws Schopenhauerian calm to the winds when she leaps to her high G-sharp on the word *Welt-Atem*, "World-Spirit." The lovers' volcanic energy adds credence to Nietzsche's remark that Love in *Tristan* "is not to be interpreted as Schopenhauerian, but as Empedoclean."[31]

Nietzsche's remark, however, though apt, is too simple. The Schopenhauerian strain of *Tristan*, love as curse, is not to be denied or minimized. It is the emphatic subject of Act 3, and Isolde's Bacchic exultation comes on the scene only after we have been subjected to Tristan's seemingly interminable love-agony.[32] If Wagner had wanted to, he could have had the lovers die in each other's arms at the end of Act 2 "in the spirit of early romanticism."[33] But, inspired by Schopenhauer, he wanted a musical-metaphysical depiction of eros as the pain of endless longing, the pressure of the Will.[34] Writing to Frau Wesendonck, Wagner gives the stark contrast between these two psychic modes, Tristan's and Isolde's, when he describes the final act of the opera as "real intermittent fever:—the deepest and most unprecedented suffering and yearning, and, immediately afterwards, the most unprecedented triumph and jubilation."[35] In Wagner's formulation, these extreme states are juxtaposed but not connected, at least not in one character. One commentator regards this fact as pointing to the philosophic incoherence of Wagner's drama.[36] Whether or not this is true, from a dramatic and experiential standpoint, Isolde's transfiguration music in B major, though decidedly not Schopenhaurian, satisfies and in addition harmonically completes the opening A-minor phrase of the opera.[37] Through its soaring beauty and evocation of the sea's sublime power, Isolde's Dionysian swan song offers emotional relief from the haunted, broken Tristan music that came before. Who would want a more doctrinally consistent but less musically gorgeous *Tristan and Isolde*? The opera is unimaginable without precisely the ending that Wagner gave it.

One Little Word

What does eros want? Isolde thinks she knows. In the lovers' duet in Act 2, Isolde is the first to make explicit that Love's *telos* is the destruction of the "little word" *and*, which both couples and separates the lovers as individuals: "Yet, how to destroy this little word 'and': how, otherwise than with Isold's very life were death to be given to Tristan?" Of course, this self-annihilation is precisely what happens at the end of the opera.

Tristan and Isolde seek a metaphysical intimacy more radical than mere being-with or even an eternal intertwining, like that of the ivy and the vine that were said to have sprouted over the lovers' shared tomb. Love, for Wagner, seeks the total merging of the lovers' separate selves, a union that spells the obliteration of the lovers as individual beings.[38] In their Dionysian love-duet, Tristan and Isolde exchange each other's names and identities. Music, in its spirituality, its transgression of spatial boundaries, allows the lovers' voices to do what their bodies cannot: merge in a musical-metaphysical unity. Erotic love seeks the sweet dissolution of the self, the loss of self in other and other in self: "No more Isolde!" "No more Tristan!" Love's desire, for Wagner, is to negate and destroy individuality, to de-create. Eros, in short, is the ultimate nihilist.

The lovers' desire for the destruction of the little word "and," which is equivalent to the desire for the destruction of the whole phenomenal world, lays bare the gnostic underpinning of the worldviews of Schopenhauer and Wagner.[39] Gnosticism, which appears in the Manichean moments of Augustine's *Confessions*, posits a strict dualism between good and evil. According to gnostic teaching, the world of determinate things, the realm of body, is evil. It is the arena of selfishness, greed, envy, love of wealth and honor, competition, hatred, war, and lies. It is also the realm of suffering, in particular erotic suffering. The underlying cause of all this evil is, for Schopenhauer and apparently for Wagner, *the principle of individuation*, the bodily world's haecceity or this-ness. Night is good—indeed, it is chaste or virginal—because it cancels all determinateness, erases all boundaries, and drowns all distinctions in the warm sea of undifferentiated feeling. Night—which the poet Novalis called "the holy, the unspeakable, the secretive Night"[40]—is a metaphysical embrace and a return to the womb-like origin of all things. Whereas Day divides, Night unites.

The paradox to which the gnostic metaphysics of love gives rise is that to love another erotically is to will the destruction not only of oneself but also of the beloved. I cannot, strictly speaking, rejoice in the beloved's being any more than in my own. All bodily being is determinate and as such inherently evil. Love's first glance, which Wagner so captivatingly sets to music with a series of increasingly tense appoggiaturas followed by a melting deceptive cadence, is in fact love's call to mystic dissolution. From Schopenhauer's reductionist perspective, the matter is simple: when lovers adore each other's identities, it is only because they are deluded, not because they have perceived anything intrinsically lovable or true. But for Wagner, erotic love, though dreamy, is the basis of mystic revelations and, as mentioned above, a call to mystic union in death. It is the ultimate enlightenment. The coveted dissolution of identity, love's voluptuous death wish, makes us wonder what Tristan and Isolde's love is love of. It seems that it is not love of the beloved, at least not primarily, but the love of love, passion for the sake of passion, which Rougemont argues is inscribed in the Tristan myth itself.[41] This view recalls the infernal realm of Dante's Francesca, who is far more consumed with her love of love than love for her adulterous lover, Paolo.[42] In the purely subjective world of love as passion, the beloved is no more than grist for the mill of self-feeling and "a great opportunity to be no longer I."[43]

But on what grounds would one conclude that individuality is evil, that limits, boundaries, and distances are evil, and that feeling surpasses thinking as Night eclipses Day? Does it not seem more reasonable, not just more healthy-minded, to affirm that goodness consists in beautiful order, in a well-ordered cosmos like the one depicted in the *Timaeus*, rather than an abyss of indeterminacy? Is the look of love, the glance, not inspired by the beloved's determinate form, which begets the desire for a keener vision, as it does for Dante in his relation to Beatrice? How could I ever want the inspiring, radiant individuality of the beloved to go away, to die?[44] And yet how could I want to preserve it without affirming, cherishing, the metaphysical distance between lover and beloved as both good and necessary?

Listening to Wagner's *Tristan and Isolde* is a ravishing, if dangerous, human experience. The opera contains music of incredible beauty and power, especially in its richly textured harmonies, although one hesitates to use the term "beautiful." "Sublime," with its intimations of the infinite and the terrible, is no doubt the more precise term. To listen to Wagner's *Tristan* is to suffer. In this *"opus metaphysicum* of all art," as Nietzsche dubbed it, we are exposed to love's violent oceanic rushes, and, in a sense, die to the music. In listening, we are under Wagner's spell and imbibe his all-too-effective tone-potion. We listen at our peril, for in listening we *are* the voluptuous music of death-bound eros. The musical potion that is *Tristan* contains much truth, terrible truth, about erotic passion, which, in some of its manifestations, does seem to be a love affair with death. But it also serves as a warning. The heady brew of *Tristan* prompts us to search for an antidote to the lovers' death wish and the gnostic nihilism it embodies, to pursue *without illusion* a love that preserves rather than destroys, celebrates rather than abolishes individuality, and seeks life rather than death, clarity rather than warmth alone, wakefulness rather than sleep, and reconciliation with the external world, in which great evil is mixed with great good.

CHAPTER SIX

Magic Circle, Magic Square

The Devil and Dodecaphony in Thomas Mann's *Doctor Faustus*

> . . . for it is only as an *aesthetic phenomenon* that existence
> and the world are eternally justified.
>
> Nietzsche, *The Birth of Tragedy*

> The ideal of morality has no more dangerous rival
> than the ideal of the greatest strength—of the most
> vigorous life—what has been called the ideal of aesthetic
> greatness . . . This is barbaric to the maximum degree.
>
> Novalis, *Logological Fragments II*

The theme of this penultimate chapter is the diabolical potential of music, as depicted in Thomas Mann's music-obsessed novel, *Doctor Faustus* (1947). My focus is Mann's appropriation of twelve-tone composition, famously fathered by Arnold Schoenberg and one of the novel's principal leitmotifs. The novel is about music and much more. In its dark and disturbing pages, we read about love, friendship, the cosmos, politics, culture, religion, and history, especially German history in the decades leading up to the Third Reich. The novel's epigraph, taken from the second canto of Dante's *Inferno*, foretells a descent into hell.[1] The descent is an exposé of the German soul—a soul most fully revealed for Mann by the demonic spirit of music.

The chapter has two main parts. In the first, I describe twelve-tone composition or dodecaphony, the music of the so-called

Second Viennese School. In the second, I turn to Mann's novel, in particular the parts that deal with twelve-tone composition. Mann's brilliant transformation of Faust into a musician will give us a further opportunity to explore music and the idea of a world.

Part One: A Brave New World

What follows is by no means an adequate account of twelve-tone music or serialism, as it is also called. It is a brief "summary of first principles" that will pave the way for my discussion of Mann's Faustus novel.

Twelve-tone music arose in response to a perceived crisis, often described as the breakdown of structure in the works of late Romantic composers like Richard Strauss, Gustav Mahler, and others. The breakdown occurred because the music of this period, though still officially tonal, had drifted in its harmonic adventures further and further away from the establishment of the tonic triad or I-chord and the cadence formulas that had been so effectively used by composers from Bach to Beethoven.[2] Wagner's highly chromatic, tonally elusive *Tristan and Isolde* was the first of these harmonic adventures.

Serialism was the fruit of a sustained effort on the part of Schoenberg and his students, Anton Webern and Alban Berg, to restore music to a condition of order and health.[3] It was preceded, in Schoenberg's case, by a period of so-called atonality, which dispensed with the tonic but had no intrinsic principle of order.[4] To use a central term from Mann's novel, twelve-tone composition was the *breakthrough* that would lead music out of the dark wood of enfeebled tonality to a better, reconstituted world in which music would be both rigorously disciplined and artistically free. It would be a new classicism. Hence the name: the Second Viennese School (the first comprising Haydn, Mozart, and Beethoven).

Twelve-tone composition is based on a set of twelve tones derived from the equal-tempered semitone or chromatic scale, although the set itself in no way functions as a scale. Its elements are not degrees or steps. The set is unique to each individual work. Below is the set for Anton Webern's *String Quartet*, Opus 28:[5]

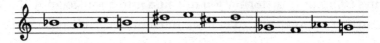

The set is based on Bach's name, B-A-C-H, where B in German is our B-flat and H our B-natural.[6] Webern's set has an evident rationale and illustrates the tonal mirroring that fascinated the serialists. The set is divided into three tetrachords or groups of four tones. The second group is an inversion, the third a transposition, of the first.[7] The row is strict in that no tone may be repeated before the whole set has appeared. This condition in no way dictates what the composer might do with the row, how he is to compose.

Twelve-tone music replaces the governing role of a $\hat{1}$, more precisely the tonic triad or 1-chord, with the fixed sequence in which tones appear in the chosen set. As Adorno puts it, there is no longer any "free note."[8] Twelve-tone composition banishes the tonal and chordal dynamic qualities that I discussed in Chapter Two and that we examined in the arias of Bach and Mozart. Tones are no longer waystations of a journey-like scale and are not related to a dynamic center of action. They are related, as Schoenberg states, "only with one another."[9] The result is tonal egalitarianism: "the regular application of a set of twelve tones emphasizes all the other tones [other than the traditional tonic] in the same manner, thus depriving one single tone of the privilege of supremacy."[10] With the elimination of the dynamic qualities inherent in the major scale, tone ceases to be tone in the strict sense and regresses to the status of acoustical pitch.[11]

Coordinate with this tonal egalitarianism is the "emancipation of the dissonance," as Schoenberg called it.[12] In Renaissance polyphony and tonal harmony, dissonance was a bridge from one consonance to another. Its function was to facilitate smooth transitions between voices and to heighten the consonance that followed. Dissonance was a tension that needed resolution. To emancipate the dissonance is to free it from the need to resolve to consonance. The avoidance, or at least postponement, of resolution was already present in the works of composers like Wagner and Debussy. In twelve-tone music, dissonances are used freely and rise to the status of consonances. The old polarities—consonance and dissonance, the major and minor modes,[13] tonic and dominant (1 and V)—are gone. Gone, too, is the division between the horizontal and vertical dimensions of music, melody and harmony, which now fuse into a single integrated tonal space. This fusing of the horizontal and vertical is the most interesting feature of the new music, which, in the absence of traditional chordal structures and its corresponding emphasis on individual lines, resembles pre-harmonic counterpoint.[14]

One downside of the "emancipation" is that dissonance now becomes something unexceptional and even risks becoming a cliché. Even granting that some dissonances are more dissonant than others, since dissonance is the norm, it is no longer an event that stands out and piques our interest, like the *Tristan* chord or the diminished seventh chord when the crowd in Bach's *St. Matthew Passion* screams "*Barabbam!*"[15] There are no suspensions, tonal knots that need to be untied. Nor are there leaning tones, like the appoggiatura at the end of the Bach *Passion*, since leaning presupposes a leaning toward a tone that is stable. Moreover, there can be no deceptive cadences, like the one we saw in Tamino's aria, since there are no cadences at all. We cannot be surprised by twelve-tone music, at least not tonally, or put on hold, since no tonal expectations have been aroused. Music no longer has a narrative structure but lives in the moment. Still less can it be, like tonality, the pure form of narration. Tension still exists (indeed, it is there all the time), but it is not directed to a goal. It is more like free-floating unsettledness and unease—when, that is, it does not take the form of outright violence. For all its dissonances, twelve-tone music cannot be the tonal analogue of desire, as it is in Tamino's aria and the tonal-erotic effusions of Wagner's lovers, since desire is the desire for something or someone.

Since music without dynamic qualities has no inherent direction, no telos, the distinctness of phrases must depend largely on rhythmic patterns.[16] The metaphysical shift is radical, since motion, time, and space in the absence of a tonal force-field all become static. Since tone is no longer dynamic, motion is simply transition from interval to interval; time is no longer an arrow; and space is no more than the acoustical domain in which tones are located. There is no need for Zuckerkandl's mysterious "third stage," since tone, now reduced to acoustical pitch, is no longer an instance of material transcendence.

This is not to say that music can no longer be humanly meaningful. On the contrary, the practitioners of serialism, especially Schoenberg, laid claim, not unreasonably, to an increase in emotional expressivity. The emotional *range*, however, is much narrower than in tonal music and tends toward the expression of angst, hysteria, frustration, melancholy, and other modes of psychic distress.[17] It can accommodate emotions in response to erotic longing but not, as mentioned above, longing itself. In any case, meaning is now the result not of dynamic qualities but of physical factors: pitch, interval, volume, tone color, tempo, and rhythm.[18] In contrast with Zuckerkandl's transcendence of materiality, twelve-tone music is the total materialization of music, the exploitation of sound and sound effects.

The materiality of musical means, the reduction of tone to pitch, must not be taken as a sign that the serialists were not interested in a spiritual, transcendent "sense of music." But this transcendence is not inherent in the tones themselves, which have been reduced to acoustical pitches. A concern for transcendence is especially evident in Schoenberg, who read Schopenhauer avidly when he was young and was no doubt attracted, like Mann, to the philosopher's cosmic pessimism.[19] Reflecting on the attempt to express musical meaning in language, Schoenberg criticizes Schopenhauer's attempt to translate tonal into conceptual, verbal meaning ("he loses himself").[20] But he praises Schopenhauer's claim, which I quoted in Chapter One, that "the composer reveals the inmost essence of the world and utters the most profound wisdom in a language which his reason does not understand." Schoenberg, too, no doubt believed in a cosmic will; and he certainly believed that life was suffering. He differs from Schopenhauer in this decisive respect: whereas Schopenhauer regards music as contemplative refuge from the passions that besiege us, music for Schoenberg is the raw *expression* of passion, especially the violent emotion of the moment. For Schoenberg, we are very much the stretched string. Also, unlike atheistic Schopenhauer, Schoenberg was religious, though it must be admitted that in his religious works he depicts biblical characters like Jacob and Moses more as alter egos, fellow artists struggling for illumination and self-expression.

Earlier, I said that the twelve-tone row does not dictate how the composer is to use the row in his composing. There are, however, rules of the game—postulates, as George Perle calls them in his *Serial Composition and Atonality*. The rules are guarantors of coherence in the absence of tonality. I quote Perle's concise formulation of the four postulates of twelve-tone composition:[21]

1. The set comprises all twelve tones of the semitonal scale, arranged in a specific linear order.
2. No note appears more than once within the set.
3. The set is statable in any of its linear aspects: prime, inversion, retrograde, and retrograde-inversion.
4. The set, in each of its four transformations (i.e., linear aspects), is statable upon any degree of the semitonal scale.

We have already discussed the first two postulates, though an additional observation is in order. By a tone in a set, we are to understand not necessarily the tone that appears on the staff. The twelve-tone set is not an order of pitches but rather of so-called pitch-classes. What matters is the interval. In the Webern tone-row quoted above, the A that follows the initial B-flat refers to any A whatsoever. It designates the class to which every A belongs. Wherever the A sounds in the original set within the piece, whether above or below the B-flat, it will be functionally a semitone away.[22]

As for the third postulate, the permutations of the original set allow for a variation and complexity that could be absent if a work were confined to a single row in its prime aspect.[23] Inversion occurs when the tones of the original set appear upside down, when, for example, an upward second in the original set becomes a downward second. Retrograde occurs when the tones appear in reverse order, and retrograde-inversion when they appear in reverse order *and* upside down. Combinations of these four aspects can, of course, occur simultaneously, as they often do in twelve-tone music.[24]

The fourth postulate may be called the Postulate of Non-Literalness. In the Webern set, what is given in the opening tetrachord is not the literal pitches that spell B-A-C-H. It is rather the signature *order of intervals*: downward minor second, upward minor third, downward minor second. The order E, D-sharp, F-sharp, and E-sharp would do just as well and is allowed, indeed invited, by postulate four, which for this reason can also be called the Postulate of Intervallic Absoluteness. According to this postulate, a given set of twelve tones, or any of its permissible variations, can start on any tone of the chromatic scale. Since the set can appear in four different forms (prime, inversion, retrograde, retrograde-inversion), there are altogether *forty-eight* possible forms of the prime set.

In their theoretical writings, Schoenberg and Webern stress the importance of the musical *idea* and the successful articulation and communication of this idea. All art, for them, aims above all at "comprehensibility."[25] This goal is maximally achieved in music in the thoroughgoing, every-which-way unity of a twelve-tone work. Unity, here, consists in the relative self-identity of the row in its four aspects or transmutations, which are all mirror images of one another. At the very end of his lecture series, *The Path to the New*

Music, Webern uses an ancient Latin word-square to convey the identity in difference in what he calls "the round of twelve notes":[26]

SATOR
AREPO
TENET
OPERA
ROTAS

One possible translation is: "The sower Arepo keeps the work circling."[27] The square is a fourfold palindrome that reads the same from top to bottom, bottom to top, left to right, and right to left.[28] It is clever, devilishly clever, and is the brother of the numerical "magic square" that plays a central role in *Doctor Faustus*. According to Webern, the word-order of the Sator square, like that of twelve-tone music, is "ever different and yet always the same."[29] The implication is that the task of the composer, like that of the sower Arepo, is to keep the circling going, to sow seeds of free creativity in the fatefully recurring circles of the row and its permutations.[30]

For the ordinary human listener, twelve-tone music is a hard go. In addition to its overall disjointed sound, it is difficult to discern by ear what is often an intricate and carefully planned order and to detect the row on which the music is based. I find this next to impossible, which does not prevent me from enjoying some serial works more than others (Berg's *Violin Concerto* comes to mind), or at least finding them interesting as curiosities and grotesques on which great skill has been perversely lavished. In the next part of this chapter, we shall return to twelve-tone music in the context of Mann's novel and how this forbidding music born of calculation relates to human meaning and feeling.[31]

Part Two: Summa Demonologica

My title is from Erich Heller's *Thomas Mann, The Ironic German*. Heller observes that the Faustus novel, a "*summa demonologica* of Thomas Mann's imagination," brings together ideas from Mann's earlier works, now explicitly under the sign of Satan: the dissolution of life by music (especially the music of Wagner) in *Buddenbrooks*, the ascetic artist's surrender to Dionysian chaos in *Death in Venice*, the spiritually heightening effect of disease in *The Magic Mountain*, and the musical Germany intent on military breakthroughs in Mann's early *Reflections of a Nonpolitical Man*.[32]

Mann's novel appeared in 1947. Its full title is *Doctor Faustus, The Life of the German Composer Adrian Leverkühn As Told by a Friend*.[33] The friend and fictional biographer is Serenus Zeitblom, a Catholic humanist and amateur musician[34] who serves as the devoted witness of Leverkühn's tragic fate.[35] Serenus begins writing in 1943, in the middle of the war, and ends in 1945. His biography covers the years from 1885, the year of Adrian's birth, to 1940, when Adrian dies. The novel is, in Heller's phrase, "the tragic parody" of the *Faust Book* of 1587, which Mann closely follows and brilliantly translates into the sphere of music.[36]

Of the many influences on Mann's novel, the most important by far is Nietzsche, who is never mentioned by name. Mann explains why in his *Story of a Novel*: "the euphoric musician [Leverkühn] has been made so much Nietzsche's substitute that the original is no longer permitted a separate existence."[37] We see the pervasive presence of Nietzsche in the events of Leverkühn's life (which mirror those in Nietzsche's own), the novel's reflections on the artist and the degraded state of Europe, and quotations from Nietzsche's works.[38]

Another major influence is Arnold Schoenberg, who is also never named. The omission enraged the composer, who failed to see that the novel was not an historical statement about the origin of twelve-tone composition but a poetic appropriation. To placate his friend, Mann added the *Author's Note* that now appears at the end of the book. Eventually, the two men were reconciled.[39]

Finally, there is the influence of social critic and musicologist Theodor Adorno, who served as Mann's major source for the teachings about music in the novel. Mann regularly quotes passages from Adorno's *Philosophy of New Music* (of which Mann had an advance copy) and puts them into the mouths of Leverkühn and his teacher, Wendell Kretzschmar. Of special importance to Mann was Adorno's pointing out "the dire consequences that must flow from the constructive Schoenbergian approach to music."[40]

The story centers on the composer Adrian Leverkühn's pact with a devil who promises twenty-four years of inspired musical creativity in exchange for the composer's soul, or rather his capacity for human love. The pact consists in Adrian's having deliberately contracted syphilis from a prostitute he once met at a brothel in order to unleash the animal spirits that incite genius. Mann adopts Nietzsche's idea that the modern artist suffers from an excess of rational awareness and the consequent depletion of life and creative energy. Adrian needs the Dionysian jolt that will liberate the ironically objective composer-thinker from the sterile business of mere games and musical parody and allow him to soar. The satanic encounter, modeled on Ivan's similar meeting in Dostoevsky's *Brothers Karamazov*, explicates and makes official a path already taken.[41] Adrian's disease takes its toll and, in the language of the *Faust Book*, "fetches" him in the end.

TEARS AND LAUGHTER

The cosmos plays a central role in Mann's novel. In Chapter One, I contrasted the cosmologies of Timaeus and Schopenhauer. For Timaeus, the cosmos is the best of possible worlds, mathematically constructed by a good and generous craftsman. It is animated by an intelligent soul that has a musical, diatonic order. The world of the likely story is a genuine *kosmos*, a beautifully ordered whole. For Schopenhauer, the external world is the tragic realm of infinite desire and the phenomenal incarnation of the will. In *Doctor Faustus*, the cosmos receives yet another pessimistic depiction. No longer a cosmos in the true sense, the natural world is wedded to mischief and monstrosity. Its strangeness attracts the daring Adrian (whose last name, Leverkühn, suggests "to live boldly") but repulses the humanistic and wary Serenus.

Cosmic oddity first appears in Chapter 3, in the natural inquiries of Adrian's father, Jonathan Leverkühn, who has a desire to "speculate the elements" (16).[42] The phrase is inspired by the original *Faust Book*. There we learn that John Faustus was a *Speculierer*, a speculator who turned away from theology to concentrate on the forbidden study of "figures," "characters," and "conjurations."[43] Adrian recapitulates this apostasy when he gives up the study of theology for music. He inherits from his father the Faustian fascination with hidden things and a "thirst for the cosmic." He inherits his musical proclivity from his warm-voiced mother, Elsbeth. Despite her inner musicality, she does not espouse music, as Serenus tells us in Chapter 4, but modestly suppresses her musical potential.[44]

Jonathan Leverkühn shares his scientific findings with Adrian, Adrian's brother Georg, and Serenus, when they are young boys. The episode introduces us to the demonry of nature. According to Serenus, "nature produces such a plethora of things that have a puzzling way of spilling over into the realm of magic—ambiguous moods, half-concealed allusions that insinuate some eerie uncertainty" (16–17). A case in point is the butterfly named *Hetaera esmeralda* (Emerald Courtesan), "whose transparent nakedness makes it a lover of dusky, leafy shade," and whose deceptive coloring allows it to mimic perfectly a windblown petal. The mimicry is just one example of mischievous nature, which sometimes, as in the case of the leaf butterfly, combines "poison and beauty" (19). *Hetaera esmeralda* will be the magic name that Adrian assigns to the prostitute who infected him, the name inscribed in his compositions as their deepest personal secret.

Jonathan Leverkühn personifies the quest for meaning in the wordless realm of nature. He is like one who hears instrumental music and strains to decipher its elusive message. Leverkühn searches for meaning in the tiny hieroglyphic-like markings on the shell of a Caledonian conch. "Their meticulous complexity," Serenus admits, "gave every appearance of intending to communicate something" (20). Leverkühn knows that his search is in vain. But he refuses to separate ornament and meaning, which are combined, as he observes, in the ornate symbols of ancient scripts. Undaunted by nature's indecipherability, he stubbornly clings to his fascination with a meaning he knows he will never find. "For the message to be inaccessible, and for one to immerse oneself in that contradiction," he tells the boys, "also has its pleasure" (20). His obsession with the hermetic will be further developed in his son's far more advanced Faustianism.

The elder Leverkühn also has an interest in "the unity of animate and so-called inanimate matter." The lifelike behavior of the inorganic is strikingly revealed in the store-bought crystals that develop through osmotic pressure into "a grotesque miniature landscape of different colored growths." Serenus describes them as especially remarkable because of their deep melancholy. The growths seem to strive pitifully to be what they can never be. The boys suspect that the entities are plants. But no, the elder Leverkühn explains, they only pretend to be (23). He goes on to show how "these woeful imitators of life" turn toward the sun with what seems to be a desperate longing for warmth and joy. "Even though they're dead," the father laments. As tears come to his eyes, his son Adrian shakes with suppressed laughter.

This early scene is telling in several ways. It brings the cosmos to the fore as a central theme; it introduces the *hetaera* as a leitmotif; and it gives an inkling of Adrian's demonic leanings, manifested in his cold-hearted laughter at the pitiful mimicry of longing and his father's sentimentality. It also sheds light on Serenus, who forswears cosmic oddities: "Phantasms of this sort are exclusively the concern of nature, and in particular of nature when she is willfully tempted by man. In the worthy realm of the humanities one is safe from all such spooks" (33).

THE TEACHINGS OF WENDELL KRETZSCHMAR

Adrian is initiated into music by "barnyard Hanne," a floppy-breasted milkmaid who works on the Leverkühn farm. An earthy Dionysian, she teaches the boys to sing folk songs and rounds. Serenus comments on Hanne's exuberant love of singing: "And strangely enough, whereas Elsbeth Leverkühn, with her lovely voice, abstained from singing out of some kind of chaste modesty, this creature still smelling of her animals would go at it with abandon" (31). The singing of rounds (the equivalent of our "Row, Row, Row Your Boat") is Adrian's raucous introduction to the high and subtle art of counterpoint or polyphony, which Serenus describes as "a temporal intertwining with imitative entrances." This art will play a central role in Adrian's compositional life.

Adrian's theoretical relation to music begins when he discovers the circle of fifths while visiting his uncle Nicholas, a violin maker (43). Adrian uses an old harmonium to show Serenus how the magic circle works: "when you figure it out for yourself for the first time, it seems curious how it all hangs together and goes in circles" (50). The circle shows how keys are related to one another through the perfect fifth. Keys a fifth apart, like G major and D major, are harmonic next-door neighbors. The key signatures of neighboring keys differ by only one sharp or flat. This allows music to move easily from one key to the other. Adrian plays an F-sharp, A-sharp, C-sharp. The triad appears to signal the key of F-sharp major. But when you add an E above, as Adrian does, the once stable triad is "unmasked" as the unstable dominant seventh chord of B major, the key a fifth away. The circle of fifths and the revelation that a chord has no inherent key lead Adrian to an insight: "It's all relationship [Beziehung]. And if you want to give it a more exact name, then call it ambiguity" (51). Music, he proclaims, is "ambiguity as a system." The relativity that Adrian relishes contrasts with the worldview of Serenus, whose commitment to the ethical realm rests on the belief in "absolute values" (49).

In Chapter 8, Serenus recounts the lectures of the eccentric church organist, Wendell Kretzschmar, whose teachings, general ideas, and mannerisms are those of Theodor Adorno, Mann's musicological advisor. Serenus makes much of Kretzschmar's fatal stutter: "how tragic, since he was a man with a great wealth of urgent ideas and a passionate desire to communicate them in speech" (54). The stutter symbolizes the tragic fate of music when it struggles to translate its world of tones into the world of words.

The Kretzschmar lectures are a feast for lovers of music theory and history but the despair of the uninitiated. They introduce many of the oppositions that recur in the novel: asceticism versus sensualism, cult versus culture, objectivity versus subjectivity, polyphony versus harmony. The recurrence of interrelated leitmotifs in the novel (and there are many) is the sign of Mann's imitation of music in the sphere of words. His tightly organized novel is like twelve-tone music, where, as Adorno says, "there is no 'free' note,"[45] no note that is not integrated into the structure of the whole. Similarly, in Mann's contrapuntal montage, there is no "free" theme, no motif or symbol that is not intimately related to all the others.

The first two lectures are on Beethoven's heroic struggles with composition. Beethoven is the prototype of the lonely artist, all the lonelier because of his isolating deafness. In the first lecture, Kretzschmar explains that the late piano sonata in C minor (Opus 111) lacked a traditional third movement because the second was an extended farewell to the sonata as a form. It expressed in tones Beethoven's awareness of coming death. The second lecture is about Beethoven's struggle with the fugue, which "belonged to an age of liturgical music which lay far in the past." (64).

Music in the west began with the cult, that is, Christian liturgy. It took the form of Gregorian chant and, later, polyphony. In time, with the rise of opera, music desired emotional expressiv-

ity. It liberated itself from worship and asserted its secular autonomy, ultimately even freeing itself from words. It became *culture* as
a counter-cult devoted to aestheticism and the expression of feeling. The music of great composers was no longer for the church
but for the concert hall. Kretzschmar explains that Beethoven's
attempt to write fugues, especially for his monumental *Missa solemnis*, embodies the homesickness of music, which, having freed
itself from the cult, longs to return to its cultic origins (65).[46] The
claim is related to a recurring image in the novel: time's *revolving
sphere*, which causes the old to become new again. The circling
path of time accounts for why, in music and in history at large, the
reactionary and the revolutionary tend to coalesce.

Adrian has a fatal attraction to the medieval age, in which the
cultic spirit reigned supreme and the individual was immersed in
a community of belief. He displays that attraction here. Moved
by Kretzschmar's claim that music's secular liberation was only a
passing phase, Adrian fantasizes about music's imminent return
to the role of serving "a higher fellowship, which did not have to
be, as at one time, the Church." Serenus balks. "But the alternative
to culture," he says, "is barbarism." Adrian's cool response contains
the beginnings of a Nietzsche-inspired ideology, which affirms the
ascendancy of instinct and will over reason: "Our level is that of
civilized behavior—a very praiseworthy state, no doubt, but neither can there be any doubt that we would have to become much
more barbaric to be capable of culture once again."

The fascinating topic of Kretzschmar's third lecture is "Music
and the Eye." Recalling the medieval system of ornate symbols or
neumes, Kretzschmar praises the purely optical effects of written
music. This appeal to the eye, the symbol of the mind, argues for
music as the most intellectual of the arts. The reason is that in
music form and content are perfectly intertwined. In direct opposition to Kierkegaard, who identified music with sensuality,[47]
Kretzschmar maintains that music in its essence is anti-sensual,
indeed ascetic. Music's deepest desire, he muses, is perhaps "not to

be heard at all, not even seen, not even felt, but if that were possible, to be perceived and viewed in some intellectually pure fashion, in some realm beyond the heart even." But music, alas, does not live in this ideal realm. Wedded to the bodily world, it must seek its realization there, especially in the sensual orgy of orchestral music.[48] Kretzschmar finishes his reflection by praising the piano as "the direct and sovereign representative of music *per se* in all its intellectuality" (69).

This brings us to the fourth lecture. It, too, is about a return to origins. Its theme is music in its relation to the elemental. Kretzschmar calls attention to music as a time-honored cosmic metaphor. He recalls how Wagner, at the beginning of his *Ring* cycle, equates the elements of music, represented by the E-flat major triad, with "those of the world itself." He goes on to speculate about how music throughout its history, sometimes without any knowledge of its past, desires "to rediscover itself, to regenerate." A prime example of this naïve genius for renewal is the real-life Johann Conrad Beissel, who emigrated to Germantown, Pennsylvania, and founded the Seventh Day Baptists. Beissel boldly set out to compose hymns and to invent his own system of singing. In a Luther-like spirit that combined reaction and revolution, he wanted to "begin anew, do things better," by devising a musical system that was more suited to the simplicity of his followers' souls. He wanted to return to elements. To do so, Beissel invented a system of "master" and "servant" tones. If the hymn was in C major, then the tones of the C-major triad (C, E, and G) would be the master notes that all the other notes of the scale had to serve. Accented syllables of a text were to be represented only by master notes, unaccented syllables by servant notes. Kretschmar describes the otherworldly way in which Beissel's rigidly composed hymns were sung: "It had all been sung falsetto, the singers barely opening their mouths or moving their lips—a most marvelous acoustic effect." It was as if the tones "had descended from on high to float angelically above the heads of the congregation" (74).[49]

After the lecture, Adrian expresses admiration for the reforms of Beissel, whom Serenus derides as a "backwoods dictator" (75). He admires what Serenus finds ridiculous: the crude distinction between master and servant notes, which Adrian regards as a praiseworthy commitment to *law*. Adrian's praise of law prefigures his invention of twelve-tone composition as the pinnacle of musical rigor. Law corrects what the austere Adrian contemptuously calls music's "bovine warmth," which could use some cold-minded intellectual discipline. Music, in fact, desires this discipline. Serenus reminds Adrian that although there was discipline at the beginning of Beissel's project, in the end the heartfelt singing of the congregation restored to music its bovine warmth. Echoing Kretzschmar's claim that music combines asceticism and sensuality, Adrian responds in religious terms: "Music always does prior penance for its sensual realization" (76).

Serenus recoils from Adrian's depiction of music as a paradoxical union of rigor and self-indulgence. With his characteristic disdain for the demonic, he defends music as a gift of life and of God. Instead of mocking music's paradox, one should see in the opposites that music unites "the fullness of its nature" (77). One should *love* these opposites. Adrian responds with a question: "Do you believe that love is the strongest emotion?" When Serenus asks in return whether there is any stronger, Adrian responds in the affirmative: "Yes, interest." Interest, Serenus suggests, is "love that has been deprived of its animal warmth." Adrian agrees. The substitution of interest for love foreshadows Adrian's willingness to part with love's warmth in exchange for a brilliant future as a composer of rigorously disciplined, anti-Romantic music.

A WEDDING, A STRICT STYLE, AND A MIGRAINE

Twelve-tone composition first appears in Chapter 22, where Adrian informs Serenus of his musical brainchild.[50] Their conversation about this austere method is occasioned, ironically, by two happy events: Adrian's sister's wedding and Serenus's announcement of his plans to marry. Adrian's description of a "strict style" (a term Kretschmar had applied to pre-harmonic counterpoint) draws on many of the features of twelve-tone composition I summarized in Part One.[51]

By this point in the story, much has happened. I must leap over many crucial past events in Adrian's life and development. These include his private composition studies with Kretzschmar, his failed attempt to flee his musical destiny and humble his pride by studying theology, and his encounter with two bizarre theology professors: Kumpf, a lusty reincarnation of Luther, and the demonic Schleppfuss, who teaches that evil, the Evil One himself, "was a necessary outpouring and inevitable extension of the holy existence of God Himself" (109). In Chapter 16, a porter who physically resembles Schleppfuss plays the role of Mephistopheles by leading the unsuspecting Adrian to the brothel where he first meets his *Hetaera esmeralda* (150). The scene closely follows a similar event in the life of Nietzsche.[52] In Chapter 19, Adrian returns to his poisonous butterfly, this time with fatal intent.

Most worthy of mention is Adrian's fascination with the number square in Dürer's *Melancolia I* in Chapter 12. The drawing depicts a sad angel, an Adrian figure, sitting dejectedly among various geometrical solids, measuring devices (including an hourglass), and a magic square. The magic is that the numbers in the square are so arranged that when they are added, whether from the top or bottom, horizontally or diagonally, the result is always 34—an accuracy Serenus finds annoying. Adrian is so taken with this mystic symbol of flawless symmetry that he places a reproduction of the square above his piano, as if it were his god or beloved. Like the Sator square, it is the emblem of the tonal perfection to which twelve-tone composition aspires, especially in its integration of the horizontal and vertical dimensions of musical space.

By the time we see Adrian in Chapter 22, he has turned away from Lutheran theology and is the composer of several musical works. These include a parodic farewell to the symphony (*Phosphorescence of the Sea*) and musical settings for poems by Clemens Brentano. His two masterpieces lie ahead: the *Apocalypsis cum figuris*, an oratorio inspired by Dürer's woodcuts of that title, and the *Lamentation of Dr. Faustus*. He has already begun to inscribe in his compositions the secret name "that haunts his works like a rune" (165). The letter-tones are, in German usage, "H-E-A-E-Es: *Hetaera esmeralda*," that is, B-E-A-E-E-flat. The five-note theme proceeds in healthy reliable consonances before sinking chromatically, as if falling ill, to E-flat at the end. The *hetaera* tone-code is more than a personal reminiscence. It symbolizes the mystic unity of sensual impulse and intellectual contrivance. It is the paradox of music expressed in musical terms.

Chapter 22 dramatizes the sensual/intellectual opposition from Kretzschmar's lecture in the two parts of the conversation between Adrian and Serenus. In the first part, the friends discuss the sensualism that marriage sanctifies but cannot erase. The idea draws on Nietzsche's view that high things have low origins. Marriage is like music: it aspires to the pure and holy but fulfills itself in the flesh. The second part is a sudden modulation, as Adrian, in the heat of enthusiasm, describes the unprecedented intellectual "cold" of the twelve-tone method.

After some sexual banter about Serenus's upcoming marriage, the conversation turns to Adrian's opera version of Shakespeare's *Love's Labour's Lost*—a parodic play about the attempt to abstain from sex. In this context, Adrian fondly recalls Beissel, "that strange lawgiver and renewer of music" (202). He admires the man for his will to power in establishing a strict style that combines restoration with revolution. He sees in this project the solution to a current crisis, "a remedy in a time of ravaged conventions and the dissolution of all objective obligations" (203). The formulation echoes Schoenberg and especially Adorno regarding the current state of music, whose subjective freedom of expression caused it to degenerate into platitudes and sterility. Also suggested is the need for a cultural revolution that will bring about a return to a rigorous organization of life.

Freedom, when left to itself, Adrian asserts, despairs of being creative on its own and seeks protection and security in objectivity. It tends to dialectical reversal and "finds fulfillment in subordinating itself to law, rule, coercion, system." Serenus objects: there is no freedom at all in dictatorship born of revolution. Adrian dismisses this worry as no more than "a political song." His claim about the dialectical nature of art is worth quoting in full:

> In art, in any case, the subjective and objective are intertwined beyond recognition; each proceeds from the other and assumes the character of the other, the subjective takes shape as the objective and is awakened to spontaneity again by genius— 'dynamized,' as we say—and all of a sudden is speaking the language of subjectivity. (203)

The claim echoes similar formulations by Schoenberg and Adorno. It finds support in the case of a poet like Baudelaire, who expresses the strongest emotions through the strict form of the sonnet, or a composer like Bach who does so through the fugue. When Adrian discovered the circle of fifths, he declared that in music, "It's all relationship" (51). In the present chapter, he utters another absolute: "Organization is everything" (204).[53] Combining the two pronouncements, we get "Everything is organized relationality." This is the goal of twelve-tone composition. Tones, as Schoenberg says, are related only to one another and not to a central tone or key. And although the twelve-tone method rejects the circle of fifths, the principle of the magic circle is retained: "Relation is all."

Adrian describes the general principles of strict style in terms reminiscent of Schoenberg. The new strict style is "the total integration of all musical dimensions, the neutrality of each over against the other by means of complete organization" (204). We detect in this totalitarian formula a will to power that risks reducing music to a mere medium for the establishment of a perfectly rational, quasi-mathematical scheme—a tonal utopia. Adrian strongly affirms what we saw in Part One about the new music, that it would be a new, radicalized version of the old counterpoint that goes all the way back to Perotin in the thirteenth century. It would break free of the soft tyranny of chords and harmony, so dear to composers like Wagner, Strauss, and even the polyphonic Bach, who in the novel is regularly demoted to the status of a mere "harmonist."[54] In its reactionary zeal, the new music will be true counterpoint as the simultaneity of independent voices, with no concern for consonant combinations. It will overcome the antithesis of the "polyphonic fugue" and the "homophonic sonata" (205).[55]

But can it be done? Can music be made subject to a rational total organization? Adrian tells Serenus that he has already taken a step in that direction. In a song based on the Brentano poem "Oh sweet maiden," he used the *hetaera* tone-row, B-E-A-E-E-flat, as a "musical word" capable of variations.[56] But the five-tone row is too confining. For greater flexibility, one would have to build longer words using all twelve tones of the equal-tempered semitone alphabet: "Each tone in the entire composition, melodic and harmonic [i.e., horizontal and vertical] would have to demonstrate its relation to this predetermined basic row" (205). When Serenus worries that the confinement to a single row might lead to musical impoverishment, Adrian tells him what we already know about twelve-tone method, that the row can start on any pitch and can be inverted as well as played backwards to produce forty-eight different forms. Moreover, a single piece can use more than one row, just as a fugue can have more than one subject. The important thing is that a tone strictly preserves its position in the row or in one of its alternate iterations. This ensures the coveted "neutrality" of harmony and melody, of the vertical and horizontal dimensions of music. Neutrality, here, means that neither dimension is subject to the other, just as in the tone-row there are no master and servant notes. As Serenus correctly observes, what Adrian has just described is a magic square.

Will people be able to hear the order? Adrian coolly responds to Serenus's question by repeating what Kretzschmar had said: not everything in music needs to be heard. Just as we are not aware of the precise methods by which the course of the stars has been ordered, we will not hear the method of twelve-tone composition. Nevertheless, Adrian claims, people will hear "the order itself, and the perception of it would provide an unknown aesthetic satisfaction." The assurance echoes the official (and dubious) claim of Schoenberg and his followers.[57]

Serenus notes that twelve-tone composition is a kind of composing prior to composing. Would not the composer, then, severely limit his creative freedom by binding himself to a pre-selected row as if to a predestined fate? But the composer is free, Adrian insists, because the restraint is self-imposed. It is a fate freely chosen, a free subjection. If restraint is imposed on the melodic dimension, Serenus worries, what would happen to the vertical dimension of music? Wouldn't chords be the result of mere chance? Adrian responds again with something we already know: the new music represents the "emancipation of the dissonance." This gives unlimited freedom to what counts as a chord. But what if a chord, produced by the collision of vocal lines at a given moment of time, turns out to be one of the old traditional chords like the diminished seventh? Well, says Adrian, in that case something old will have been given new life. The musical work will have renewed what was worn out, breathed new life into a cliché.

Adrian's interweaving of old and new prompts Serenus to observe that his friend's brave new world contains an element of restoration. Adrian responds in terms that recall the circle of fifths as the symbol of ambiguity. Life's interesting phenomena, he says, are Janus-faced and tend to combine progress and regression. When Serenus tries to apply this idea to the current state of Germany, Adrian objects. He returns to the aesthetic realm of music and the "ancient desire to impose order on every sound and to resolve music's magical essence into human reason" (207). For Serenus, however, it's the other way around: "your system looks to me as if it's more apt to resolve human reason into magic."

At this point, Adrian puts a fist to his temple in response to one of his migraines, an affliction he inherited from his speculating father. The gesture resembles that of the sad angel in Dürer's drawing. It also suggests the birth of Athena from the forehead of Zeus. In this case, the birth is that of Adrian's brainchild: the strict style of twelve-tone composition, the symbol of tonal severity. "Reason and magic," Adrian says, as he presses against his head, "surely meet and become one in what is called wisdom, initiation, in a belief in the stars, in numbers. . . ." On this ambiguous word that combines reason and magic, his speech breaks off. Serenus observes that everything his friend has said "bore the stamp of pain, stood under its sign, however brilliant and worthy of consideration it might be" (208). For Adrian, ingenium and pain are wedded. We hear more about this tragic union in Adrian's conversation with the devil.

As the friends continue their walk home from the wedding, they stop beside the Cattle Trough on the family farm and gaze at the nearby pond. "Cold," Adrian says, pointing to the pond with his still-aching head, "much too cold for swimming now." "Cold," he repeats with a shudder. The word is often used to describe Adrian, who applies it to himself in his letter to Kretzschmar: "I fear I am a mean fellow, for I have not warmth . . . I am decidedly cold" (139). The scene in the present chapter is a prophecy of Adrian's later attempt, after the self-inflicted disease has ravaged his nervous system, to drown himself in the pond's cold depths. His shudder is a presentiment of that attempt.

AN INTERVIEW IN PALESTRINA

At the end of Chapter 23, we hear that Adrian's work on his parodic opera version of Shakespeare's *Love's Labour's Lost* has stalled. "Parody of artificiality," as Serenus observes, "was difficult to maintain as a style" (224). The artificiality refers to the play itself, which is a parody of Renaissance humanism and the high-minded but foolish attempt to forego the pleasures of love. Adrian seeks refuge from the world and the renewal of his creative energy in Palestrina, the town from which the famous composer gets his name. It is referred to as Penestrino in *Inferno* 27, in the realm of the evil counselors. Here, in this once-pagan, now-Catholic city, Adrian meets his Lutheran devil.[58] Serenus reports the fatal interview in Chapter 25, the bulk of which is Adrian's own documentation of the event. The text is written on music paper and transcribed by Serenus, who is unwilling to entrust the manuscript to a printer.

The long interview with the devil, located at the novel's center, is a literary tour de force. Mann incorporates many details from the *Faust Book*. He also draws on assertions by Nietzsche, Dostoyevsky, Kierkegaard, and Adorno. As one commentator notes, the chapter is "the apotheosis of what has gone before, and it sows the seeds of all that is to follow."[59] The dialogue is written in the archaic Luther-style German that Adrian used in his letter to Kretzschmar. Adrian and his devil, in other words, not only speak the same language but even prefer the same dialect. The tone throughout is that of banter and mockery.

During the interview, the devil takes on various forms. First, he looks like a *strizzi* or pimp, whose verbal mannerisms mimic those of the crude Luther-figure Kumpf, then a "better gentleman" who resembles Adorno, then the demonic theologian Schleppfuss, and finally the pimp again. The string of personae is like variations on a theme, with the theme returning at the end. The devil enters Adrian's room in the evening, after Adrian has spent the day nursing a migraine. He is reading Kierkegaard's praise of Mozart's *Don Giovanni* in *Either/Or*, the work in which Kierkegaard identifies music with sensualism and sin. Adrian addresses his visitor in Italian but is corrected: "Speak only German, good old-fashioned German . . . my favorite language" (239). The devil tells Adrian that he has come to offer time—"mad time, devilish time"—for Adrian to rise to the heights of which he is capable, to "transcend himself by high illumination."

Hell has known for a while that Adrian was capable of much. The devil even quotes passages from the Brentano poem in which Adrian first used his ingenious letter code. It was this ingenium that attracted Hell's interest. But for Adrian to soar in his genius and transcend parody, he needed "a little kindling, incitement, and inebriation" (244). This intoxicating poison was provided by the *hetaera*, whom the devil at a later point calls "my little one" (263).

The devil reminds Adrian that great suffering will be required, as with all artists who aspire to greatness (246). He compares Adrian's condition to that of Hans Christian Andersen's little mermaid, who in her longing for an immortal soul willingly endured the knife pains in her newly sprouted legs. The devil then gives a chillingly clinical description of the disease that Adrian inflicted on himself four years ago. Here, Mann effectively translates the theological ideas of the *Faust Book* into the cold and pitiless facts of modern pathology. Adrian's sin, we should recall, was not against God but against his own nature—his body, mind, and wellbeing. The sin's wages are in his brain, the cerebral workshop and forge that is simultaneously blessed and cursed with excitation. The clinical account of the disease recalls the impishness of nature in the speculations of Jonathan Leverkühn. The devil even uses the osmosis involved in syphilis to taunt Adrian for having mocked this process when he was young (251).

Finally, the devil-pimp reminds Adrian that ingenium cannot be separated from its relation to hell: "The artist is the brother of the felon and the madman" (252).[60] The devil sets the record straight: he is not the intellectual skeptic, "the man of ravaging criticism," as many believe. On the contrary, he comes to cure great souls of being "sicklied o'er with the pale cast of thought." He despises criticism and its ravages and prefers "the shining want of thought (*die prangende Unbedenklichkeit*)." No, the devil is no critic. He is, on the contrary, "the Lord of Enthusiasm."[61] As the devil glides into a discussion of music, he morphs into his next guise— that of an Adorno doppelganger.

The revised devil launches into Adorno's métier, criticism, which is what the new music has become. He expounds on the degenerate state into which music has fallen and praises the inaugurators of new music for at least being undeluded. Composition, says the devil, echoing Schoenberg and Adorno, "has become difficult." He proceeds to rail against the illusory character of the self-contained "work," which wants to be taken as a perfect organic whole but is in fact no more than a patchwork that falsifies current reality, smooths over the suffering and dissonances of the age.[62] The objective work is something Adrian himself had criticized earlier as a pretense and sham (192). The new music tolerates no such games and fictions, no idealizing of emotion and suffering in the artificial terms of Romantic harmony. Instead, it expresses, says the Adorno-devil, "the unfeigned and untransfigured expression of suffering in its real moment" (256).

In defense of his cold intellectualism, Adrian mocks the devil's appeal to emotion: "Touching, touching. The Devil waxes poetical . . . he beshits his way into art" (256). Adrian suggests that another way to escape what has become stale, flat, and unprofitable would be the parodying of outmoded musical forms. This is, of course, Adrian's specialty. But no, the devil tells him, tricks of that sort will hardly bring much greatness. The only path to genius is through sin, as the Christian Kierkegaard rightly affirmed. Only through a violent breakthrough, a transgression, will Adrian raise himself to dizzying heights. Adrian mockingly infers that he is to grow "osmotic vegetation," like the chemicals in his father's crystal garden (258). He will, indeed. But this will happen only if he forgoes his insistence on objectivity and "so-called truth" and yields to the wild promptings of subjective impulse. Adrian's skepticism regarding the devil's real presence is a case in point: "Does it pay to ask whether I really am? Is 'really' not what works, and truth not experience and feeling?" Echoing Nietzsche, he asserts that "an untruth of the sort that enhances energy is a match for every profitably virtuous truth" and that "creative disease, genius-bestowing disease . . . is a thousand times dearer to life than plodding health." In a dark prophecy of the Hitler Youth, the devil extols the fiendish enthusiasm this robust disease inspires in the young:

> A whole horde and generation of receptive lads, all healthy to the core, throw themselves upon the work of the diseased genius whom disease has made a genius, admire, praise, and exalt the work, carry it away with them, refashion it among themselves, bequeath it to the culture, which does not live by homebaked bread alone, but equally by donations and poisons from the apothecary of the Blessed Messengers. (258)[63]

Yes, the devil offers time enough for Adrian to soar to the new "enthusiastic surge of health" that will come after the pains of the little mermaid. But to satisfy Adrian's inveterate craving for objectivity, he offers an additional transcendence. Adrian will lead [führen] and "set the march for the future" (258–59). The devil here sounds like Zarathustra, as he tells Adrian that "lads will swear by your name, who thanks to your madness will no longer need to be mad." Adrian as an aesthetic Führer will break through the age.[64] Through his will to power in the mystic realm of tones, he will bring about a double barbarism, double because it comes after liberal humanitarianism. The devil adds that mystic passion and true religion lie outside of bourgeois experience and that it is he, the devil, not the liberal theologian, who speaks on behalf of religion. He echoes Kierkegaard, who took aim at the easy superficialities of cultural Christianity.

During the latter part of his tirade, the devil was already beginning to assume a new form: that of the demonic theologian Schleppfuss, who played on Adrian's taste for the knowledge of hidden things. Adrian now indulges that fatal curiosity. He wants to know about hell, as Faust did in the original story: "What is life like in Old Scratch's house?" The devil confesses that it is not easy to put hell into words. Hell, like music, lies apart from all language, so Adrian must be content with *symbolis*. Hell is the place "'where all things cease,' every mercy every grace, every forbearance" (260). It combines gruesome pain and obscene pleasure, pitiful groaning and mocking laughter. These opposites will later be combined musically in Adrian's *Apocalypsis cum figuris*.

When Adrian presses the devil to say more about what the damned can expect in hell, the devil accuses him of asking only to find a way out of the deal through *attritio cordis*, the wearing down of the obstinate heart through fear of punishment. But no, this will not save a soul, which can escape hell only through the *contritio* of "true Protestant remorse for sin" (262). In any case, Adrian can expect nothing new in hell—nothing, that is, beyond his own extreme-seeking nature.

Adrian tries again to best Old Scratch, this time in matters concerning redemption. He suggests the possibility of "a prideful remorse." This is *contritio* in which grace and forgiveness come from the proud sinner's having gone all the way to the bottom of despair and come out on the other side (as Dante does at the end of the *Inferno*). The idea is that the deepest guilt is "the last and irresistible provocation of infinite goodness" (263). Here Adrian speaks for Mann's hope, expressed at the end of the novel, that his country's descent into hell will somehow be redeemed through a grace induced by despair. The devil is unimpressed by this prospect. Hell, he says, is filled with such theologians, who, like Adrian's father, gave themselves to speculation.[65]

The devil now assumes his fifth and final guise. He appears again as bawd and actor. In this concluding phase of the interview, the devil sums up Adrian's life, drawing extensively on elements of the *Faust Book*. The pimp-devil continues to emphasize the speculative drive and cosmic thirst, the desire to know the absolute, that Adrian inherited from his father. Hell sought out Adrian precisely because of his ingenium and fascination for hidden things. It was in large part this fascination rather than any religiosity that led Adrian to theology, which he soon abandoned for the Faustian figures, characters, and incantations of music.

The devil connects this interest in figures and spells with Adrian's twelve-tone method, which combines reason and magic. The strict twelve-tone style, the tonal counterpart of Dürer's magic square, is the work of cunning and calculation. It seems to be rational but is in fact "daringly aimed against reason and common sense" (263). It is, in other words, a madness. Adrian's longing for the cosmic ordering of elements was not enough to enable him to use his cold method in an inspired way. To cure his dull chastity and asceticism, Adrian needed union with Esmeralda, who supplied "the aphrodisiac of the brain." Continuing to use the Faust legend as his playbook, the devil reminds Adrian that no ritual or meeting in the woods is necessary to seal the bargain, which had already been secured by the *hetaera*. Adrian will indeed be given, as Faust was, twenty-four years of "high flying time." After this, he will be fetched.

One thing alone remains to be mentioned: the price. Adrian must forswear love. "Love," says the devil, "is forbidden you insofar as it warms. Your life shall be cold—hence you may love no human" (264). For Adrian this is nothing new, since Cold is his element. The "small folk" that have invaded his brain, the devil says, do nothing new. They merely magnify what Adrian already was and is. In place of human warmth, Adrian will warm himself in the flames of artistic creation, into which he will flee from the coldness of his life. But then, as Adrian observes, he will go from his artistic heat back into the ice, which is his hell on earth. In the second half of the novel, Adrian will try, unsuccessfully, to flee his fate by seeking refuge in human love. Like the pathetic crystals he once mocked, he will long for warmth and joy. His effort will take the three forms that Serenus listed at the very beginning of the novel (8). Adrian will love an artistic woman (Marie Godeaux), an angelic child (Adrian's nephew, the boy Echo), and a "lightweight dandy" (the friend and violinist, Rudi Schwerdtfeger).

When the interview ends, Adrian feels the intense cold and loathing he felt when the devil first appeared. He swoons in disgust and then hears the voice of his friend and collaborator, Rudiger Schildknapp, who had accompanied him to Palestrina. Adrian finds himself once again sitting in his summer suit with Kierkegaard's book on his lap. But where is the tight-trousered bawd? Adrian speculates that he must have chased the devil away in a fit of indignation before his friend arrived.

Was the devil real or only a projection of Adrian's mind? The ambiguity lingers. What can be said is that the fiend that dwells in Adrian's mind is experienced by Adrian and by the reader as an all too real person, an Other with whom one can converse. Thanks to Mann's genius for vivid storytelling and taste for the uncanny, we share Adrian's experience of the reality, the mocking personality, of evil.[66]

REVELATIONS

In the second half of the novel, Adrian continues to indulge his thirst for the cosmic. In Chapter 27, he relates a fantastical Faustlike undersea adventure which he narrates as if it really happened. He tells Serenus about the sense of indiscretion and sinfulness he felt as the diving bell that was his vehicle went deeper and deeper into realms meant to be kept hidden (283). He then relates a similar adventure beyond the earth "into the ocean of the worlds." These imagined excursions repel Serenus, who sees no goodness, beauty, or even greatness in this "monster" that is the universe (286). He cannot understand the cries of "hosannah" that these so-called works of God evoke in some people: "Can a production ever be declared a work of God, if one's response to it can just as well be 'so what' as 'hosanna'?"[67]

The fruit of Adrian's cosmic transgressions is the orchestral fantasy, *Marvels of the Universe*. Serenus calls the sarcastically named work "a Luciferian travesty" that mocks not only "the dreadful clockwork of the world" but music itself as the cosmos of tones. The description recalls what Adrian says of himself at an earlier point as he comments on his proneness to laughter, that everything to him is its own parody (143).

Adrian's next musical work is based on the *Gesta Romanorum* (*Deeds of the Romans*), a medieval collection of legends, which Adrian writes as an opera for puppets. The odd idea is inspired by Heinrich Kleist's essay, "The Puppet Theater." Puppets are the embodiment of unconscious certitude. They move with grace because they do not think. Humankind lost grace, here understood as assured effortless movement, when Adam and Eve ate from the Tree of Knowledge and became conscious beings, whose reliance on knowledge makes them gravity-bound and prone to ineptness. The essay ends with a paradox: grace will return, along with lost innocence, only after we eat again of the Tree of Knowledge.[68] The paradox may be Mann's way of reminding Germany that after its unspeakable sins, any recovery of health will require a full recognition of its descent into hell. It will need to take another bite of the apple.

We hear about Adrian's desire to compose his *Apocalypsis* in Chapter 34, which Serenus divides into three parts, as if it were a sonata. In the first, Adrian, in great pain, starts work on his Dürer-based oratorio. In the second, Serenus reports the conversations about violence and dictatorship that he heard at the apartment of the graphic artist, Sixtus Kridwiss. In the third part, Serenus completes his description of the *Apocalypsis*. The work is an oratorio, like Bach's *St. Matthew Passion*, and is based not just on the Book of Revelation but on the entire visionary tradition. Serenus calls Adrian's cosmic synthesis "a new apocalypse of his own" (377). The curious division of the chapter stresses the continuity between Adrian's musical work and the fascist ideology of the Kridwiss circle.

At the beginning of the chapter, Serenus reports his dread at the coming of an imminent apocalypse: the passing away of bourgeois humanism, the age in which Serenus had made his intellectual home, and the rise of a new, post-humanist epoch. The world, he says, seems to be entering "a new, still unnamed sign of the zodiac" (372). The events about which Serenus writes take place in 1919, not long after the defeat of Germany in the first World War. Serenus connects his dread with the reactionary discussions about culture and politics that he heard in the Kridwiss circle. This was during the time that Adrian was giving birth to his *Apocalypsis*, "a work that did not lack certain bold and prophetic connections to those discussions, that confirmed and realized them on a higher, more creative plane" (372). The correspondence consists, as we shall see, in Adrian's having projected the unleashing of terror and chaos onto the theological plane through tones.

At this point in his life, Adrian, in the middle of birthing a masterpiece, suffers from the stabbing pains of his migraine, which he continues to compare with the knife pains of the little mermaid, who longed for an immortal soul. But he now adds a new comparison that Serenus finds remarkably precise. Adrian compares his torment to that of John the Martyr in his cauldron of oil, depicted in the first of Dürer's woodcuts. As John was tortured for his faith, Adrian suffers from the creative fire that burns within him and that will soon give rise to a dark revelation. He will be a martyr for art. The likeness confirms Serenus's sense that genius "is a form of the life force that is deeply versed in illness, that both draws creatively from it and creates through it" (374).

The range of sources on which Adrian draws is immense. Clearly, he means to write music that will be a final musical-theological revelation, a summa of the cosmos in its most terrifying aspect. The work is in stark contrast with his cosmic parody, *Marvels of the Universe*. Adrian's sources include, in addition to John's *Apocalypse*, the *Vision of St. Paul* and the prophetic writings of Ezekiel and Jeremiah. His goal is to gather all the elements of the ecstatic tradition into "a single focus, compressing them into a menacing latter-day artistic synthesis, as if under an implacable injunction, holding the mirror of revelation up to humanity's eyes, so that it may see what is approaching and near at hand" (376). Adrian enters this tradition as a modern prophet of doom armed with the power of music as the ultimate truth-teller and revealer of hidden things.

One of the most distinctive features of Adrian's synthesis is its reliance on "visual objectivization." This includes, of course, the fifteen Dürer engravings that inspired the work and title. But to this Adrian adds a tonal depiction of the images of torment in Dante's hell and most especially those of Michelangelo's *Last Judgement*. In describing Adrian's sonorous painting, Serenus singles out for special mention the sinner in Michelangelo's fresco who puts a hand over one eye and with the other stares in horror at eternal damnation (377). The harrowing image will be applied to Germany in the final paragraph of the novel.

At the end of the first part of Chapter 34, Serenus reports that Adrian was working at fever pitch in fear that his devil-bestowed illumination might be withdrawn before he is able to finish the work. The dreadful culmination, which will require all of Adrian's courage, was "far removed from any Romantic music of redemption" and "ruthlessly confirmed the theologically negative and merciless character of the whole." It was to be, as Mann described it, "something satanically religious, diabolically pious."[69]

In the middle part of Chapter 34, we meet German intellectuals and artists who champion Nietzsche's will to power. Their ideas are fueled by the widely read *Reflections on Violence* (1908) by Georges Sorel, whose socialist rhetoric made violence a thing of beauty enhanced by myth.[70] Here we return to the idea that old and new, reaction and revolution, are often united by time's eternal return. One of these figures is a poet and self-appointed prophet, the clerically attired Daniel Zur Höhe (Daniel on High), who adds to the infernal brew of ideas the Sorelian theme of the *aesthetic*. His only poem ends with the exhortation: "Soldiers . . . I entrust to you the plundering—of the world!" It was all beautiful, says Serenus, "in a cruel and utterly beauty-bound way . . . the sheerest aesthetic mischief I have ever encountered" (383). The talk of these proto-fascists is made even more satanic by their amusement in imagining a court of law in which critical reason and its defense of bourgeois humanism are crushed by mass-myth propaganda, bolstered by the testimony of "scientific witnesses" (386). At the end of this middle section of the chapter, Serenus recognizes in everything he has heard "an old-new, revolutionary atavistic world." It is a dictatorship of belief that wants to take the world back to the theocratic Middle Ages and even before that to the Dark Ages.

In the concluding Chapter 34, Serenus acknowledges that the ideas he heard at Kridwiss's, though repellent, were prophetic of the (then) coming age: "I could not, even for one moment, conceal from myself that they had laid their fingers with remarkable sensitivity on the pulse of the age and were foretelling truth at its best" (390). It is against the background of this prescient revelation of coming terror and the rise of the Blond Beast that we hear about the music of Adrian's demonic *Apocalypsis*.[71] Before proceeding to describe this daring work, Serenus marvels at the proximity of aestheticism and barbarism, and how the former, in its mindless enthusiasm for a Great that is in Nietzsche's phrase "beyond good and evil," paves the way for the latter.[72]

The point of contact between the ideas of the Kridwiss circle and Adrian's composition is the renewal of the violent cultic spirit and the mystic unity of opposites. The music begins with "magical, fanatical African drums and booming gongs, only to attain to the highest music" (393). Music is apocalyptic, since it reveals what had been safely hidden beneath the surface of easy-to-hear formulas and mannerisms. In bringing to light the beast and the god in man, the composition, writes Serenus, is nothing less than "the life-history of music." Adrian's unflinching exposure of extremes, his totalism, incurs contradictory critical reproaches of bloody barbarism and bloodless intellectuality.

Serenus dwells, interestingly, on one musical feature in particular: the glissando or sliding tone, often played by the trombone. Adrian's frequent use of this device in the *Apocalypsis* is a regression to the pre-art state of nature. The "gliss" in modern music is the vestige of the primitive stage of human life. It is a naturalistic atavism that Serenus calls "anticultural, indeed anti-human, even demonic" (393). The slide, which is a tonal howl, negates distinct tones and the steps of a scale. Used in a modern work, it represents nihilism and the destruction of order. In Adrian's oratorio, the glissando, we are told, is used for the voices of the four avenging angels (the Four Horsemen) who embark on mass slaughter.[73] "The howl as a theme," Serenus says, "—how ghastly!"

Other shocking aspects of this terrifying work include the strange use of the chorus, which finds its classical model in the shout "*Barabbam!*" from Bach's *St. Matthew Passion*. The chorus takes on an orchestral character that blurs the distinction between tones and words. It is the transgression of a boundary. Most striking is the "extreme polyphonic harshness" of the work, which is entirely governed by the intellectual dissonance of *paradox*.

Presumably, Adrian in this composition uses his magic square, the strict twelve-tone method. One of its features is evident in the complete integration and even identity of opposites. The best example of this integration is Adrian's vocalization of the orchestra and instrumentalization of the voice. This enhances artistic unity but also, as a musical transgression, produces the effect of something "oppressive, dangerous, and malevolent," in short, demonic. An example of the work's shocking use of paradox is the music for the whore of Babylon, who is given "the most graceful coloratura soprano." Her tones, like those of Mozart's Queen of the Night, merge into those of a flute (394). On the other side of the integration, muted trumpets and saxophones eerily imitate the human voice.

There is also a rhythmic atavism in the work's transgression of bar lines, which are preserved in the score in a mockingly conservative way. Adrian's following the natural accents of speech causes Serenus to recall Beissel, whose ghost seems to haunt the *Apocalypsis*. Other disturbing aspects of the work include the setting of the narrator ("I, John") as a near-castrato rather than the traditional tenor and the use of loud speakers for infernal sound effects. The tone of the narrator is that of a detached reporter, a feature that adds to the horrors he recounts. All these explain why critics accused the work of barbarism.

Serenus goes on to defend Adrian's oratorio against the reproach of soullessness (396). He points to lyrical passages that are like "a fervent plea for a soul" that would bring tears to the eyes of a man harder than he. They are Adrian's longings for an immortal soul, "the longings of the little mermaid" (397).

Serenus's account of Adrian's composition ends with the work's dialectical depiction of laughter. Serenus here recalls his fear of his friend's laugh, which has the sound of the demonic. He feels the same fear in listening to Adrian's music in the *Apocalypsis*. The laughter of hell, "the sardonic *gaudium* of Gehenna," appears at the end of part one of the oratorio (397). It starts with the giggle of a single voice and spreads quickly to the chorus and orchestra to become "the mocking, triumphant laughter of hell." Serenus loathes the episode in itself but values it as having revealed to him what he would never have seen for himself: "the deepest mystery of music, which is a mystery of identity." The mystery is music's dialectical essence, its terrifying ability to reveal a transgressive identity of opposites. This appears in Adrian's treatment of the children's chorus at the beginning of part two. The chorus and small orchestra are a "cosmic music of the spheres, icy, clear, transparent as glass." In its very dissonance, it is so sweet and otherworldly "that it fills the heart with hopeless longing" (397). Nevertheless, in this heavenly sound the attentive listener will hear "a reprise of the Devil's laughter."

The musical-mystic identity of opposites leads Serenus to a revelation of Adrian's nature: "At every turn, Adrian Leverkühn is great at making unlike what is in essence alike." This Hegelian sorcery is present in all of Adrian's works but nowhere as magnificently as here in the *Apocalypsis*, which is the grand revelation of Adrian as composing magician: "Every word that suggests the idea of 'moving beyond,' of alteration in a mystical sense, of mutation—that is, of transformation, transfiguration—is to be understood here literally."[74] The laughter of hell and that of the celestial children mirror each other, are inverted images of each other, just like twelve-tone rows.

Serenus sums up his vivid description of the *Apocalypsis* with a summation of Adrian himself. Again, he uses his friend's full name:

> That is Adrian Leverkühn in his entirety. It is the music that he represents in its entirety; and correspondence is, in its profundity, calculation elevated to mystery. That is how a friendship marked by pain taught me to see music, although, given my own simple nature, I would perhaps have gladly seen something else. (398)

The phrase "calculation elevated to mystery" recalls Dürer's magic square and its mystic 34, the number of Serenus's three-part chapter.

A COSMIC LAMENT

I now turn to Adrian's final masterwork, the *Lamentation of Dr. Faustus*, which Serenus movingly describes in Chapter 46. Unlike the *Apocalypsis*, it is based on a single text: the *Faust Book* of 1587. Once more I must leap over many important events in the novel and in Adrian's life. These include Adrian's desire to marry the artistic and naturally beautiful Marie Godeaux, his tragic decision to send his intimate, Rudi Schwerdtfeger, to be his surrogate wooer, and Rudi's death at the hands of Inez Rodde, who had been Rudi's lover and whom Rudi betrayed by wooing Marie on his own behalf.[75] I must also leap over the musical works of the period between the *Apocalypsis* and the *Lamentation*. These include a violin concerto, which the flirtatious Rudi "wooed" Adrian into writing for him,[76] and a barely playable string trio. The trio is Mann's nod to Schoenberg, whose late string trio depicted in tones the composer's brush with death.[77]

The decisive event in Adrian's life before he writes the *Lamentation* is the time he spends with his nephew, Nepomuk—or rather Echo, as the child called himself. Serenus laments the inability of language to do justice to this winsome fairy-like child: "Words are made for praise and tribute, they have been granted the power to admire, to marvel, to bless, and to characterize a phenomenon by the emotion it arouses, but not to conjure it up, not to reproduce it" (484). It is one of many passages in which Mann's novel, through Serenus, comments critically on itself and laments the inability of words to do what tones alone can do—put us in immediate touch with the thing itself.

Echo in his innocence has the magical power to break through Adrian's coldness, melt his heart, and draw him out of his lonely existence. He is like a visitor from some higher and purer realm, an angel: "He brought something close to bliss, a constant cheering, and tender warming of the heart, not just to the farm, but to the village as well, even to the town of Waldshut" (486). Although Adrian never fawns on the child, he enjoys walking hand in hand with him across the fields. Inspired by Echo, Adrian secretly begins to compose songs based on the *Tempest*. Serenus reports that merely hearing with the mind's ear Adrian's ethereal music for the play's enchanted isle would lead one to ask, with Ferdinand, "Where should this music be? I' th'air or th' earth?"

Adrian is moved by Echo's prayers, which he and Serenus overhear. They are religious poems in old German that the boy seems not to have learned from anyone. In one poem, he prays for the redemption of all mankind, among whom he includes himself

(494). It is a "theological speculation" straight from the heart. While praying for himself, he prays, Serenus says, for us all. "Yes," Adrian softly echoes, "for us all."

In Chapter 45, we hear about the gruesome agony Echo endured as a result of cerebrospinal meningitis, a disease that demonically mimics Adrian's syphilis. It is the most inconceivable cruelty that Serenus has ever witnessed, one that prompts his heart to rebellion. At chapter's end, Adrian too rebels. He tells his devil: "Take him, monster . . . Take his body, over which You have dominion. But You will have to be content to leave his sweet soul to me—and that is Your impotence and Your absurdity, for which I shall laugh You to scorn for eons" (500). Adrian takes upon himself the guilt for Echo's death: "What guilt, what a sin, what crime . . . that we let him come, that I let him get near me, that I let my eyes feast on him!" He concludes: "I have discovered that *it ought not to be*."[78] By "it" he means the good and the noble, "what people call human."

And so, in a spirit of anguish and rebellion, Adrian resolves to negate that great musical celebration of humanity and brotherhood. He will *take back* the Ninth Symphony and its resounding Ode to Joy. His renunciation recalls Schopenhauer's attack on all forms of optimism:

> For the rest, I cannot here withhold the statement that *optimism*, where it is not merely the thoughtless talk of those who harbour nothing but words under their shallow foreheads, seems to me to be not merely an absurd, but also a really *wicked*, way of thinking, a bitter mockery of the unspeakable sufferings of mankind.[79]

When Echo dies twelve hours later, Adrian bids him farewell with Prospero's parting words to his beloved Ariel: "Then to the elements. Be free, and fare thou well!"

It is in April of 1945, the year of Germany's crushing defeat, that Serenus writes about Adrian's "final and ultimate work, *The Lamentation of Dr. Faustus*," which Adrian had conceived before

Echo arrived at Pfeiffering, where Adrian was staying (507). Adrian is now forty-four years old. He has grown a beard that gives him a Christ-like look of spiritualized suffering. Before describing Adrian's composition, Serenus again laments "the poor power of his words." He connects the *Lamentation* with the fate of Germany, which played the role of Faust by giving its soul to the devil for the aesthetic of power. In Beethoven's *Fidelio* and Ninth Symphony, Germany celebrated its liberation of itself:[80]

> But now only this work can be of any use, and it will be sung from our soul: the lamentation of the son of hell, the most awful lament of man and God ever intoned on this earth, which begins with its central character, but steadily expanding, encompasses, as it were, the cosmos. (509)

Serenus now describes the work in detail: "A lament, a wailing!" In the original German, it is a direct mimesis of lament: "*Klage, Klage!*"[81] "A *de profundis*," Serenus says, "that with fond terror I can say has no parallel." But the work is also an aesthetic and personal triumph. It is the *breakthrough* that Adrian and Serenus had discussed in their many conversations about art and its destiny. It is the ultimate artistic triumph in which music, precisely through its strict style and game-like formalism, recovers itself as the expression of feeling that is no falsely consoling bovine warmth but rather a direct revelation of felt meaning. Music is at last liberated and allowed to speak in a way that is neither parodic nor sentimental. It is the dialectical reversal of the magic square's calculated coldness into "an expressive cry of the soul" (509–10).

Earlier in the novel, Adrian made various absolute pronouncements about music. Now it is Serenus's turn. The lament, he says, "is expression *per se*" (*Ausdruck selbst*); "all expression is in fact lament" (510). The claim echoes Schopenhauer, for whom life is suffering and who praises the unique power of music to express suffering in an immediate, non-verbal way. Adrian's model for his *Lamentation* is Monteverdi's *Lament of Ariadne*. It is the modern beginning of expression as lament. Ariadne was abandoned by Theseus after she helped him find his way through the labyrinth. Similarly, Adrian (whose name resembles that of Ariadne) laments his cruel abandonment upon the death of Echo, the boy who offered hope for release from the labyrinth of a cold and lonely life. And just as Monteverdi in his madrigal had used the echo effect that often appeared in baroque music, Adrian uses the same device "to unutterably mournful effect" in this, his loftiest musical achievement. An echo, says Serenus, is the sound of a human voice returned as a sound of nature. It is a lament in which melancholy nature says "Ah, yes!" to grieving man. Adrian's final work is the translation of the boy Echo into the echo that is the rebellious lament for his horrible suffering and death.

The *Lamentation*, as an expressive work, mirrors the whole history of music, which across the centuries sought to express *liberation through form*. Adrian's symphonic cantata is, however, far more complex than Monteverdi's tonal madrigal. The reason is the "strict style" of twelve-tone composition, which Adrian first revealed to Serenus at the time of Adrian's sister's wedding. In that conversation, Adrian recalled having used an embryonic version of the method in his song "O sweet maiden, how bad you are!" His tone-row consisted of H-E-A-E-Es, the musical code for his *hetaera* and the elements of his magic square. This compositional method is a tonal dialectic in which continual sameness of theme is preserved, echo-like, throughout its variations. There is, as we know, no "free note," no note that is not determined by the all-conquering theme.

The identity of opposites appeared in the *Apocalypsis* in the inner sameness of the children's chorus and hell's laughter (511). Serenus calls this tonal dialectic "a formal utopia of terrifying ingenuity." In the *Lamentation*, the principle of total organization now takes possession of the entire work, which is "totally consumed by its thematic element." Like lament, the work keeps returning in waves to its theme of loss and suffering. Also, like lament, it goes nowhere. It does not develop, move into a future, and is therefore "undynamic."[82] Serenus's term recalls Zuckerkandl's dynamic qualities, which, as we know, twelve-tone music banishes. Dynamic qualities are the directed tensions that allow music to be the pure form of narration. Adrian's lament, by contrast, is no drama of tones but rather "a single immense variation" on the theme of sorrow. It is the negative image of the Ninth Symphony and its theme of joy.

Serenus describes how Adrian's music ingeniously follows the events recounted in the *Faust Book*, which he mentions by name. In the story, Johann Faustus, his hourglass running out, invites his friends and colleagues for a final feast and farewell. In a contrite but dignified speech, Faust, knowing that the devil will destroy his body, entreats his friends to bury it mercifully in the earth, "for I die as both a wicked and good Christian" (511). Faust was good, Serenus says, because he was repentant and "in his heart always hoped for grace for his soul," wicked because he must meet a horrid end and knows "that the Devil will and must have his body." How this unity of good and evil applies to Adrian will become clearer in Adrian's staged address to his friends and colleagues in the novel's final chapter. For now, we simply follow Serenus, who tells us that Adrian set the twelve syllables of Faust's words (in German, "*Denn ich sterbe als ein böser und guter Christ*") to the twelve tones of the chromatic scale. Adrian uses this perfect marriage of words and tones to form the theme that is heard everywhere in the *Lamentation*. It is tonally present long before the text is sung by a small choir, which sings the part of Faust. There are no solos in this work. All individuality has been absorbed into the communal, indeed cosmic, expression of grief.

The twelve-tone theme is the basis for every sound in the *Lamentation*, which follows the vocal rise and fall of Monteverdi's *Lament of Ariadne*. Serenus returns to *his* theme, which is the total organization of Adrian's cantata. Echoing many of the claims of Schoenberg and Adorno, he again emphasizes that in Adrian's masterpiece devoted to grief nothing is unrelated to the basic twelve-tone theme, there is no "free note," and expression is liberated precisely because the form is objectively taken care of, so to speak, by the already composed tone-row. The musical work is therefore free not just to express itself but to *abandon itself* to expression. Music in its very formalism—music as the non-verbal cosmos of tones—is "liberated as language."[83] Serenus calls this reversal in which pure form becomes an expressive gesture "a miracle" and "a profoundly demonic jest" (512). Adrian's "reconstruction of expression," as Serenus calls it, is therefore a "return to Monteverdi and the style of his era." It is another instance of time's revolving sphere, as music, through its cold and austere form, returns to its expressive origins.

Adrian's *Lamentation*, Serenus goes on to say, is the resumé of all the musical elements as bearers of expression that have appeared in music history, especially during the expressive period of Monteverdi (512). These include the sigh of the appoggiatura or leaning tone, the suspension as a rhythmic device, and the drawing out of syllables. How Adrian manages to incorporate these tonal devices into his atonal music, Serenus does not say. He leaves that to our musical imaginations. In yet another of the many echoes that appear in his description, which reads like a theme and variations in prose, Serenus returns to the *hetaera* tone-code (H-E-A-E-Es), which appears in the *Lamentation* whenever mention is made "of the pledge and bond, of the bloody pact" (513).

Serenus goes on to describe the various ways in which the *Lamentation*, Adrian's Ode to Sorrow, is the negation of Beethoven's choral symphony. One of the most striking negations is Adrian's reversal in the sequence of orchestra and chorus. Whereas in Beethoven's work the human voice bursts through at the end, the conclusion of its demonic counterpart is purely instrumental. This inversion occurs right after the "hellish gallop," the choral scherzo with which the mocking demons carry Faust to hell. The reversed order is all part of Adrian's resolve to negate, upend, and take back the optimistic humanism of the Ninth Symphony. It is the triumph of wordless ambiguous tones over determinate words.

As he moves toward the end of his reflection on Adrian's Ode, Serenus recalls the words Adrian uttered when Echo died: "Ah, it ought not to be." Adrian's musical response is a rebellion of cosmic proportions. The *Lamentation* is not just a negation of Beethoven's symphony. It is also a negation of the religious *from a religious point of view* (514). Adrian's composition is religious in that it deals with the devil and damnation. But its goal is to invert the meaning of religion by proudly rejecting the forgiveness it offers. Adrian's Faust, who is Adrian himself, refuses salvation as itself a temptation to yield to cosmic optimism and the lie of the world's "godliness," its "false and flabby bourgeois piety."

One final reversal of meaning remains. It occurs, unexpectedly, at the very end of this work of endless lament. It is a reversal, Sereneus says, that surpasses all reason and "softly touches the emotions with that spoken unspokenness given to music alone" (515). In the work's final, orchestral movement, the collective human voice is left behind, as we seem to hear in the tones of the orchestra "the lament of God for the lost state of His world." It is the sound of the Creator's sorrowful "I did not will this." In this final expression of despair, an expression that is the creature's sole consolation, we hear what Serenus calls "the religious paradox." According to this paradox, a faint glimmer of hope lies in the possibility that hope may germinate, "if only as the softest of questions," out of the deepest despair. It would be, Serenus says, "hope beyond hopelessness," the transcendence of despair through a miracle that is beyond faith.

"Just listen to the ending," Serenus tells his reader, "listen with me." His exhortation echoes the "Watch with me!" of Gethsemane. As one instrumental group after the other steps back and the work fades away, a single tone remains—a high G played by a lone cello. It is the final word of Adrian's cosmic lament. The G fades slowly in a *pianissimo fermata* before falling into "silence and night" (515).

As the soul listens to the remains of the dying note, it hears a final reversal of meaning. No longer a dying note of sorrow, it stands, Serenus says, as a light in the night.[84]

TWILIGHT OF AN IDOL

With the high G of the *Lamentation*, Adrian comes to the end of his "high flying time" as a composer. In Chapter 47, the novel's final chapter, Adrian, in a staged parody of the *Faust Book*, invites friends and associates to his residence in Pfeiffering to hear excerpts from his last work. The event expresses, Serenus says, the transformation of the "Watch with me!" of Gethsemane into the original Faust's high-minded and more manly address to his friends: "Sleep in peace and be not troubled!"

Adrian now explicitly takes on the role of Doctor Faustus. He enacts an auto-apocalypse, in which he intends not just to play music from his composition based on Faust's lament but to reveal himself as Faust. He calls his address a sermon and a confession. Adrian speaks in the Luther dialect of the *Faust Book*. To the shock of his audience, some of whom leave, he confesses his meeting with the devil. At one point in this awkward pain-ridden speech, Serenus reports his unspoken lament: "Never had I more strongly felt the advantage that music, which says nothing and everything, has over words, which lack ambiguity—indeed that art, safeguarded by being noncommittal, has in general over the compromising crudity of unmediated confession" (522).

Adrian tells the whole story. He speaks openly about his pact with Satan and the fatal union with his butterfly *hetaera*, whom he followed into "the dusky leafy shade, the which her transparent nakedness loves." On hearing this, the demonically aesthetic Daniel Zur Höhe, who had been invited to the gathering, stomps his foot in approval in a moment of dark comedy: "It is beautiful. It has beauty!" Adrian proceeds to confess his guilt for the death of Echo and compares himself to the basilisk, whose look is death. He also confesses his guilt for the death of Rudi. This death, as Adrian construes it, was satanic vengeance for his apostasy, his seeking in marriage to Marie Godeaux expiation for his sins and his sending Rudi, his friend and intimate, to be his surrogate wooer. He holds out hope that God, witnessing all the harshness and drudgery of his life as an artist, might forgive his sins. He recalls his earlier speculative calculation that a contrite unbelief in the possibility of grace might in fact provoke redemption (526). But this, he confesses, is sheer presumption, just as the devil had told him in Palestrina: "there you see that I am damned, and there is no mercy for me, because I destroy any such beforehand through speculation." In a final gesture of touching humanity, he asks his friends, whom he calls "brethren and sisters," to remember him fondly despite his sins.

Adrian then sits down at the piano to play his music, to turn his all-too-explicit lamentation into the ambiguous language of tones. Tears trickle down his cheeks and fall on the piano's keys. On the tear-drenched keys of the piano, which Kretzschmar had praised as the most intellectual of instruments, Adrian strikes a strongly dissonant chord. As he does so, he opens his mouth as if to sing and utters a piercing wail. The chord and the wail, both non-verbal, are the consummate expression of grief. In a gesture that resembles a crucifixion, he opens his arms wide, seeming to embrace the piano, and then falls sideways, as if pushed by an invisible force.

The infinitely good-hearted Frau Schweigestil, Adrian's devoted caretaker at Pfeiffering, is quick to act and comes to the fallen composer's aid, lifting him into her motherly arms. Mann gives this simple soul the last word of the novel proper: "He talked a lot about eternal grace, poor man, and I don't know if it reaches that far. But real human understanding, believe me, that reaches far enough for all!"

In the novel's Epilogue, Serenus sadly narrates the final years of his friend and idol. Intermixed with personal sadness is his horror at the now-fallen "monster state" of Germany after its last orgies

(528). Fusing his country's descent into hell with his life-long devotion to Adrian, Serenus hopes that his personal loyalty to his friend may compensate for his having alienated himself from his homeland out of horror at its gruesome sins.

The final moments of the novel are for the most part sadly quiet. Adrian's warm-voiced mother, now eighty, comes to Pfeiffering to nurse her fallen child, who, like Icarus, dared to fly close to the sun. With an implicit reference to the name Leverkühn, Serenus writes: "One cannot imagine anything more horribly touching and pitiful than when a spirit that has boldly and defiantly [*kühn und trotzig*] emancipated itself from its origins, that has traced a dizzying arc above the world, returns broken to its mother's care" (530).

Even in his ruin, however, Adrian remains proud. He dreads the "gentle humiliation" of his mother's return. This is in part why, as Serenus suspects, Adrian, informed of his mother's coming, revolts by attempting to drown himself in the cold waters of the Klammer Pool (531). Cold, Adrian's element, seems to call him to final union. The attempt is foiled by a farm hand who dives in and brings Adrian to shore. Serenus speculates that this "frustrated attempt at flight" embodied a notion of mystical salvation familiar to early Protestantism. According to this belief, someone who had invoked the devil could save his soul by consigning his body. In pondering this possibility, Serenus wonders whether it might have been better after all to have let Adrian drown, so that he might fulfill his theological intent (532).

Serenus sees his friend one more time: in 1939, after the conquest of Poland (533). He receives news of Adrian's death not long before the start of the war, whose ravages Adrian fortunately did not live to see. At that time, Serenus reports, Germany, Adrian's political counterpart, "was reeling at the height of its savage triumphs, about to win the world on the strength of the one pact that it intended to keep and had signed with its blood" (534). In the present post-war time, Germany descends ever more deeply into despair. It resembles the damned soul in Michelangelo's fresco, who holds a hand over one eye and with the other stares into the horror. The good Serenus ends his prose love-song to Adrian Leverkühn with a prayer: "May God have mercy on your poor soul, my friend, my fatherland."

Closing Thoughts and the Meaning of Mimesis

The goal of this chapter was to explore the bond between music and world in Thomas Mann's tragic tale of a Faustian *Tonsetzer*. World appeared in several guises: nature, history, the cosmos of words, and the cosmos of tones. The novel highlights music's uncanny power of revelation. As Serenus often observes, tones have the magical ability not just to express the inward motions of the soul but to reveal the hidden truth of *things*. In Adrian's compositions, truth is not Zuckerkandl's being-as-tension but a disturbing identity of opposites and an inversion of values: high and low, heavenly and infernal. Truth is apocalyptic.

Mann's novel has many connections with themes from preceding chapters. Its content owes much to Schopenhauer's cosmic pessimism, its form to Wagner's use of leitmotifs. The novel's idea of a world is related, negatively, to all forms of optimism: the Christian optimism of Bach's *St. Matthew Passion*, the secular optimism of the *Magic Flute*, and Timaeus's cosmological optimism, which affirms the inherent goodness and beauty of mathematics. The Faustian cosmos, as I noted earlier, embodies mischief and monstrosity. Its intricate designs are demonic rather than divine. Schoenberg's twelve-tone method represents the supremacy of schematic reason. In Mann's novel, it is the exemplar of order imposed through demonic ingenium. It defines the modern composer as incarnating the aesthetic will to power—the will to the total mastery of tones through the negation of tonal freedom. There is no free note. The magic square of dodecaphony is the musical symbol of totalitarianism, the total organization of life.

In his Princeton tribute to Thomas Mann, Victor Zuckerkandl addresses the pervasive role of music in Mann's opus. He cites Mann's self-description as a "musician among poets"[85] and his claim that the novel for him "has always been a symphony, a contrapuntal work, a thematic fabric, in which ideas play the part of musical motifs."[86] Zuckerkandl notes that music in Mann's works operates on three levels simultaneously: as a formal principle to be followed, as a theme, and as "a reality to be created or re-created."[87] The intertwining of these three levels is on full display in the Faustus novel.

The novel's most impressive technical achievement is its vivid description of musical works. In the case of Adrian's compositions, these are works that have never been heard and never existed. Descriptions of real works include Kretzschmar's inspired rendition of the second movement of Beethoven's last piano sonata and Adrian's poetically sarcastic description of the Prelude to Act 3 of Wagner's *Meistersinger* (which Adrian does not name).[88] Zuckerkandl calls these descriptions of music *word-images*.[89]

But what does "image" mean here? What does it mean for words—the words of Thomas Mann—to *imitate* tones? Zuckerkandl observes that although we typically regard an image as referring to some more real original, such mimesis is alien to Mann's novel. Mann's word-images of music contain their meaning completely within themselves. They represent, Zuckerkandl says, "an ideal reality" that we experience in reading the words.[90] Mann did not need to hear Adrian's fictional compositions in his head in order to describe them (to do so, he would have had to compose them), any more than Homer needed to visualize the shield of Achilles in order to describe it. The shield "is right there in all its glorious detail in Homer's words."[91] Any attempt on the part of the reader to draw a picture of what is there in the words "would interfere with the poetry and destroy its effect."[92] So too, in Mann's novel, Adrian's music is gloriously there in the words. A real performance could only ruin the effect.

The self-sufficiency of word-images is at work in Mann's novel even when the images refer to real pieces of music. When Mann, through Kretzschmar, describes the second movement of Beethoven's piano sonata, the function of the words "is not to remind the reader of a musical experience which he may or may not have had but rather *to produce the poetic equivalent of a musical experience.*"[93] Their purpose "is not the description of the real Opus 111 but the creation of an ideal Opus 111."[94] The creative power of the word-image is made explicit in the novel itself. After the lecture in which Kretzschmar discusses Beethoven's *Missa solemnis*, Serenus reports that he and Adrian, to whom the work was yet unfamiliar, had the feeling that they had heard it.[95]

Toward the end of his tribute, Zuckerkandl returns to the three levels at which music operates in Mann's works. He suggests that in the Faustus novel they are dialectically related as thesis, antithesis, and synthesis. The first, positive stage is the thesis. Here, music is an organizing principle, an Apollonian force for order. The second, negative stage is the antithesis. Here, music, as the novel's dark theme, is a Dionysian destructive force. Music is the dissonance of these two antagonistic moments. It is the paradox of Apollonian form and Dionysian flux. On this point, Zuckerkandl cites Mann's definition of music as "calculated order and chaos-breeding antireason all at once."[96]

At the third, synthetic stage, Mann as poet enters the picture. In the Faustus novel, music is transformed into word-images of music. By virtue of these images, the destabilizing world of tones by themselves is assimilated into the rational world of words and takes on a new, ideal life—a life that represents "a major victory over chaos."[97] What Zuckerkandl seems to mean here is that the stable Apollonian structures of speech save music as the play of sheer tones from the corrupting influence of Dionysian flux and its call to death. For Zuckerkandl, Mann's novel is a redemptive *Aufhebung*: "The whole antagonism of construction and chaos is transcended when music as representative of the forces of darkness becomes the protagonist in a supreme manifestation of order like a great novel. In transforming tone into word and creating music as a word gestalt Thomas Mann saved it from the very suspicion his own interpretation had aroused."[98]

If Zuckerkandl is right, then it is not the case, as I stated above, that Mann's novel negates *all* forms of optimism. In addition to the final G played by the lone cello at the end of Adrian's final work—the G that becomes in the end a hint of hope—there is the novel itself, which in its supremely ordered word-images of music transcends devil, darkness, and despair. Whatever we might think of Zuckerkandl's quasi-Hegelian interpretation of the three levels, the word-images of *Doctor Faustus* stand as an unquestionable tribute to the genius of Thomas Mann, the ironic German and the musician among poets. His musicality, fueled by his love of music and his fear, is no more apparent than in this, his polyphonic-Wagnerian masterpiece.

CHAPTER SEVEN

The Sanctity of Fear in Francis Poulenc's *Dialogues of the Carmelites*

> And the song flowed on full and clear . . . For this singing
> effaced all sense of time, it effaced *space* and the bloody
> Place de la Revolution . . . It effaced even chaos.
>
> Gertrud von le Fort, *The Song at the Scaffold*

The final stage of our journey continues the preceding chapter's reflection on music and world in the twentieth century, as we go from Germany to France, from serialism back to tonality, and from the pain-ridden *Geist* of Adrian Leverkühn to the pleasure-loving *esprit* of Francis Poulenc (1899–1963). My focus is Poulenc's radiant *Dialogues of the Carmelites*, first performed in Italian at La Scala in 1957.[1] The opera is based on an historical event. On July 17, 1794, sixteen Carmelite sisters of Compiègne were guillotined in the Place de la Révolution. As they approached and finally mounted the platform, they serenely chanted, while the hushed crowd looked on. Their music was the outward sign of an inner triumph—a victory, through grace, over the fear of death.

The event entered the Republic of Letters in 1931, when Gertrud von le Fort, a German convert to Catholicism, published her novel *The Last at the Scaffold* (*Die Letzte am Schafott*).[2] The story centers on the fictional Blanche de la Force, a young French aristocrat who seeks refuge from the world's tumult by entering the

191

Carmelite order. Succumbing to the fear that has haunted her all her life, she abandons her fellow sisters at the time of greatest peril but rejoins them as they go to their communal death. She is the last at the scaffold.[3]

In 1948, Georges Bernanos, best known for his *Diary of a Country Priest*, was asked to write the dialogue for a film treatment of the novel. But the work was judged unsuitable for this medium and the project was dropped.[4] In the meantime, Bernanos had died. The screenplay, widely regarded as his masterpiece, was discovered among his papers and made into a highly successful play.[5] In 1953, an agent of Poulenc's publisher secured for the composer a commission with La Scala. Poulenc wanted to compose an opera; it would be his second.[6] The agent suggested Bernanos's play as a source. An ecstatic Poulenc agreed: "But obviously, it was made for me, made for me!"[7] And so, in this roundabout way there was born one of the greatest vocal works of the twentieth century. As Poulenc's biographer Henri Hell observes, the opera—a fortunate "marriage of kindred spirits"—joined the similarly happy pairings of Debussy and Maeterlinck, Strauss and Hoffmansthal, and Berg and Büchner.[8]

Conversation among a group of nuns would hardly seem to be a suitable topic for an opera. Here we find no tale of romantic love or case of mistaken identity. As commentators have noted, the subject seems remote from all human interest. And yet, Poulenc's musical setting for Bernanos's screenplay is intensely dramatic—not just in the anguished death-scene of the Prioress and the concluding march to the scaffold (which includes the sickening thump of the guillotine) but throughout the work. The opera sweeps us up in a double terror: the French Reign of Terror in the external world and the internal terror of Blanche de la Force. Through the magic of Poulenc's music, we are made to experience the soul-movements implicit in Bernanos's words.[9]

Poulenc is often thought of as a composer of whimsical *jeux d'esprit*. His early works, inspired by Satie, support this view. But after his return to his father's Catholic faith, occasioned by the gruesome death of his fellow composer Pierre-Octave Ferroud in a car accident, Poulenc began to compose religious works of the most profound seriousness.[10] The greatest of these deal with the Passion and Holy Week. They include *Quatre Motets pour un temps de pen-itence*, the *Stabat Mater, Dialogues des Carmélites*, and Poulenc's last sacred work: the darkly dissonant and austere *Sept Répons des ténè-bres*.[11] An earthy man of playful disposition, Poulenc nevertheless knew intimately and profoundly the dark night of the soul.

I have chosen Poulenc's opera as my culminating musical piece for several reasons. One is that it offers a further opportu-nity to reflect on music and the idea of a world. In the opera, this is a world in which grace triumphs over the satanic will to mock, murder, and desecrate. The chapter returns us to the grace-im-bued world of *Sicut cervus*, whose praises I sang in Chapter One. Another is that having devoted much attention to German com-posers, I thought it fitting to end with one who was French, since composers in the French tradition tend to reject Wagnerism and serialism in favor of economy, clarity, and lightness of touch. I also wanted to offer my reader a tonic for the cosmic gloom and cold intellectualism of Mann's *Faustus* novel, which gives a brilliant but distorted view of music and world. The opera, to be sure, is a tragic work; but it is also, and primarily, salvific. Moreover, Pou-lenc, unlike Adrian Leverkühn, was no speculator. He was a nat-ural, instinctive composer who was relatively unaffected by the abstractions of twelve-tone composition.[12] The opera's sensuous beauty and soaring lyricism are a tribute to how fresh tonality can be, and how tonality can accommodate extreme dissonances, which in this composer's music can sound, by turns, shimmering and voluptuous.

I also have a personal reason for turning to this composer at journey's end. For decades, I have conducted Poulenc's motets with the St. John's Chorus and always find the experience exhilarating. It is a joy to introduce students to this vibrant composer and watch them come to love pieces like *O magnum mysterium* and *Exultate Deo*. My chapter is intended in part as a grateful tribute to this modern maker of sacred works who over the years has become a valued teacher and friend.

The opera is neatly divided into three acts, each containing four tableaux or scenes. The twelve-scene work is gloriously tonal. As Poulenc quipped in a letter to a fellow composer: "The Carmelites, poor things, can only sing in keys. One must forgive them."[13] More than a sly jab at the atonalists, the ironic apology expressed Poulenc's indebtedness to Monteverdi, Verdi, Debussy, and Mussorgsky—tonal composers to whom the work was dedicated. The principal key of the opera is stark A minor. It is the key of Poulenc's penitential motet, *Timor et tremor* (*Fear and Trembling*). It is also the key of the Bach aria I examined earlier ("*Aus Liebe*") and the key in which Jesus dies in the *St. Matthew Passion*, a work to which the opera is thematically connected. Poulenc's opera and Bach's oratorio begin and end in the same tonalities: E minor and C minor, respectively. It is tempting to regard the parallel as intentional.

The opera combines recitative and arioso (a mean between free recitative and formal aria).[14] The absence of arias keeps the opera close to real life and the free flow of dialogue. Recitative fits Bernanos's and Poulenc's concentration on *shared inwardness*; there is no musical equivalent of a soliloquy. The mostly light orchestration serves the same end. Poulenc wanted nothing to obscure Bernanos's lucid text.[15] He therefore followed a course that was the exact opposite of Wagner's in the composition of *Tristan*, where the whole point (as we have seen) is that tones—the incarnation of Schopenhauer's cosmic will—are meant to engulf words and the illusory world to which words belong. In the *Dialogues*, the orchestra nevertheless plays a crucial role. The brief instrumental interludes serve as effective mood-setting transitions from one scene to the next, one world of discourse to the next. Their often archaic-sounding parallel harmonies recall the French grandeur that is no more.

Finally, the opera contains gorgeously harmonized prayers sung by the sisters. Poulenc added these to Bernanos's screenplay. In real life, the prayers would have been chanted without accompaniment or harmonization. But to reproduce the chant melodies exactly, to quote them, would have placed the old modal monophony outside the opera's modern major-minor universe. Poulenc finds a way of being true to the intensely inward spirit of chant while transposing it into the idiom of tonal harmony.[16] The transposition is brilliantly achieved at the end, as the sisters mount the scaffold singing the *Salve Regina*, with the onlooking crowd providing a harmonic accompaniment.[17]

Bernanos's play, like von le Fort's novel, is the story of the ironically named Blanche de la Force (Blanche of the Strength), as she makes her spiritual journey from crippling fear to liberating martyrdom. The story is a crystallization of themes dear to Bernanos's heart: the heroism of innocence, the Communion of Saints (the union in faith of the living and the dead), the preservation of one's honor, and, most importantly, the *transference of grace*. Regarding this last theme, the very young Sister Constance plays a special role. To her is entrusted the key revelation of the screenplay and opera: "We do not die each for ourselves, but each for another, or even each in place of another."

Act One: A Death Undeserved

The opera begins with a burst: minor thirds pulsing nervously beneath a dramatic, upward-leaping theme. The theme is an insistent tonal rhyme: D to E, then D to E an octave higher:

Variations on this rising four-note theme will occur throughout the opera. The dramatic upward leap and the flourishes that follow suggest the now-threatened Old World. As we shall see, the theme is also the motif of Blanche's aristocratic family.[18] The flourishes are followed by a full measure of chromatically rising fourths. It is the sound of a dark welling up and the onset of a menacing wave.

The story begins in April of 1789, as the first stirrings of revolution begin to threaten the *ancien régime*. We are in the richly furnished library of the Marquis de la Force, Blanche's father. The backdrop of a library reminds us that the Revolution will be total. It will annihilate not only the aristocratic class but also the whole culture-world that France had built up over centuries. The Chevalier, his son, rushes in and interrupts the Marquis's nap with an urgent question: "Where is Blanche?" The question is prompted by the Chevalier's concern for his sister, whose carriage has not yet returned. The son reminds his father that these are dangerous times and that there is talk that the effigy of Jean-Baptiste Réveillon will be burned in front of his house.[19] The sleepy Marquis initially dismisses the news but then admits to visions of revolution that have haunted his dreams. He recalls the terrifying event that occurred years ago, when some fireworks accidentally exploded at the wedding of the Dauphin and the carriage bearing the Marquis and his wife was threatened by a violent mob. Later that night, his terrified wife died after giving birth to Blanche, who becomes the daughter of Fear.

But at a deeper level, the Chevalier's question refers to Blanche's state of mind. Where Blanche is—where she is spiritually—is the story's central concern. The answer will be that she is with Christ during His agony in Gethsemane. Her fear is a participation in His fear and is therefore something sacred. That Bernanos had the sanctity of fear in mind when he composed his screenplay is clear from the quotation he adopts as its epigraph. It comes from his novel *Joy*: "In one way fear is also God's daughter, redeemed on the night of Holy Friday . . . She is present at every deathbed—she is man's intercessor."[20]

The opening scene introduces us to Blanche's fear-ridden disposition, which the Marquis dismisses as a passing phase ("A happy marriage is all she needs"). But the Chevalier finds something deeply disturbing in his sister's eyes: "more than fear endangers my sister's health. You must look beneath the surface . . . A girl so noble and proud [*fière*]—yet the sickness is within her, as the worm is in the fruit."

Blanche's entrance is heralded by a spacious arpeggio, played on piano, in which all the tones are to be sustained. The rising arpeggio suggests that there is something otherworldly about Blanche, despite or perhaps because of the fear that haunts her. When it is reported that she seemed calm and courageous in her coach when it was beset by a mob, she corrects the report in a gentle passage consisting of a series of repeated dominant-tonic resolutions in keys a third apart:

Her graceful melody, with its descending up-and-down leaps of octaves and sixths, imitates repeated immersion: "*Mon Dieu*, it is with danger as with plunging into the ocean, which begins by taking your breath away, yet becomes most refreshing after you've gone in up to your neck." Fear is Blanche's element, just as Cold is Adrian Leverkühn's. It is an abiding condition, not a passing emotion.

The Marquis observes, prophetically, that a storm seems to be approaching. After Blanche turns to go to her chamber, the Chevalier recalls something that Blanche used to tell him when she was little: "I die every night, only to be born again next morning." Blanche's response points to the theological heart of the story and to the name she will choose upon entering Carmel: "There has been only one morning, my dear chevalier, that of Easter. But each night that one enters is that of the very Holy Agony." Blanche rises to her high A on "*Pâques*" ("Easter"). Her final G-flat is part of a dissonant chord played very quietly. Below this chord we hear ominous minor thirds between F and A-flat played on timpani.

After Blanche repairs to her room to rest, the Marquis and Chevalier are understandably puzzled by her parting remark. Blanche returns after having been frightened by a servant's shadow and informs her father of her decision to become a Carmelite. This is the climax of the first scene. Blanche's announcement takes the form of an arioso bordering on aria. The melodious 12-bar song in common time (4/4) is in G major.[21] The mostly diatonic harmony sounds above a stabilizing low G, as chords on the principal beats keep a measured pace (see the score on the next page). Melody, harmony, rhythm, and the repeated low G conspire to form the perfect gesture of gentle but firm resolve: "My father, there is no incident so negligible that God's will is not inscribed upon it, as the whole immensity of the heavens is in a drop of water. With your permission, I have decided to enter Carmel."

Blanche's leap to a high A at the end of the word "*Carmel*" signals the firmness of her decision and also (as we hear in the next scene) her desire for *une vie héroïque*. Blanche neither hates nor despises the world. It is rather that the world for her is like an *élément* in which she cannot live. She beseeches her father to let her hope for a remedy for the horrid weakness that has made her life unhappy and affirms her submission to God's will: "I sacrifice all to Him, I abandon all, I renounce all, so that He might restore my honor."[22] On the word "*honneur*" Blanche rises to a climactic G-sharp, the raised $\hat{7}$ of A minor. A brief coda in A minor ends the scene. The minor thirds and a variation on the Old-World theme

from the opening return. No longer agitated, they now form a slow funereal tread that foreshadows Blanche's fate. The scene ends in a hush. The lower parts of the orchestra sound a low A in octaves, and the minor third between A and C is played softly on timpani:

A slow, majestic brass fanfare serves as a transition to the crucial scene between Blanche and the Prioress, Mme. de Croissy.
It begins with a broad 3/4 sweep and highlights archaic parallel
intervals. The fanfare begins loudly in bright A major but then settles into a darkly quiet B-flat minor, the key of the instrumental
prelude that follows. In this latter section of the transition, the
timpani sound fateful and ominous.[23]

Several weeks pass before we see Blanche at Carmel in her
interview with the ailing Prioress, with whom she will have a mysterious bond.[24] A slow 2/4 prelude in B-flat minor sets the scene.
Its double-dotted rhythms played on winds suggest antiquated
nobility. After a series of muffled, ill-sounding chords, the music
settles into a slow steady 9/8 pulse in G minor—a musical ebbing away. The slow pulse leads us to suspect that the Prioress has
begun to struggle with the thought of her coming death.

As Poulenc observed, the musical setting combines gentle and
harsh moods: "calm at the beginning, fierce in the middle (rules of
the Order), calm at the end."[25] In her first speech, Blanche tells the
Prioress how sweet it must be to have advanced so far on the "road
of detachment" (la voie du détachement). But she is corrected by the
Prioress in candid C major: "What good is it for a religieuse to be
detached from all things if she is not detached from herself—that
is, from her own detachment?"

After a long pause, during which the Prioress is no doubt looking at Blanche closely, the steady pulse of triplets vanishes. At this
point, the music shifts to recitative and singing that is more like
intoned speech. The shift to plain musical speech fits what now
takes place in the interview. The Prioress remarks on Blanche's
lack of fear regarding the severities of the Order and asks Blanche
to tell her frankly what drives her to Carmel. Blanche responds:
"the attraction of a heroic life." The Prioress then warns Blanche
about the danger of personal illusions, a recurring theme in the
opera. As she proceeds to stress the purpose of the Carmelite
Order, the orchestral accompaniment returns, this time in march-

ing 4/4 time with a combination of eighth-note scales and arpeggiated chords. The purpose of the Order, the Prioress affirms, is not to mortify the soul or to safeguard human virtue but to pray: "We are houses of prayer." Her fortissimo affirmation (marked *très violent*) consists of a repeated rising tritone in the melody (C-flat to F), underscored by the same tritonal relation of chords in the orchestra (C-flat major to F major). She sings her conclusion in measures without accompaniment: "Prayer alone justifies our existence."

In calmer tones, the Prioress elaborates on the centrality of prayer. Whoever doubts prayer, she observes, must regard the Carmelites as no more than "impostors or parasites."[26] In another stretch of unaccompanied measures, she stresses the universality of prayer: "If belief in God is universal, must this not be true of prayer as well?" Now in triple time and accompanied by lush dissonant chords on the opening beat of each measure, she sings with quiet intensity about the little shepherd, whose simple prayer is the prayer of the human race. What he does from time to time, says the Prioress, the Carmelites must do day and night. Her inspired, sublime-sounding meditation suggests that prayer has been much on her mind—that she has perhaps been praying, and continues to pray, for a good death.

At this point in the interview, the Prioress turns her attention back to Blanche, this time more personally. Addressing Blanche as "my child," she admits that although tenderness is not the way of Carmel, now that she is old and ailing, she can allow herself to pity Blanche and to fear for the great trials that await her. When Blanche expresses confidence that God will give her strength (*la force*), the Prioress corrects her: it is her weakness, not her strength, that God wants to test. Blanche begins to weep—less from sorrow than from joy. Even if the Prioress's words were harsher, she says, they could never break the *élan*, the lively force, that brings her to Carmel. She adds: "I shall in fact have no other refuge than this." The Prioress bristles at the word. She responds in a fortis-

simo passage marked *rude* ("harsh") and "punctuated with a single
dissonant chord" (Nichols, 234): "The Order does not guard us, my
daughter. It is we who guard the Order."

At the end of the interview, the Prioress, now calmly and without harshness, asks Blanche what name she has chosen, if she were
to be accepted. Blanche responds very softly: "I would be called
Sister Blanche of the Agony of Christ." Her simple melody is supported by a mystical-sounding descent of seventh chords in sharp
keys over a chromatically descending bass. On the name of Christ,
melody and harmony form a gentle deceptive cadence, as Blanche
sings an unexpected B-flat and the harmony goes to a warmly
shimmering ninth chord on E-flat (a tritone away from the preceding seventh chord on A). Her music does not express agony, but
rather mystic consolation. The Prioress then gives an imperceptible start. She does so because, as we learn in her deathbed scene,
this was also her chosen name. The scene ends with a brief return
to the ebbing 9/8 pulse in G minor, and on a very softly played
G-*major* chord. The chord recalls the key of Blanche's announcement in the previous scene. Here, it points forward to the Prioress's blessing. Blanche will indeed become a Carmelite.

A slow rhythmic transition in C minor takes us to the next
scene. It features rich chords over a staccato bass that bounces
along lightly in octaves and fifths. The overall sound is that of the
passing of time. The music broadens at the end to become a slow
procession of very quiet dissonant chords. The bass, no longer
leaping, becomes a repetition of the half-step between B and C.
The repeated half-step is a recurring theme in the opera. It is a
musical gesture of worry and wavering.

Scene 3 brings us back to Carmel, where Blanche is now a mem-
ber. The slow, medieval sounding prelude in B minor alternates
between the pointed rhythms of a two-part canon (an old form)
and rich harmonies played by brass. The prelude, which includes
the ringing of the convent bells and haunted-sounding chords,
exudes a quiet grandeur tinged with darkness.

The scene takes place in the workroom of the convent. It introduces the young childlike Sister Constance, who says whatever comes into her mind. She is the constant bright spot in the opera and, like the Prioress, a conduit of grace. She is the opera's upbeat. After another archaic-sounding opening, the music erupts in an exuberant Mozart-like A-major allegro (played *giocoso*) in which Sister Constance displays her sunny disposition. Her melody sounds like a tune that could be sung by the soubrette Despina from Mozart's *Così fan tutte*. Constance chatters on about lentils, bread, and a pressing iron. She recalls the good time everyone had at her brother's wedding—how, before entering the convent, she danced through the night, and how close she, an aristocrat, felt to the peasants who were there: "These poor people loved me to distraction, because I was always gay and danced as well as they did." We hear the dancing in Constance's carefree melody and the laughter in her repeated high As. Her music, like her, is a sheer delight.

Downbeat Blanche, however, is not amused: "Are you not ashamed to chatter like this, while our Reverend Mother. . . ." Constance responds in her lighthearted way that she would be glad to die in order to save the Prioress's life and adds: "But, really, when one is fifty-nine, is it not high time for one to die?"[27] The conversation then turns to death and the fear of death, as Blanche asks: "But have you never feared death?" Constance responds that early on she did but then came to the realization that since life was so amusing, death had to be as well. In bright C major and on repeated Cs, she explains that she finds it amusing to serve God humbly and to do whatever she is told, cheerfully leaping way up to a high C on the word "*amuse.*" When Blanche asks whether Constance is not afraid that God will tire of her good humor, the latter responds softly and in a childlike way: "I can't prevent myself from thinking that you've come expressly to do me harm." Blanche admits to her ill will: "Indeed, you're not wrong. It's only that I envied you." Returning to her sprightly music and over a lively sixteenth-note accompaniment, Constance joyfully turns the tables: "You envied *me*? When it is I who deserve to be punished for having spoken so lightly of our Reverend Mother's death. . . ."

Constance then suggests that in atonement for her sin, she and Blanche should kneel together, pray, and offer their lives for that of the Prioress. When Blanche derides this as a piece of childishness (*enfantillage*), Constance replies that, on the contrary, it is "an inspiration of the soul." In radiant E major, she then reveals to the still-disapproving Blanche that she had always wished to die very young, that the arrival of Blanche convinced her that her wish would be granted, and that she and Blanche would *die together*. This series of revelations is punctuated by objections from an increasingly angry Blanche. Her final outburst is especially harsh: "Are you not ashamed of believing that your life could ever redeem the life of someone else? You are proud as a demon." Exasperated, she rises to her high B: "You . . . you . . . I forbid you . . ." In response to this outraged reprimand, Constance tells Blanche sweetly and with a poignant dignity that she did not think that her words would give offense.[28] As the scene ends, the opening grace note of Constance's A major melody returns as its own little theme, now in pastoral F major. The pace is more measured, since Blanche has succeeded in deflating Constance's perky mood. After two measures of peaceful F major, the ending shocks with a blunt A minor chord played fortissimo. It is a stark reminder of the terror-world outside the convent walls. The chord also points ahead to the tragic-heroic fulfillment of Constance's premonition of a shared death.

A lone pastoral-sounding English horn begins the interlude that takes us to the finale of Act 1. It is the harrowing scene in which the Prioress, after prolonged suffering in body and mind, dies. Poulenc called it the crux of the whole play.[29] In this scene, we hear how tonality, no less than serialism, can express the extremes of anguish, suffering, and terror. The horn's disjointed tune darkly mimics the spritely ornament associated with Sister Constance.[30] The now-morbid grace note seems to mock her gaiety. It is the tonal metamorphosis of Constance's love of life into the Prioress's fear of death.

The orchestral prelude to the final scene of Act 1 begins with the discordant clanging of the convent bells in B minor—a foreshadowing of the tonality that will be spelled out at the end of the scene. In the scene's first part, the Prioress—attended by Mother Marie (the Assistant Prioress) and accompanied by rocking octaves on E—berates herself for her lack of courage. She wishes she could summon sufficient composure to appear before her daughters, but the pain is too great. Her comparison to someone drowning recalls Blanche's immersion in the sea of fear. Mother Marie, who throughout the opera is the voice of practicality and good sense, tries in vain to calm the Prioress, who agonizes over the horror of watching herself die and feels that she has been abandoned: "God has become a shadow!" Her melody is accompanied by oscillating octaves on E that sound like the ticking of a clock and the beating of a pulse, as she confesses: "I have been thinking of death each day of my life, and now it does not help at all."

The Prioress's thoughts now turn to Blanche. Over a quickened pulse of minor thirds in sixteenth notes, she asks whether Blanche still holds to her chosen name, Sister Blanche of the Agony of Christ. When Marie reports that she does, the Prioress reveals that this was also her chosen name. She then recalls her old Prioress's warning, which applies to Blanche: "Question your strength [*vos forces*]. Those who enter Gethsemane may not leave it." She sings her simple, diatonic melody line quietly over straightforward chords in A minor and staccato octave leaps in the bass. The phrase ends with a half cadence on an E-major chord, in anticipation of the terrifying question to come: "Have you the courage to remain to the end the prisoner of the Holy Agony?" In stark contrast with the quiet simplicity of the warning's first part, the Prioress sings a chromatic melody fortissimo over a wavering accompaniment in A major. The harmony, here, vacillates between major and minor chords a half-step away from A major: down to A-flat, up to B-flat. The wavering harmony is the sound of a will teetering on the knife edge between weakness and strength. As the Prioress sings the last syllable of the crucial word *Agonie*, the orchestra repeats the descending chordal pattern of the previous phrases, this time with very harsh dissonances. The question ends with a repeat of the questioning half cadence on E.

After expressing concern for Blanche, the Prioress, in her last official act, solemnly entrusts Blanche to the care of Mother Marie, who has the firmness of judgment and character that Blanche lacks: "It is in the name of obedience that I entrust to you Blanche de la Force. Do you answer for her before God?" Over a sparse but radiant accompaniment, her song rises dramatically at the very end to a high G on "*Dieu*," sung very loudly over a G major chord.

Blanche enters the room and falls to her knees at the bedside. Her entrance is preceded by a ghostly descending series of chords. It is the sound of both the haunted scene and Blanche's inner state. The Prioress calls Blanche the dearest of her daughters, "just like the child of one's old age." She tells Blanche that she fears for her and wishes she could die for Blanche in order to avert the danger, the weakness, that threatens her. This is in fact what happens in the story and, for Bernanos, in reality: through the mystery of transferred grace, the suffering and death of one human being can redeem the life—or in Blanche's case the *honneur*—of another.[31] In the end, Blanche will find the strength for martyrdom through the mediation of both Constance and the Prioress, both of whom, in different ways, are instruments of grace. In the Prioress's terms, Blanche will join the ranks of God's "heroes and martyrs."

After Blanche leaves having received the Prioress's blessing, we are exposed to the latter's horrible death agony. The Prioress asks the doctor for more pain medication but is told that she cannot take any more. Marie urges the Prioress not to think about her daughters but about God. The word causes the Prioress to cry out in pain: "Who am I at this moment, wretched as I am, to concern myself with *Him*! Let Him first concern Himself with *me*!" As Roger Nichols observes, this outburst is not to be interpreted as blasphemous (235). It shows rather that the Prioress is suffering the full measure of anguish as a prisoner of Gethsemane. She is experiencing the God-abandonment that Christ, too, suffered.

While Marie tries to prevent the sisters from being scandalized by this last outburst, we hear the Prioress's groans over repeated worrying half-steps in the bass (D and E-flat). She then utters a prophetic vision of the chapel empty and desecrated: "Alas, God is deserting us! God has abandoned us!" Marie urges the Prioress to control her tongue and to say nothing scandalous, but to no avail. For much of the scene, the Prioress is accompanied by dissonant chords and oscillating eighth notes in the bass. This oscillation is now quickened in the form of sixteenth notes that express increased torment. The sixteenth notes then form descending chromatic scales followed by a descent of gratingly dissonant sets of thirds, as the Prioress cries out: "Anguish clings to my skin like a waxen mask.... Oh, if I could but scratch off that mask with my nails!" Her desperate outcry in F minor ends with an upward octave leap on G-flat over a mysterious-sounding half-diminished seventh chord:[32]

The clanging of bells from the opening of the scene returns ominously, as Mother Marie tries to restore calm to her fellow sisters. The sound of the bells is the outer counterpart to the Prioress's inner anguish.

A calm quiet instrumental section provides the transition to the Prioress's final moments. It is marked by steadily pulsing chords above a rising and falling bass. Having been summoned by the Prioress, Blanche enters the room petrified and haggard. The Prioress addresses Blanche by name and struggles to tell her something, but all she can manage is a final tormented outburst that will have special meaning for Blanche: "Beg forgiveness . . . death . . . fear . . . fear of death!" She leaps up to a high A on the word "death." The accompanying chord is a clash between an F major triad and a diminished seventh chord on D-sharp. On this last word, the Prioress falls dead. Blanche does not know what the Prioress wanted to say, nor do we. The scene ends calmly, as a shaken Blanche struggles to find the right tense: "Our Reverend Mother wants . . . wanted . . . would have wanted . . ." After a brief fortissimo burst, the scene ends very quietly, as the orchestra spells out a final B-minor triad in octaves and the convent bells sound a lone B.

The death of the old Prioress marks the first stage of Blanche's spiritual journey. The question now is whether fear-afflicted Blanche will recapitulate the Prioress's agony or be saved through it.

Act Two: God's Logic

The second act begins with a florid instrumental prelude in C minor marked *très calme*. It is a baroque-style three-part canon played by strings. The scene is the convent chapel, where the body of the Prioress lies in state. It is night. Blanche and Constance stand watch over the deceased. We hear them sing an excerpt from the Latin Office for the Dead. Their restrained, chant-like music fits the calm meditative prayer for eternal rest. Constance leads with the verse about Jesus's raising Lazarus "stinking from the grave." Blanche responds with the plea for rest and pardon for the dead. Then Constance sings about Jesus as the one who will come to judge the living and the dead. Blanche then repeats the previous plea for rest. Both sisters join for the plea for pardon.[33] The duet ends with an *Amen* in parallel thirds followed by parallel sevenths. It resolves on the major third between A and C-sharp. Mellers rightly calls it seraphic (113):

The final chord is one of Poulenc's shimmering dissonances. Built around the A-major triad, the chord allows Blanche to share momentarily in Constance's radiance. The opera's regular pairing of the two sisters suggests the eventual intertwining of their fates.

At the sound of the clock, Constance leaves to find the sisters who are to replace them. But as Blanche, now alone with the Prioress's body, tries to pray, broken tritones undercut her calm and reveal inner stabs of anxiety. After a fixed gaze at the body, she rises terror-stricken and moves toward the door, where she meets Mother Marie and explains that her replacements have not yet arrived. Marie, ever aware of what needs to be done at a given time, harshly accuses Blanche of having yielded to fear—of having abandoned her post. She then assumes a gentler, more understanding tone, as she advises Blanche to get some sleep and, in the morning, to ask God for forgiveness. The scene ends with a brief statement of the opening flourish, now in A minor. At the very end, the somber mood is dispelled by a quiet consoling cadence in A major.

The interlude that follows is the pivotal scene in which Sister Constance, in her childlike way, gives voice to the mystery of transferred grace. The scene begins with the convent bells tolling quietly, as Constance and Blanche make a cross out of flowers. Constance sadly observes that the large cross made to honor the deceased Prioress is out of proportion with so small a grave. She suggests that the leftover flowers be presented to the new Prioress, who Constance hopes will be her fellow aristocrat, the practical Mother Marie. When Blanche asks her whether she really thinks that God will grant whatever Constance asks of Him, Constance responds: "Why not? What we call chance is perhaps God's logic." The offhand response acknowledges the often strange and to our minds incomprehensible workings of grace.

As Constance approaches her inspired thesis, her recitative becomes an arioso in sober A minor. She is accompanied by a rising ostinato bass that marks off the minor third between A and C, as the harmony oscillates between the A minor triad and its tense diminished seventh chord on G-sharp: "Think of the death of our dear Mother, Sister Blanche! Who could have believed that she would have such a hard time dying, that she could die so badly?" As Constance moves into her final phrase about dying badly, her harmony shifts from A minor to C minor—the key in which Blanche will die and the opera will end. With touching simplicity, Constance speculates that God must have made a mistake, and that just as sometimes one is given the wrong coat from the cloakroom, the Prioress's death in fact belonged to another. Throughout her speculation, which she sings *très doux*, her accompaniment gently descends in support of her simple and beautiful melodic arc. The ostinato bass, now in C minor, returns as she concludes forte: "Yes, it must be that it was the death of another."

At this point in her arioso, the music, still supported by the persistently rising bass, shifts suddenly to dark B-flat minor, as Constance sings: "It was a death too small for her." By "too small" she means "unworthy of the Prioress's great *honneur*." To this, Blanche asks anxiously: "The death of another—what can that mean, Sister Constance?"

Constance continues her comic metaphor of the mistaken cloak: "I mean that this other, when it is *her* time to die, will be astonished that she will enter into it so easily, and will feel that it is comfortable." She sings these words sweetly, with a melody line that consists of falling octaves and rising sixths. The key (G major), melody, and underlying harmony of the first three measures are identical to those of Blanche's arioso in Act 1, when she announced that her native element was fear—that fear *suited* her. The harmonic motion, here as in the earlier passage, combines smoothness with pleasant surprise, as it modulates by thirds through a series of dominant seventh chords that immediately resolve:

Tones, here, express a meaning that is not yet explicit in words and plot. Blanche, because of the Prioress's sacrificial death-agony, will transcend the fear that is her element and her fate. Indeed, her elemental fear, which she finds strangely comfortable as well as oppressive, is a presentiment of that transcendence. What Constance naively announces turns out to be truer than she realizes. The tale, in any case, has already been told by the tones in a wordless statement of things to come.

The smoothly flowing sequence then shifts to a diminished seventh chord on D-sharp—the enharmonic equivalent of the E-flat with which the phrase began. The abruptness of this chord is softened by Constance's sweetly rising sixth at the end of the word *facilement,* "easily." The chord is part of a carefully designed transition to a half cadence on E (on the word *confortable*) that sets up the concluding phrase in A minor, the key in which we hear the mystery of transferred grace in its full generality: "We do not die each for ourselves, but each for another, or even each in place of another, who knows?" As Constance sings the first half of her statement very quietly, the underlying descending chords gently stress the principal beats of the measure and the syllables of the proclamation. Then, more strongly and with a graceful flow of triplets, she utters the second, more important half about substitution. Her casually appended *"qui sait?"* ("who knows?"), sung with a rising sixth, hovers. The final cadence of the interlude echoes the quietly haunting chords with which the interlude began, as the key slides from A minor to D-sharp, a tritone away. The scene ends as it began: with the clock sounding a lone, quietly ominous A.[34]

Scene 2 begins with an orchestral andante in B-flat minor that has the sound of a gently measured march. The noble tread of the opening introduces us to the new Prioress, Mme. Lidoine, who gives her fellow sisters their marching orders. She urges them to move forward in an undistracted andante of the spirit. Her melody stays close to the degrees of the B-flat minor scale and keeps within a limited tonal range—in imitation of the strict boundaries she recommends to her "dear daughters." The one exception is her octave leap up to a high B-flat on the word *vivre,* to live: "What the years we are going to *live in* will mean to us, I do not know." The central theme of her arioso is courage, the courage that fits "poor daughters who have gathered to pray to God." She cautions her daughters to beware of thoughts and aspirations that might distract them from their humble vocation. Especially dangerous is the aspiration to martyrdom: "Prayer is a duty, martyrdom a reward." As Mme. Lidoine sings these words, the orchestra accompanies her with heroic-sounding double-dotted chords in a crescendo that rises to fortissimo. If a mighty king invites one of his woman servants to sit beside him on his throne, as if she were a well-beloved wife, is it not wiser, Mme. Lidoine asks, "that she first refuse to believe her eyes and ears, and go on working in house and garden?" When she finds herself unable to find the right ending for her speech, she appeals to always-dependable Mother Marie, who reinforces the counsel already given: "Let us obey, not only with our tongues but with our hearts, the wishes of Her Reverence."[35]

Poulenc then regales us with one of his most celestial choral settings in the opera, as the sisters, led by Marie, sing *Ave Maria* in F-sharp minor. Once again, we hear a tonal-harmonic mimesis of chant produced by chords in roughly parallel motion, embellished with the shimmering dissonances that make Poulenc's music immediately recognizable. Marie begins the second half of the prayer with a soaring melodic arc built on the F-sharp minor triad:

The scene ends in a hush, as the sisters leave the chapel to subdued exit music.

The interlude that follows contrasts sharply with the previous scene of calm and prayer. It is the transition to the dramatic dialogue between Blanche and her brother. The music is frenetic, as the sound of a doorbell sends the sisters into a panic. There's a *man* at the gate! We hear the Old-World motif, now played four times, as if to emphasize that it is the tonal symbol of Blanche's aristocratic family. Mme. Lidoine infers that since he is at the gate in the alley and is eager to conceal himself, he must be a friend rather than one of the revolutionary rabble. The mystery man, Mother Marie explains, is Blanche's brother, here to see his sister. Mme. Lidoine accedes to his request ("Circumstances warrant this infraction of the rules") and instructs Marie to be present during the interview. The interlude ends in extreme agitation, with a series of abrupt flourishes in B-flat minor and a final loud B-flat minor chord from the interlude's opening. The chord no doubt signals that the interview will not end well.[36]

The orchestral prelude to Scene 3 brings us to the midpoint of Poulenc's twelve-scene opera. It is a calm extended refrain of the Old-World theme in 3/4 time. The piece is a good example of Poulenc's fondness for symmetry and the traditional four-bar phrase. It has a clear-cut ABA structure: a twelve-measure first section that spells out the A minor triad in the bass with loud dissonant chords above, a warm eight-measure middle section played by strings (the music, here, sinks rather than rises and ends on a half cadence), and an almost twelve-measure concluding section in which the rising family theme returns, this time played in the higher register with dissonant chords above and below. It ends with a simple spelling out of the minor third between A and C, before leading into the first measure of the scene. The composed-sounding music may be the sound of the Chevalier waiting for his sister to say something.

Scene 3 dramatizes the clash of two worlds: the outer secular world beyond the walls of Carmel and the inner sacred realm of prayer. The scene is intensely, even alarmingly, passionate. Here we see and hear the Chevalier trying relentlessly to get Blanche to leave Carmel for the safety of home and the care of her old father—to break her spiritual resolve through a heartfelt assault. Poulenc described the scene as "a mixture of anxiety and tenderness."[37] Throughout the opera, we hear how deeply Poulenc had *felt himself* into the souls of his characters. In the present scene, through the power of tones in time, we feel the intense love that the Chevalier has for his sister and the ambivalence of Blanche, who resists her brother's worldly temptations by putting up a brave front, all the while concealing her abiding fear.

The scene continues the prelude's somber key of A minor. The recurring thirty-second note upbeats will soon metamorphose into the scene's signature rhythmic gesture: a double-dotted note followed by a thirty-second note. It is a heaving of the heart with a double meaning. The rhythmic push signals the violence of the Chevalier's pleas and of Blanche's disrupted inner state.[38]

Blanche's brother asks: "Why have you been sitting like this for twenty minutes, your eyes downcast, hardly responding? Is this the welcome one owes a brother?" His question, which begins the painful conversation, is followed immediately by the thirty-second note theme that will intensify as the interview proceeds. When Blanche responds that she had no wish to cause any displeasure, the Chevalier informs her of their father's judgment that it is no longer safe for her to remain in Carmel. Blanche tells her brother that although she may not be safe, feeling so is enough for her.

The conversation then shifts to a deeper and more personal concern, as the Chevalier observes that Blanche has changed from the sister he once knew, since she now seems constrained and ill at ease. As the key shifts from A minor to C-sharp minor, Blanche gently explains that her demeanor is the result of her not yet being accustomed to living happy and free (*délivrée*). Throughout this reassuring speech, the now-denser accompaniment betrays signs of anxiety that undercut her words. During the Chevalier's retort, the double-dotted figures that appeared in Blanche's preceding speech now come in pairs and with more passionate insistence: "Happy you may be, but not free. It is not in your power to rise above nature."[39] Blanche responds with a rhetorical question: "Come now, does it appear to you that life at Carmel conforms to nature?" Her half cadence on a C-major dominant chord (a standard device for questions in tonal harmony) sets the stage for her brother's response in F minor.

The Chevalier addresses Blanche with increased urgency: "In times such as these, there is more than one woman, once envied by all, who would most gladly change her place for yours." Blanche should jump at the chance to come back home to a loving family! Catching himself, the Chevalier explains in calmer tones that his harshness is caused by the image of their father, alone among the servants. As he sings, the family-theme, now in B-flat minor and descending, sounds in the orchestra.

The conversation then turns to the opera's main theme, fear, as a now confident-sounding Blanche asks: "Do you think I am kept here by fear?" "Or the fear of fear," the Chevalier perceptively adds. Now voicing Bernanos's own conviction, he calmly reminds Blanche of the need to "run the risk of fear as you would run the risk of death." He speaks of the need for "true courage," not realizing how this might apply to Blanche's higher, supernatural calling. Blanche gently responds to her brother's summons in terms that the secular Chevalier cannot understand: "From this day on, I am only the poor innocent victim of His Divine Majesty."[40] Addressing Blanche by name, the Chevalier resumes an impassioned tone. Accompanied by the double-dotted figure, he recalls their childhood: "It is probably through clumsiness that we have come to almost throwing challenges at each other. Have they changed my little hare (*mon petit lièvre*)?" As he utters his sentence about clumsiness, his melody rises with great tenderness to a high A—his highest note in the scene. The mention of his pet-name for his sister recalls Blanche's first speech in the opera: "My brother is too kind to his little hare."

Blanche responds harshly in C minor: "Ah! Why do you wish to throw doubt into me like a poison? I all but perished once from this poison." Rising to her high A-flat, she adds: "It is true that I have changed (*que je suis une autre*)." An unexpected C-major chord signals a change of mood, as the Chevalier asks: "Are you no longer afraid of anything?" Blanche, in a toneless voice, answers: "Where I am, nothing can reach me." The Chevalier capitulates: "Well then, farewell, my dear." As he moves toward the door, Blanche laments in C-sharp minor and accompanied by anxious sixteenth notes: "Oh! Do not leave me with an angry farewell!" Rising to her high A on "Alas!", she expresses her frustration at being constantly treated with pity rather than with "that simple esteem that you

would give the least of your friends!" The passionate double-dotted figure then returns, as the Chevalier accuses Blanche of being
the harsh one. Confessing her respect and tenderness for her
brother, she tells him with admirable directness that she is now no
longer his "little hare" but "a daughter of Carmel," who will suffer
for him. Her final plea stresses the militant character of the life of
prayer and sacrifice (a topic close to Bernanos's heart and beliefs).
She asks only that her brother think of her not as a weakling but
as a companion in battle (*un compagnon de lutte*). Her eloquent,
gently falling *portando* (in which the voice glides from one note to
another through the intervening tones) seems to express her mode
of engaging in battle: through prayer and submission to God's
will. Her brother will fight in his way, she in hers. Having failed in
his attempt to "free" his sister, the Chevalier gives Blanche a long
look—and leaves. A shaken Blanche clings to the grille in order not
to fall.

In a coda to the scene, Mother Marie, who has heard everything, comes to Blanche's aid: "Compose yourself, Sister Blanche!"
Blanche confesses, with a trembling accompaniment in B-flat
minor, that she has lied in pretending to a strength she does not
possess, all because she could not endure being pitied. On the word
"Alas!" she leaps up to a high C and asks God for pardon. After a
long pause, she quietly admits that the kindness of it (the compassion) sickened her soul (*écœurait l'âme*): "Oh! Shall I never be more
than a child in their eyes?" She confesses that she has been proud
(*orgueilleuse*) and will be punished for it. To this, Marie responds
(on a persistent C) that there is only one way to put down pride:
one must raise oneself above it.[41] Her accompanying music in C
minor consists of a very low pedal C, repeated dissonant sevenths,
and an ornament that mimics a trumpet call.

As Mother Marie leaves, she gently straightens Blanche's bowed
figure and issues a bracing command with a leap of a diminished
seventh: "*Tenez-vous fière!*" ("Stand proud!"). Marie's command to
fight the sin of pride with a virtuous pride, a demeaning fire with

an ennobling one, recalls the theme of *honneur* that pervades Bernanos's screenplay. It also stresses the militarism that is characteristic of Mother Marie and that will be further emphasized by Sister Constance in the next scene. In a resounding postlude, the orchestra plays very loudly E-flat major triads and a variation on the four-note theme that has been a leitmotif for the *ancien régime* and Blanche's family. The scene ends on a resplendent E-flat major chord over the still-sounding pedal on a low C. As Mellers observes, the postlude "transforms the Old World theme into potential heroism" (119). Thanks to the persistent deep-sounding C (an echo of the preceding C minor music), the heroic tone is melded with the deep-set anxieties and turmoil that have been heard and felt throughout the scene.

The final scene of Act 2 will culminate in a more brutal invasion of Carmel's inner life, as the revolutionary crowd converges on the sacred place and commissioners of the Revolution demand entry. The drama at this point gains considerable momentum.

The scene opens in the sacristy of Carmel, as we go from the heroic E-flat at the end of the last scene to the opera's principal key of A minor—a dissonant tritone away. It begins with a violent burst: an A minor chord played sforzando. We then hear the ostinato bass that is one of the opera's principal themes, as the Chaplain informs the nuns that the Mass he has just said will be his last: he has been forbidden to perform his duties and will now "partake of the grief of our early Christian fathers." He then leads the sisters in singing a gorgeously harmonized *Ave verum corpus*, which ends with a plea for mercy in the trial of death. Blanche fears that the Chaplain will be killed after he leaves, but he gently urges her not to yield to her fearful imaginings. He will be in disguise and will return as often as he can. He then leaves.

Sister Constance, angered by what she has just heard, comments on the times: "Is it believable that our priests are allowed to be hounded like this in a Christian country? Are the French now so cowardly?" During this last question, she is accompanied by two sets of agitated descending tritones (in thirty-second notes) that express Constance's patriotic indignation and, simultaneously, the faltering of French courage. Bernanos's most beloved saints were Thérèse de Lisieux (the Little Flower) and Jeanne d'Arc (the Maid of Orleans). He combined their spirits in Sister Constance, the simple child-nun who utters mysteries and has the heart of a warrior-patriot. Sister Matthilde answers Constance in terms that recall the central theme of the opera: "They are afraid. Everybody is afraid. They infect each other with fear, as they might in a time of epidemic with plague or cholera." The observation touches Blanche personally. She responds in flowing triplets over a very slow sequence of chords that vacillate between sharp and flat keys: "Perhaps fear is in fact an illness [*une maladie*]."

Constance, true to her name, is unimpressed by this appeal to fear: "Are there no longer decent Frenchmen to take up the defense of our priests?" The new Prioress, lowborn Mme. Lidoine, observes that when there aren't enough priests, there will be plenty of martyrs, "and the balance of grace will thus be restored." Her statement ends on a C-major chord that leads (as a dominant) to the dark key of F minor, in which Mother Marie interprets the Prioress's claim in her own way, as a call to martyrdom: "So that France may again have priests, the daughters of Carmel have only to give their lives." Marie's accompaniment includes heroic double-dotted rhythms and a glorious, if quiet, ascent of D minor and F major chords that mimics the resurgence of the priesthood. But the Prioress reprimands her and recalls her earlier injunction: "You have misheard me, Mother, or at least you did not understand me." In a gentler mode, she reminds her: "It is not for us to decide whether our poor names will be inscribed among the martyrs [*dans le bréviaire*]." The Prioress then leaves, followed by Sister Jeanne, as the other nuns, dumbfounded, look at Mother Marie.

The calm is broken by the doorbell. It is the Chaplain, who has returned to escape the crowd and the patrol of soldiers that have gathered outside. He enters through a small door, as disso-

nant syncopations signal the crowd's approach. As he explains his
situation, the muttering crowd intones an "Oh!" with a menac-
ingly dissonant chord over the persisting jagged syncopations. As
a trumpet call sounds and the crowd (now louder) draws near, the
sisters are thrown into an outright panic: "Listen! Listen! They are
here!" After the terrified Chaplain escapes (again), there is knock-
ing at the door to the sound of officials who demand entrance:
"Open the door! Open the door!" The sisters huddle in a corner
(all but Mother Marie) and cry out with an antistrophe in octaves:
"Don't open! Don't open!" The banging on the door grows louder
and finally stops, as the harmony shifts momentarily to B-flat
minor. It is a moment of high drama. After a long silence, Mother
Marie, always in control, calmly but firmly urges Constance ("*ma
petite fille*") to do as they say. Two *commissaires* enter, while two
others remain near the door. The crowd is held back by armed
guards with long pikes.

Mother Marie is marvelous throughout the scene, as she proudly
confronts the swaggering flunkies of the Legislative Assembly. The
first commissioner—in F minor and to the sound of bluntly stated
chords in the orchestra—wants to know where the sisters are.
Mother Marie responds just as bluntly: "You see them over there!"
The commissioner then announces, with descending notes in the
accompaniment, that they must be made aware of the "decree of
expulsion." The second commissioner then reads the decree over a
low pedal F, descending chords, and a pompous oom-pah bass.

The first commissioner then ridiculously asks whether there
is anything to which the sisters object. "How can we object," asks
Marie, "since there is nothing at all left for us to decide?" She adds:
"But it really is necessary that we obtain some clothes, since you
prohibit us from wearing these." Her appeal to common decency
is met with mockery, as the commissioner sings a taunting parody of unadorned C major: "Are you then so eager to leave these
religious frocks and dress like everybody else?" Unruffled Marie
reminds him that it is not the uniform that makes the soldier, and

that regardless of what clothes they wear they will always be nothing but humble servants. When the commissioner asserts that the people have no need of servants, Marie sounds her earlier theme: "But there is a great need of martyrs, and that is a service we can assume." Resuming his mocking tone, the commissioner dismisses martyrdom as insignificant: "Bah! In times like these, to die is nothing." Marie shoots back at him: "To *live* is nothing, when life is thoroughly debased and has no more value than your *assignats* [paper money]."

The commissioner then explains himself. "These words," he says, "would have cost you dear, if you had said them to anyone but me!" He then tells Marie, in an aside, that she should not take him for one of these "drinkers of blood." He was once sacristan (one in charge of a sacristy) and loved the parish priest as a brother. But what can he do now except "howl with the wolves"? Marie then asks him to prove his good will by helping the sisters escape danger. No longer in a mocking tone, he promises (over a constant pedal C) to lead the patrol away. Before leaving, he warns Marie not to trust the ironically named blacksmith, Blancard: "He's an informer."[42]

The commissioners then withdraw and the crowd leaves amid noise and laughter. Mother Marie closes the doors and returns to her daughters, who are left dumbfounded. Blanche, "like a poor wounded bird," has dropped down on a little stool. Throughout the scene, she has kept herself hidden behind the other nuns. After a brief orchestral introduction in A minor, Sister Jeanne arrives to tell them that the Prioress is coming to say good-bye, since she has been called away to Paris. She will return in the next act.

As the key moves from A minor to F-sharp minor (the key of the *Ave Maria* sung earlier), Jeanne turns to Blanche with a pitying look and tells her that every Christmas Eve, the figure of "our Little King" is carried from cell to cell. Sister Jeanne entrusts the figure to Blanche in the hope that it will brighten her spirits. "Oh! How little He is! How frail," Blanche says and takes the figure in her arms. "No," Marie corrects her. "How little He is, and how power-ful!" At the sound of the mob's "*Ça ira!*", Blanche cries out in terror and drops the figure, which shatters on the flagstones.[43] Bereft of orchestral accompaniment, she laments in B-flat minor: "The Lit-tle King is dead! Nothing remains to us but the Lamb of God." The dissonant shattered chord on "*Dieu*" hovers softly, as the "*Ça ira!*" doubles in speed and grows louder. The breaking of the Little King points to Christ's power over death and sin—a power that consists in the will not to break but to be broken. It is a power that dwarfs the Revolution, whose diabolical high spirits, heard in the rousing orchestral conclusion of Act 2, only apparently win the day. In the end, the serenity of chant will triumph over the mind-numbing jingle of the "*Ça ira!*" Act 2 ends with a frenzied march of violently assertive chords in B-flat minor.

Act Three: The Last at the Scaffold

The final act opens with a grand gesture: a *Tempo de Sarabande* in A minor. Normally a dignified dance in triple time, the sarabande here oscillates between double and triple meter to give the rhyth-mic figure a broader and more flexible sweep. Its opening measure features dramatically rising and then falling octaves in the bass and noble-sounding double-dotted notes in the upper parts. The thirty-second-note flourishes echo those heard at the beginning of the opera. The sarabande is to be played *fièrement*—proudly, nobly. The marking echoes Marie's command to Blanche: "*Tenez-vous fière!*"[44] The moment to stand proud has arrived.

The sisters and the Chaplain have gathered in the devastated sacristy. In the absence of the cautious Prioress, martyr-minded Mother Marie now assumes a leading role. Before she speaks, the sarabande shifts from A minor to C minor. The shift of a minor third foreshadows the same modulation that will occur in the concluding march to the scaffold. Marie tells the Chaplain: "Speak to them, *mon Père*. For a long time, they have been ready to take this step." The Chaplain defers to Marie: "That is not one of my

duties, and I think that in the forced absence of Her Reverence
you yourself should speak to the Community." Marie, in candid
C major, does not hesitate to do as she is bidden: "My daughters,
I propose that together we take the martyr's vow, in order to win
the continued existence of Carmel and the salvation of our country." The orchestra responds with the heroic double-dotted chords
from the prelude.

When the sisters look from one to the other "without enthusiasm," Marie is pleased. Her proposal, she says, should be accepted
as coldly (*froidement*) as the Lord inspires her to make it. The sarabande returns over a pedal B, as Marie reminds her daughters that
they should have no illusions about what their lives are worth.[45]
Moreover, no one should be forced to act against her conscience.
Marie therefore decides that a single dissenting voice would make
her abandon her plan. Now in dark F minor and over a stabilizing
pedal F, she announces her intention: the matter will be decided
by a secret vote. The Chaplain will receive everyone's response
under the seal of the Sacrament. He then asks the sisters to pass
one by one behind the altar.

Sister Mathilde, with a slight movement of her chin in Blanche's
direction, whispers to a sister next to her: "We can be sure there
will be one vote against." The noble tread of the sarabande returns,
as each sister disappears behind the altar and reappears "almost
immediately." Blanche reappears, her face haggard. Constance follows her with her eyes. The Chaplain then approaches Marie and
utters a few words in a low voice, as the sarabande's flourishes, over
a pedal G, end in a muffled dissonance (an A diminished seventh
chord)—in effect, a deflation. "There was only one vote against,"
Marie announces. "That is enough." When Sister Mathilde says
that they know whose vote it was, Constance speaks up: "It was
I! The Chaplain knows I speak the truth." In a measure without
accompaniment, Constance leaps to a high B-flat and asks for
another chance: "*But . . . but . . . I am now ready to declare myself
in accord with all of you.*" In a follow-up measure without accom-

paniment, she asks, in lower tones and very slowly, that she be allowed to pronounce the vow: "I beg of you, in the name of God."

Constance has covered for Blanche—not by lying about her initial vote but, having supposed that Blanche voted against, by voting *with her*. To Constance's prophetic mind, she and Blanche must suffer a common fate. She refuses to let Blanche stand alone. Now that it has been revealed that hers was the only dissenting voice, she wishes to stand with Blanche again—this time in death. The Chaplain accedes to Constance's request. Putting on his vestments, he asks the sisters to come forward and take their vow of martyrdom before the book of the Holy Gospel, which has been placed open on the prayer-stand. "First, the youngest," he says. "Sister Blanche and Sister Constance, I pray you." Accompanied by the sarabande's flourishes in F-sharp minor, the two kneel side by side and offer their lives to God. The accompaniment reaches the dominant of F-sharp minor (a C-sharp major triad), but the expected cadence turns out to be a deception. Instead of a resolution, we hear a diminished seventh chord on E (the raised $\hat{7}$ of F minor), followed by low quiet octaves on C. As the *religieuses* jostle one another to take their places according to age, Blanche flees.

The C just heard signals the dominant of dire F minor, the key in which we hear once more the double-dotted motif of the sarabande, this time with harshly dissonant chords. It is the sound of noble intent undermined by crippling fear. The sequence ends with the unexpected statement of an F *major* chord played very loudly. The chord is a prophecy of Blanche's later fulfillment of her vow and her return to Gethsemane as Sister Blanche of the Agony of Christ.

The first interlude of Act 3 takes us from the dark grandeur at the end of the preceding act to the calm of humble acquiescence. As the sisters leave the convent,[46] they are accompanied by a sparse instrumental duet: a worrying repeated half step between E and F below and a simple melody above.[47] The key is A minor. The sisters are met by three municipal officers, one of whom comments sarcastically on the sisters' discipline and public spirit and pronounces the edict: no more living in Communities, no more relations with "the enemies of the Republic or with refractory priests, henchmen of the Pope and of tyrants." The sisters are to appear one by one before the Court and receive the *certificat* that will allow them to enjoy anew the benefits of freedom under the watchful eye of the laws.

As the officers depart, the music rises from A minor to B-flat minor. The Prioress, having returned from Paris, holds the sisters back with a gesture and counsels prudence. She urges Sister Gerald to warn the priest not to celebrate Mass today as originally planned, since it would endanger both him and the sisters. She then turns to Mother Marie, who, in the earlier absence of the Prioress, had pressed for the vow of martyrdom: "Don't you think so, *Mère Marie?*" Marie responds forcefully (*très violent*) to the sound of heroic double-dotted chords over a pedal F: "I rely on Your Reverence from now on for all I must think and believe." She adds in her practical way: "But if I was wrong to act as I did, it is no less the case that what is done is done." She turns to leave but then stops: "How can we reconcile the spirit of our vow with this caution (*prudence*)?" The Prioress calmly responds in B-flat minor over a pedal B-flat and addresses her fellow *religieuses*. Rising above Marie's practical attitude, she tells them that each will be accountable to God for her own vow, but that she, the Prioress, will answer for them all, adding: "and I am old enough to know how to keep my accounts in order." Throughout her speech, the orchestra, in support of the Prioress's equanimity, stresses the first beat of each measure with a full rich chord. The interlude ends, disconcertingly, on an E diminished seventh chord, which paves the way for the F minor transition to the following scene.[48] The unexpected chord no doubt signals the uncertainty and possible violence to which the sisters are now exposed.

I have dwelled on the details of this interlude because it highlights a central theme of the opera, dramatized in the opposed

views of the Prioress and Marie on the topic of martyrdom. Earlier, the new Prioress had reminded her daughters, and especially
the headstrong Mother Marie, that martyrdom is a reward to be
accepted, not an achievement to be sought out. As Marie shows
us in the interlude, the striving for martyrdom remains a strong
temptation for the heroic-minded and is always in need of the Prioress's sober reminder.

The orchestral transition to Scene 2 is in F minor and marked
"calm and sorrowful." Its main function is to provide a strong statement of the theme of Blanche's family. The statement fits, since
we now find Blanche, having absconded from Carmel, back in her
father's house. The scene opens in F minor with agitated dotted
figures that are now "distraught rather than heroic" (Mellers, 122).
The offbeat rhythm in the bass signals that something is indeed
"off." Having obtained the Prioress's permission, Mother Marie, in
ordinary clothes, has come to Blanche's home, where Blanche has
sought refuge, to persuade her to return to the safety that her sisters can offer. It is the inverse of the scene in which the Chevalier
tried to liberate his sister from Carmel. Marie finds Blanche in her
father's library, where the story began. The pillaged room, once
sumptuous, now has a low stove in the large fireplace and a folding
bed. Aristocratic Blanche is watching a pot on the stove. She has
been reduced to the status of a servant in her own home. "It's you!"
Blanche exclaims, as Marie appears, in civilian clothes. "Yes," says
Marie. "I've come to find you. It is time."

A haggard Blanche tells Marie that she is not free to follow
her now and asks for more time. Marie, undaunted, tells Blanche
that she must come immediately. In a few days it may be too late.
The "pushy" dotted figure of the opening punctuates her statement. "Too late for what?" Blanche asks, as the same rhythmic
figure returns. "For your safety," says Marie. Blanche insists that
no place could be safer than where she is right now: "Where I am,
who would think of looking for me?" Leaping up to her high A on

the word *mort*, she adds: "Death strikes only above me." Then certainty gives way to confession: "But I am so tired, Mother Marie!"

Blanche suddenly realizes that her conversation with Marie has caused her to neglect the pot on the stove: "Look! My stew is burned! It's your fault! *Mon Dieu! Mon Dieu!* What will become of me?" She ends on a high C-flat. As she kneels at the stove to tend her stew, Marie kneels beside her and quickly transfers the stew to another pot.[49] Accompanied by slowly descending thirds, fourths, and tritones, Marie consoles Blanche, who is reduced to tears by Marie's kindness.

The conversation then turns, once again, to fear. Blanche is ashamed of her tears and wishes that her companions would just leave her in peace and never think of her again: "Why must they all reproach me? What harm have I done? I do not offend God. Fear does not offend God." Her first two questions are underscored by a strongly affirmed pair of chords: F minor, followed by a diminished seventh chord on E over a dissonant A-flat. The stress on the second beat of the 3/4 measure tragically echoes the dance gesture of a sarabande. It is a sad reminder that the woman who suffers the unjust reproach of others is of aristocratic origin and has an inborn sense of *honneur*.

Blanche then recalls her back-story: "I was born in fear, I lived in it, I still live in it. Everyone despises fear, so it is only right that I, too, should live in contempt. *That* I have believed for a long time." With an upward octave leap on F, Blanche fondly recalls her father, the only one who could prevent her from speaking like this. But he is dead. In a choked voice, she adds: "They guillotined him a few days ago." Throughout this passage, the family theme sounds in the orchestra in dark B-flat minor (the key associated with the Revolution). As Blanche now reflects on her horrid falling off, she throws herself on the folding bed: "In his own house, what other role should I have, I who am so unworthy of him and of his name, than that of a wretched servant?" Her reference to her father's name has a double meaning. It is an aristocratic name that also celebrates strength: *de la Force*. Blanche then recounts the lowest point of her humiliation: "Only yesterday they struck me. Yes, they *struck* me!" Her pained admission is accompanied by the pushy dotted figure we heard at the opening of the scene. Here, it expresses both the insult to Blanche and her proud defiance.

Marie responds to Blanche with one of Bernanos's central teachings: "The misfortune, my daughter, is not to be despised but to despise oneself."[50] Marie begins in C minor and then modulates to a half cadence in A minor. The noble rhythm of the sarabande (stress on the second beat) momentarily returns, as Marie, a fellow aristocrat, attempts to rouse Blanche with her chosen name: "*Soeur Blanche de l'Agonie du Christ!*" Blanche rises, as if to a general's summons, to face Marie with dry eyes: "*Ma Mère?*"

To the sound of a simple accompaniment in half-note chords, Marie gives the address of a friend, one Rose Ducor, who will offer Blanche safety.[51] As Marie gives the address, she leaps dramatically from F to a high A.[52] The address, which promises safety, is punctuated by a straightforward harmonic cycle in A minor over a pedal A, ending on a hopeful A major chord. Continuing in A major, and with noble flourishes from the act's opening sarabande, Marie promises to wait there for Blanche until the following night. Blanche mournfully refuses: "I will not go. I cannot go there." "You will go," Marie responds. "I know you will go, my Sister." The rasping voice of a woman off-stage breaks the mood: "Blanche, your errands!" The interruption is followed by the "pushy" dotted figure. Blanche then flees through a small door. Marie, dumbfounded, steals away through the large one. The scene ends with a slow procession of sad trochees in F minor.

The second interlude is marked "lugubrious and quite slow." Its dark limping motion begins with offbeat B-flat major chords in triple time over a pedal D, as a lone clarinet plays a gloomy variation on the dotted rhythms from the previous scene.[53] The music is the sound of mournfully passing time.

The penultimate scene of the opera takes place at dawn in the Conciergerie prison, where the Carmelites have been confined. The E-minor music that opens the scene is calm, flowing, and quietly noble.[54] The Prioress gently consoles her daughters with music that is "not arioso but fully fledged aria."[55] Supported by a steady heartbeat pulse in the orchestra, the Prioress sings what is perhaps the most sublime music in the entire opera. Her vocal line soars effortlessly in tonal space in a variety of inflections, as if it were the embodiment of the Holy Spirit. She consoles her daughters with the observation that the worst is over. They have endured their first night in prison and now will easily adapt to their new condition. Besides, she tells them reassuringly, their confinement is nothing new—no more than a change of scene. "No one," she says, "can deprive us of a liberty that we shed long ago."

The song then ascends to luminous E major, as the Prioress recalls the martyr's vow, which her daughters have taken but she has not. Whether or not the vow was a mistake, the Prioress tells them, God cannot now allow such a noble act to trouble their consciences. As the key moves from E major to A-flat major (four sharps to four flats), she resolves to assume the vow herself: "Henceforth, I am responsible for it. I am and will be, whatever happens, the sole judge of the vow's accomplishment." Heroic double-dotted chords support her resolve. "Yes!", she says, rising forcefully to her high B-flat, "I take the burden of the vow and leave you the merit, since I did not pronounce the vow myself." Her song then moves to the realm of D major, as she resumes her gentler, reassuring tone over an accompaniment that alternates between diatonic and chromatic chords. She reminds her daughters once again that she has always been ready to answer for them all and has no desire to avoid what is to come.

The Prioress ends her soaring address with a momentary shift to D minor: "Put your minds to rest!" ("*Soyez tranquilles!*"). The parallel minor and noble flourishes played by the strings support the Prioress's call for untroubled endurance. Low-voiced Sister

Jeanne then re-introduces the theme of fear: "With Your Reverence, we will fear nothing." The lowborn Prioress then rises to the heights of mystery, as she stresses the sanctity of fear: "In the Garden of Olives, Christ was no longer master of anything. He feared death."[56] The Prioress is no doubt recalling the passage in which Christ tells his disciples: "My soul is troubled, even unto death" (Matthew 26:38). The sanctity of fear is to fear *in Him* and to be consoled *by Him*. As Mellers observes, "the key teeters between pastoral F major and tenebrous B-flat minor" (123). The Prioress's simple melody is supported by chords in iambic rhythm in 3/4 time over a pedal F. The effect is almost that of a very slow siciliano. The upper strings play the opening ascent of the Prioress's melody: C, D, E-flat, E-natural, G. The harmony features the reverent-sounding vi-chord and an alternation of half-diminished and full-diminished seventh chords—the former celestial-sounding, the latter anguished.[57] The music suggests the intimate union of the divine and the all-too-human. The last word, "death" (*"mort"*), is accompanied by an E diminished seventh chord—a tense pointer to the serene F-major chord to which it quietly resolves. The Prioress's utterance of mystery ends with an orchestral recapitulation of the opening ascent, this time played a celestial octave higher. It features a slow iteration of the four-note theme of Blanche's family. The often dark-sounding theme is here an ascent to the divine—a musical transfiguration.

As if in response to the rising family theme, Sister Constance asks abruptly: "And what of Sister Blanche?" Contrary to what the others think, she is certain that Blanche will return. Why? "Because . . . because . . ." she stammers, "I had a dream." All the sisters, except for the Prioress, then burst into laughter.

But the hilarity is soon dispelled by loud jarring chords in B-flat minor: the jailer has come to read the sisters their death sentence. He recites (or rather barks out) the edict of the Revolutionary Tribunal over a violent accompaniment with rhythmically jarring chords played by the piano. In a shift to C minor, he rattles off the names of the accused with mocking insouciance. To him, as to the Revolution, the women are not human beings, only obstacles. Tension builds as the jailer lists their crimes: meeting in secret to defy the Revolution,[58] corresponding with its enemies, and seeking to re-enslave the French people to tyrants, and drowning their liberty in the torrents of blood that their plots and treachery have brought about "in the name of heaven." Finally, the jailer comes to the condemnation: "The Revolutionary Tribunal in consequence has declared that the aforementioned are condemned to death." He sings the declaration over a tremor of widely spaced octaves on C. Just before the final "*mort*," the music drops to a deflating pianissimo. The word of death is approached through a ghostly arpeggio that outlines a seventh chord on C. The jailer rolls up the edict, as the sisters lower their heads. He clumps off to the sound of heavy, dead-sounding chords and a brief transition to heroic E-flat major.

The Prioress then resumes her gentle tone and returns to the theme of the vow. She addresses the sisters with an accompaniment which echoes that of her previous assurance ("Do not, then, burden yourselves with any worry, my daughters"). She tells them that from the very first day that she met them, she loved them with a mother's love: "What mother agrees to the sacrifice of her children, even if it be to His Majesty himself?" Supported by heroic double-dotted chords that affirm E-flat major, she tells them that they are her only possession. On this last word, she rises again to her high B-flat, her highest note in the opera. When she adds that she is not one of those women who throw their wealth out the window, the key area shifts from E-flat to F-sharp minor (three flats to three sharps). She then moves to her final official act as Prioress. She does so in F-sharp *major* (a key of transcendence) over a pedal F-sharp and the gradually descending thirty-second note flourishes that were heard earlier: "My daughters, I now solemnly put you under obedience for the last time, once and for all, with my maternal blessing." She means their vow of martyrdom. On her final "*bénédiction*," she rises to the tonic F-sharp, as the orchestra plays a heavenly-sounding F-sharp major chord.

The third interlude, which takes place in front of the curtain, opens with a B-flat minor chord played fortissimo. It is followed by an agitated flurry of sixteenth notes. We are to imagine that the scene is the safe house that Marie recommended to Blanche in Act 2. The Chaplain has come to give Mother Marie the bad news: "They have been condemned to death." "All of them?" Marie asks. "All of them," he responds. "It will doubtless happen today, or tomorrow." On a noble flourish in the orchestra, Marie turns to leave with the intention of joining the condemned sisters. She is stopped by the Chaplain, who reminds her that God chooses or holds back whom He pleases. "I have taken the martyr's vow," she says. The Chaplain reasonably responds: "It was to God that you made it, it is to Him that you must answer for it, and not to your companions. If it pleases God to relieve you of it, He takes back that which belongs to Him." "I am dishonored!" Marie cries, leaping an octave to her high B-flat.[59] "Their gaze will seek me in vain." The Chaplain gently reminds the heroic-minded Marie: "Think only of Another's gaze, on which you should fix your own." The interlude ends, quietly, on a half cadence (an E major chord) that paves the way for the opera's final scene.

The scene, we should note, has a thematic connection with the scene in the prison. The Prioress, who cautioned against heroism, did not take the martyr's vow but will nevertheless die a martyr. Hero-minded Mother Marie did take the vow but will be saved, perhaps in order to tell the tale. It is the second transference of grace in the story (the first being the death of the former Prioress) and another instance of chance as "God's logic."

We now arrive at the opera's final, emotionally devastating scene: the march to the scaffold in the Place de la Révolution. It is preceded by "a barbaric revolutionary march, transformed into a funeral march as the nuns line up to face the guillotine" (Mellers,

124). The thudding march includes an ostinato bass that oscillates heavily between A and C—the minor third in A minor. The music soon modulates to minor thirds in G minor before settling back into its original key. This pattern will be repeated as the sisters go to their death. The most striking feature of the march is Poulenc's juxtaposition of A major chords in the upper parts and A minor triads in the bass to produce one of the harshest dissonances in the whole opera—a persistent grating of C-sharp against C-natural. Toward the end of the march, the crowd gathers to witness, and to relish, the slaughter.

Poulenc manages the culminating scene with breathtaking attention to words and drama. As each sister is executed, the remaining sisters continue their miraculously untroubled singing. They are arranged in sequence from eldest to youngest, the Prioress first and Constance last.[60] The crowd forms a second, accompanying chorus that murmurs "oh," "ah," and "ooh," in octaves and then in multi-part harmony. Their music makes clear that they have been momentarily transformed by what they see and hear into wonderstruck participants in a sacred drama. The thumps of the guillotine occur unexpectedly and brutally disrupt the serene flow of song—sometimes on a strong beat, sometimes not.[61] Here, as elsewhere in the opera, Poulenc conceives the overall motion as a three-phase wave: first subdued, then strong, then subdued again.

There is no dialogue in the scene, only harmonized chant: the whole of the *Salve Regina* and the final, doxological verse of *Veni, Creator Spiritus*.[62] The former is a prayer of "tender, helpless abandon" (Bush, 201). It is a cry to Mary, Mother of Mercy, and is traditionally chanted at the bedside of a dying sister. The latter is praise to the Triune God: "All glory to the Father and the Son, who rose from the dead, and to the Holy Spirit, forever and ever."

Poulenc divides the chorus of fifteen nuns (Blanche will make sixteen) into two sections: eight sopranos and seven mezzo-sopranos. The score carefully tracks the decreasing number of voices in each section. The nuns sing the first phrase of the *Salve Regina* pianissimo in A minor: "Hail, Queen, mother of mercy. Hail, our life and sweetness and hope." The Prioress, the first victim, is killed near the end of the first phrase. The thump of the guillotine falls on the last syllable of the word "*salve*," "hail." The key then shifts to C minor, as the remaining nuns start the phrase again, this time fortissimo. The second gruesome thump falls in mid word (on "*dulcedo*," "sweetness"), as if to say "Enough, already!" The nuns start the same phrase a third time, now in G minor, and get as far as "*in hac lacrimarum valle*" ("in this valley of tears"). Along the way, there are more thumps of the guillotine, as the number of victims diminishes.

The music then goes to the very dark key of A-flat minor: a half-step above G minor and below the original A minor. Dropping to pianissimo, the remaining sisters proceed to the prayer's supplication: "Therefore, our greatest advocate, turn toward us your eyes of mercy. And after this, our exile, show us the blessed fruit of your womb, Jesus. O clement, O loving, O sweet Virgin Mary." The crowd here, also pianissimo, sings in split parts, eight in all, to produce a harmonic thickening that signals growing awe. The key then shifts to F minor, as the number of victims falls to four.

Eventually, only one voice remains: that of the youngest, Sister Constance.[63] On the repeated word "*clemens*" ("merciful"), she leaps to her high A—the note on which she celebrated her love of life and joyful service to God—and pauses. Who is this she sees in the crowd? It is Blanche! As Constance beams with gladness at the sight of a prophecy fulfilled, we hear a heartrending recollection of Constance's celebratory music from Act 1: a modulation from a C major to an A major chord. After a return to somber A minor, Constance resumes her march to the scaffold with a gentle smile to Blanche. Her melody consists of a single tone: a constant C, supported by dissonant chords in the orchestra and the now quiet ostinato bass. She softly picks up the chant where she left off: "O loving, O sweet Virgin Mary." The guillotine stops her in mid word, as it did the other Carmelites. She dies in the middle of Mary's name.

As the key moves away from A minor, a calm miraculously transformed Blanche emerges from the crowd, which is astonished at the sight. She mounts the scaffold, quietly singing the final verse of *Veni, Creator Spiritus* (*Come, Holy Spirit*). We are not told how Blanche's transformation has taken place. Nor could we be, since it is a matter of supernatural rather than natural causality.[64]

The sublime culmination of the opera deserves to be quoted in full (see next page). Blanche's chant-like melody picks up on Constance's repeated C. It consists entirely of thirds and fourths. The absence of steps (the momentary lowering of A to A-flat is an inflection rather than a stepwise move) makes the melody sound uncannily still, as if it lived in an eternal Now. The lower parts of the orchestra, over a sustained C in the bass, gently echo the sarabande rhythm with which the final act began. This noble dance figure, with its stress on the second beat of the 3/4 measure, lends subdued grandeur to Blanche's ascent to martyrdom. It signals the fulfillment of the vow Blanche made in the opera's first scene: "I sacrifice all to Him, I abandon all, I renounce all, so that He might restore my *honneur*."

The sarabande rhythm in the accompaniment is further stressed by a barely perceptible melodic alternation (played by cellos and bassoons) between C-D-E and C-D-E-flat, which reinforces Blanche's alternation between C-E and C-E-flat. Throughout the opera, Poulenc uses the major-minor opposition to great effect. The shifts from major to minor, or the other way around, are sometimes abrupt, even violent. But here, in the moment of grace, Blanche is beyond the stark opposition of Dark and Light, which now mysteriously fuse to form a gentle untroubled wave. The fear of death has been changed into tranquil acceptance.

A carefully constructed harmony supports and interprets the tones of Blanche's simple song. We are reminded once more of Wagner's observation that harmony gives melody its full depth

of emotional meaning. The progression eschews the minor triads that were prominent in the *Salve Regina*. It consists entirely of
chords of the seventh and ninth: C7, D9, A-flat7, D9, C7, A-flat7, D9,
A-flat7, and finally D9. The smooth sequence of unresolved domi-
nants seems never to touch the ground. It is the sound of a shimmer upon a shimmer, where dissonance functions as a felt symbol
of peace and light.

As Blanche attempts to repeat the final phrase of the prayer ("*In
saeculorum saecula*") and the crowd falls silent, she is interrupted
before she can utter the final word of eternity. We hear the brutal sound of the guillotine in a measure without music, "a bar of
stunned silence" (Nichols, 242). It is finished.

The opera then proceeds to its quiet end. The crowd begins to
disperse with a final murmured "ah." And for the last time we hear
the four-note theme associated with Blanche's aristocratic family:

In being true to her martyr's vow, Blanche has also redeemed her
family's *honneur*.[65] The quietly stated theme is in sharp contrast
with its agitated mood at the start of the opera. The final sound
is a brief burst: a very quiet C minor chord that has been distilled
to its minor third between C and E-flat. It is the last beat of the
opera's passionate heart.

Closing Thoughts

Dialogues of the Carmelites is a world of worlds. As a work of art, it
is a world unto itself, a world we inhabit feelingly and perceptively
as listeners. We enjoy the work as music. The opera has an historical world as its backdrop: the French Reign of Terror and the

real-life martyrdom of the sixteen Carmelites on the seventeenth of July, 1794. This is the external world of the opera.

The work's deepest concern, however, is the inner world of thought and feeling, anguish and transcendence, fear and spiritual calm. This inwardness befits Carmel, a house of prayer. The vocation of music is to reveal, in tones and rhythms, the inner truth of all things. To echo the *Timaeus*, music presupposes that the world is ensouled. In the *Dialogues*, Poulenc, as I noted earlier, feels his way to the interior of his characters and lets us hear the invisible music of their souls. In all this, the external world—the central concern of Zuckerkandl's inquiry into music—is far from absent. It is in response to this world that we see, hear, feel, think, suffer, and rejoice. Whether natural or historical, the external world is part of our inner life, our existence, our world—just as our inner life is part of the cosmos as a whole. As Schopenhauer reminds us, the external world is the object (for him, the very embodiment) of our abiding care.

Poulenc called the opera terrifying and said that it would make us "weep and weep."[66] He was right on both counts. But he also said this: "If it is a play about fear, it is also—and above all, in my opinion—a play about grace and the transference of grace. That is why my Carmelites go to the scaffold with an extraordinary calm and faith. For are not faith and calm at the heart of all mystical experience?"[67] The opera, like the novel and screenplay that came before it, focuses on the spiritual journey of a fictional character: Blanche de la Force. But the inspiring real-life event was thoroughly communal. As we hear in Blanche's own final song, the event was a tribute, not to human heroism but to the Triune God. It was, in truth, a theophany, that is, a shining forth of God's glory.[68]

The *Dialogues* invites, perhaps even compels, our tears. Yet, like Bach's *St. Matthew Passion*, it also invites us to see beyond our tears that we may contemplate the heart of Christian mystery: the mystery of sacrifice and substitution. Through the uncanny power of music, a power both emotive and revelatory, Bach and Poulenc point beyond woe to wonder, acknowledgement, and in the end joy. Their profound musical dramas echo what Jesus tells his disciples in the gospel of John (16:33): "In the world you have tribulation; but be of good cheer, I have overcome the world."

Afterword

In writing a book, an author makes discoveries. While writing this one, I discovered that one of my book's most pervasive themes was death. Oddly, the realization dawned on me only after I had begun work on the final chapter.

As we saw in the first chapter, Timaeus's likely story is the exemplar of cosmic optimism. For Timaeus, the cosmos is adorned with beautiful mathematical structures and endowed with an intelligent, musically ordered soul. Death is present in the dialogue's prelude: in Socrates's desire to hear about the best city made mortal in war (19B–C) and in Critias's story about the destruction and rebirth that civilizations periodically experience (22B–23B). In the likely story, death pervades Timaeus's account of the corruptible parts of body and soul. The natural death of the composite being is a breakdown of the body's elemental triangles; and the soul, having been released from the body, "flies out with pleasure" (81D). The Minotaur of the *Phaedo*—the fear of death—is absent. Music is a form of therapy and a participation in the world's eternally self-same order. We partake of the deathless above all in the music of mathematical astronomy, which binds our souls to the cosmic whole to which we belong.

For pessimist Schopenhauer, what we call the cosmos is an illusion. Life is suffering, and to live is to be perpetually unsatisfied. The problem is not the will as such, but the will incarnated as *this* individual. Love as desire, especially sexual desire, is the fiery wheel of Ixion. Death is the ultimate cure for erotic love and the correction of an error. This is the original sin of having been born.

Music plays a crucial role in this gnostic cosmology. By offering intuitive apprehension of the modes of will, music is momentary refuge from the fiery wheel of infinite desire. Alone among human endeavors, it reveals the will in its pure, non-pictorial glory.

Zuckerkandl's account of music stands apart from the theme of death and the bearing music has on our mortality. His focus in *Sound and Symbol* is music as a source of cognition, a window into nature. Zuckerkandl discusses music in relation to human experience in the first chapter of *Man the Musician*. There, we hear that music, in tandem with discursive reason, defines the human essence. It is thoroughly life-affirming.

In Bach's *St. Matthew Passion*, death is the manifestation of divine love: "Out of love is my Savior willing to die." In the arias of his Great Passion, Bach explores various modes of human willing. But the crucial act of will, as Bach's soprano makes clear, is that of Jesus. Love shows itself in willingness to die on behalf of the beloved. The death on the cross—the ultimate symbol of divine love—saves humankind from death and sin. It thereby brings rest to the tormented conscience, the Christian wheel of fire.

Mozart's *Magic Flute* takes us from Christian faith and sacrifice to a secular idea of the world. From the opera's enlightened perspective, nature rather than God reigns supreme. Through Mozart's sublime music, we hear the reflective stirrings of first love in the soul of Tamino, as he gazes at the image of Pamina. Such love aims at marriage, the bond in which Man and Woman "touch unto divinity." It is an earthly, immanent transcendence. As in the *Timaeus*, death is not a cause for fear, especially if one trusts in the magical power of music, symbolized by Tamino's flute. As Pamina observes, she and Tamino, protected by the flute's wordless song, will "walk joyously through death's dark night."

Wagner's *Tristan and Isolde* celebrates love's intimate, Dionysian bond with death. Gone is the world as a noble construct fashioned by a good craftsman; gone the Christian story of grace as divine suffering and death; gone the apotheosis of marriage and the ideal of a humane social-political order. Schopenhauer's pessimistic idea of the world provides the cosmological foundation for Wagner's story of the archetypal lovers. But there is a twist. *Erotic love is now the path, through intense suffering, to the highest wisdom and the highest bliss.* Its goal is death as the coveted annihilation of individuality, the destruction of the "and" that keeps the lovers apart. Music alone does justice to the love-death bond, whose wordless sound is darkly evoked in the opening measures of the opera's Prelude.

Twelve-tone music proclaims the death of tonality and of Zuckerkandl's dynamic qualities. In its rage for a new order, it posits dissonance without direction and has the sound of perpetual disjointedness. Serialism is the idea of a world marked by anxiety, frustration, and fragmentation. It is music that is perfectly (dare I say, beautifully?) suited to the violent emotions and events depicted in Alban Berg's *Wozzeck*.

In his symbolic appropriation of twelve-tone music, Thomas Mann takes us into the tragic world of the musical *Übermensch*, Adrian Leverkühn. The narrative path is strewn with death. Most crucial is Adrian's death, brought on by his will to disease—the Nietzsche-inspired precondition for ecstatic artistry. Other tragic deaths include the suicide of Clarissa Rodde and the murder of Adrian's intimate, the violinist Rudi Schwerdtfeger. Most important is the death of Echo. In reaction to the angelic boy's gruesome end, Adrian conceives his twelve-tone masterpiece, the *Lamentation of Doctor Faustus*, as a "taking back" of the Ninth Symphony's Ode to Joy. It is a Schopenhauerian attempt to kill the mocking spirit of cosmic optimism, which through Echo's death has been shown to be a cruel joke.

Poulenc's *Dialogues of the Carmelites* is part of the exuberant rebirth of the tonality that serialism had pronounced dead. Tonality is given new life by an infusion of Poulenc's quirky harmonies, shimmering dissonances, and breathtaking lyricism. The opera takes its cue from the Passion and is, as Mellers rightly called it, metaphysically death-celebrating (102). It focuses on Blanche de la Force's fear of life and death. After abandoning her Carmelite sisters, Blanche rejoins them, graced by the old Prioress's bad death and Sister Constance's cheerful faith. She goes to her death miraculously transformed and no longer fearful, thanks to a not-so-mistaken cloak.

What, then, of music in relation to death? It might be said that through music we celebrate our bond with body, time, and change, and therefore also with death, since all change is a kind of death. This is the view put forth by Wallace Stevens in his anti-Christian poem *Sunday Morning*: "Death is the mother of beauty." Stevens replaces the purposeful descent of the Holy Spirit and divine grace with "casual flocks of pigeons" that "make / ambiguous undulations as they sink, / Downward to darkness, on extended wings." His celebration of earthy eroticism is explicit in *Peter Quince at the Clavier*, where we hear that music "is feeling, then, not sound" and that beauty "is momentary in the mind— / The fitful tracing of a portal; / But in the flesh it is immortal."

It is arguable, however, that music is, or at least can be, a temporal participation in the eternal. Math-minded Pythagoras, Plato, Kepler, and Leibniz certainly thought so. But in addition to the intellectual participation in the eternal through number and ratio, there are the non-discursive, vital phenomena of singing and listening. Do we not experience the sense of being lifted outside of time, change, and mortality by the pre-tonal radiance of *Sicut cervus*? Do we not experience this even more in the music that the historical Carmelites sang as they went to their death—in the passionate stillness of Gregorian chant? These experiences of music are surely more than mere feeling, more even than the immanent transcendence that Zuckerkandl posits. They point to the likelihood that music in its greatest moments—especially moments in which tones take their cue from sacred words—is a life-celebrating point of contact with things that do not come to be and pass away but *are*.

Appendix: Scores

Aus Liebe
Recitativo and Aria

J. S. Bach

Lyrics:
Er hat uns al-len wohl - ge - tan. Den Blin - den gab er das Ge-sicht, die Lah-men macht er ge-hend; er sagt' uns sei-nes Va-ters Wort, er trieb die Teu-fel fort; Be-trüb - te hat er auf – ge-richt't; er nahm die Sün-der auf und an;— sonst hat mein Je-sus nichts ge - tan.

58 Aria

248

Lie – be will mein Hei-land ster-ben, aus Lie – be will mein Hei – land

ster – – – – ben, von ei–ner Sünde weiß er nichts, nichts, von

ei–ner Sün-de weiß er nichts,

daß das e –

249

250

ster - - - - ben von ei-ner Sün-de weiß er

nichts, nichts, von_ ei - ner Sün-de weiß er nichts,

Dies Bildnis ist bezaubernd schön

W. A. Mozart

Dies Bild - nis ist be - zaubernd schön, wie noch kein Au - ge je ge - sehn! Ich

fühl es, ich fühl es, wie dies Götterbild mein Herz___ mit neu - er Re-gung füllt, mein Herz__ mit

neu - er Re-gung füllt. Dies Et - was kann ich zwar nicht nennen; doch

fühl ich's hier wie Feu-er brennen. Soll die Emp-fin - dung Lie-be sein?

Soll die Emp-fin - dung Lie-be sein? Ja, ja! Die lie-be ist's al - lein, die Lie-be, die

Lie-be, die Lie - be ist's al - lein.

o wenn ich sie nur fin-den könn - te! O wenn sie doch schon vor mir stän - de!

Ich wür-de, wür-de warm und rein, was wür - de ich?

ich wür-de sie   voll___ Ent - zük - ken   an diesen

hei - ßen Bu - sen   drü-cken, und e-wig wä-re sie dann mein, und e - wig wä - re sie dann

mann,   und e - wig wä-re sie dann mein, e - wig wä-re sie dann mein, e-wig wä-re sie dann

mein.

254

Notes

CHAPTER ONE

1. I have slightly modified the translation by Allan Bloom, *The Republic of Plato*, Basic Books, 1991.

2. For a discussion of the difference between seeing and hearing, see Hans Jonas, *The Phenomenon of Life: Toward a Philosophical Biology*, Chicago: University of Chicago Press, 1966: "For the sensation of hearing to come about the percipient is entirely dependent on something happening outside his control, and in hearing he is exposed to the happening . . . he cannot let his ears wander, as his eyes do, over a field of possible percepts, already present as a material for his attention, and focus them on the object chosen, but he has simply to wait for a sound to strike them: he has no choice in the matter" (139).

3. For a more detailed discussion of the tension between Socrates and Timaeus regarding the role of mathematics in education, see the interpretive Essay in my translation of the *Timaeus* (second edition, Indianapolis: Hackett Publishing Co., 2016), and my lecture "Plato's *Timaeus* and the Will to Order," published in *The St. John's Review*, Vol. 47, number 1, 2003, 137–167.

4. Quoted by Socrates in *Republic* 4, 424C, translation by Allan Bloom.

5. It is an instance of what Kepler, the other modern Timaeus, would call the *mysterium cosmographicum*. This is the mystery or secret with which the biblical God inscribed His work. See *Mysterium Cosmographicum, The Secret of the Universe*, translated by A. M. Duncan, New York: Abaris Books, 1981. For Kepler, the first stage of this *mysterium* is God's use of the five regular Platonic solids. The second is God's use of mathematical music. See *Harmonies of the World*, translated by Charles Glenn Wallis, Amherst NY: Prometheus Books, 1995.

6. In an Appendix to his essay, "Is God a Mathematician?", Hans Jonas articulates the Pythagorean understanding of ratio as applied to

the cosmos: ". . . *logos* as applied to reality is a selective standard which some phenomena come up to and others do not. . . . The tones of a harmony come and go, and it may be impure: the *logos* which makes them a harmony is imperishable, and the same each time the imperfect material harmony occurs. As its eternal truth, the *logos* is the measure of, and at the same time the reason for, each instance of temporal harmony" (*The Phenomenon of Life*, 93)

7. For a fuller account, see Appendix A in my translation for Hackett Publishing Co., second edition, 2016, 157–162.

8. Translations of the *Timaeus* are from my second edition for Hackett Publishing Co.

9. The second volume consists of supplements to the four books in Vol. 1.

10. "Schopenhauer," *Thomas Mann: Essays*, tr. H. T. Lowe-Porter, New York: Random House, 1957, 283.

11. I have emended the sentence to include a phrase that the translator omits.

12. Numbers in parentheses refer to page numbers in *The World as Will and Representation*, translated by E. F. J. Payne, New York: Dover, 1969.

13. The best example is Timaeus's witty account of the liver and spleen, which the god-endowed intellect uses to produce psychic order by controlling (through images) the lower, desirous part of the soul (71A–72D).

14. *Parerga and Paralipomena*, Vol. 2, translated by E. F. J. Payne, Oxford: Clarendon, 1974, 430.

15. "The heart, that *primum mobile* of animal life, has quite rightly been chosen as the symbol, indeed the synonym, of the *will* . . ." (*WWR*, Vol. 2, 237). The atheist Schopenhauer says at one point: ". . . like God, [music] sees only the heart" (ibid., 449). He is referring to 1 Samuel 16:7.

16. It is easy to reject the claim that music is the universal language. After all, different peoples across the globe and throughout human history have had different scales and different kinds of music. One might nevertheless wonder whether some scales and kinds of music are more universal than others, whether there is something in the music of Mozart, for example, or perhaps in diatonic music generally, that reaches out to all human beings insofar as they are human.

17. In her book on will, Eva Brann remarks that Schopenhauer's will "has a character that I have not come across in any writer I know of before him: It is *unfriendly* to human happiness" (*Un-Willing: An Inquiry*

into the Rise of Will's Power and an Attempt to Undo It, Philadelphia: Paul Dry Books, 2014, 122).

18. The title of Miguel de Unamuno's book.

19. Schopenhauer quotes from Calderón's *Life Is a Dream*: "For man's greatest offence is that he has been born" (*WWR*, Vol. 1, 254). This is "the guilt of existence itself"—original sin. Death is, in effect, the correction of an error. Schopenhauer would say to the dying individual: "You are ceasing to be something which you would have done better never to become" (ibid., Vol. 2, 501).

20. Ovid, *Metamorphoses* 10, 42.

21. Schopenhauer makes this point in *The Fourfold Root of the Principle of Sufficient Reason*: "In just the same way, the succession of sounds in a piece of music is determined objectively, not subjectively by me the listener; but who will say that the musical notes follow one another according to the law of cause and effect?" (127, translated by E. F. J. Payne, La Salle: Open Court, 1974). Also see Victor Zuckerkandl: "In music no step necessarily follows from the preceding in the sense of being deducible through keen listening" (*Man the Musician*, Princeton: Princeton University Press, 1973, 297).

22. The Ideas for Schopenhauer differ from how Plato describes them. For Schopenhauer, the Ideas cannot be genuine beings, which would undermine the ultimacy of the irrational will. They are simply eternal modes or ways in which the will objectifies itself.

23. These archetypes recall Vico's imaginative universals. See *The New Science of Giambattista Vico*, tr. Thomas Goddard Bergin and Max Harold Fisch, Cornell NY: Cornell University Press, 1988. See Paragraphs 381 and 460.

24. *Nichts*, Nothing, is the last word (in more than one sense) of Schopenhauer's book (Vol. 2, 412).

25. "Music charms us, although its beauty consists only in the agreement of numbers and in the counting, which we do not perceive but which the soul nevertheless carries out, of the beats or vibrations of sounding bodies which coincide at certain intervals" (*Principles of Nature and Grace, based on Reason, Philosophical Papers and Letters*, ed. Leroy E. Loemker, Holland: Reidel, 1976, 641).

26. Translations of Aristotle's *Politics* are from the edition by Joe Sachs for Hackett Press, Focus Philosophical Library, 2012.

27. "... soul signifies an individual unity of consciousness which obviously does not belong to that inner being ... The word should never be applied except in a metaphorical sense" (Vol. 2, 349).

28. Leviathan XI.1.

29. On this point Schopenhauer writes as follows: "Hitherto the concept of *will* has been subsumed under the concept of *force*; I, on the other hand, do exactly the reverse, and intend every force in nature to be conceived as will" (*WWR*, Vol. 1, 111).

30. "Tonality is not, as is sometimes claimed, a system with a central note but one with a perfect central triad" (Charles Rosen, *Arnold Schoenberg*, Chicago: University of Chicago Press, 1996, 27). In Schoenberg's twelve-tone system, the twelve equal-tempered chromatic tones are related not to a governing "one" but only to each other. The result is tonal egalitarianism.

31. *The Sense of Music*, Princeton: Princeton University Press, 1959, 18–28.

32. "Richard Wagner in Bayreuth" (8), *Untimely Meditations*.

33. See Carl Dahlhaus: "It is not that Wagner anticipated Schoenbergian atonality; there was never any question of his abandoning the principle of tonality, and he used to attribute emotive and symbolic significances to tonal relationships. Yet the harmonies of *Tristan* point the way to the dissolution of tonality, the emancipation of melody and counterpoint from preformed chordal associations" (*Richard Wagner's Music Dramas*, Cambridge: Cambridge University Press, 1971, 64).

34. For a fascinating reflection on the resolution of the Tristan chord to a dominant seventh chord, see Zuckerkandl, *Sound and Symbol: Music and the External World*, Princeton: Princeton University Press, 1973, 50–51.

35. The sketch occurs on the frontispiece of *Nietzsche and Music*, Georges Liébert, Chicago: University of Chicago Press, 2004. For a facsimile of Strauss's hand-written version, see *Richard Wagner: Theory and Theatre*, Dieter Borchmeyer, Oxford: Clarendon Press, 1991, 367. The natural that appears on the D in the final chord appears to have been a slip—an interesting one, given Strauss's claim that the final B-*major* chord of *Tristan* is "the most beautifully orchestrated chord in the history of music" (ibid., 367).

36. "The longing of the lovers is merely objectified in the poem and plot: it is expressed directly in the music" (Elliott Zuckerman, *The First Hundred Years of Wagner's Tristan*, New York: Columbia University Press, 1964, 17). In Kant's terms, the words and images function as the schematism of a pure concept (*Critique of Pure Reason*).

37. *Birth of Tragedy* 6. David Cartwright puts the problem very well:

"Schopenhauer's account of music ended, however, with a dissonance. Music was said to be the copy of something that cannot be copied—a mirroring of an original that cannot be reflected, a representation in tunes of that which cannot be represented" (*Schopenhauer: A Biography*, Cambridge: Cambridge University Press, 2010, 318).

38. *Parerga and Paralipomena*, Vol. 2, 432.

39. See *Wagner on Music and Drama*, selected by Goldman and Sprinchorn, New York: Da Capo Press, 1988, 171.

40. In the *Phenomenon of Life*, Hans Jonas critiques the thinker's claim that "through him speaks the essence of things itself" (257). In his chapter "Heidegger and Theology," Jonas connects Heidegger with Gnosticism and finds in Schopenhauer's theory of music the sole philosophic precedent for Heidegger's claim that poets and philosophers embody "the voice of Being" (257). Jonas comments: "Schopenhauer's fantasy [unlike Heidegger's] was innocent, for music is nonresponsible and cannot suffer from the misconception of a duty it does not have" (258). There is good reason to think that music is not as "innocent" or "nonresponsible" as Jonas thinks.

41. *Parerga and Paralipomena*, Vol. 2, 430.

42. Overtones or "partials" are the sounds produced simultaneously by the segments of a sounding body, such as a vibrating string or column of air. The tone produced by the vibration of the whole string or column of air is the "fundamental." The overtones form the "overtone series," the first members of which (including the fundamental) outline the major triad: octave, fifth, fourth, major third.

43. Tragedy depicts conflict as occurring among individuals. But it is more deeply understood as "the antagonism of the will with itself." In tragedy, "[it] is one and the same will, living and appearing in them all [all the individuals involved], whose phenomena fight with one another and tear one another to pieces" (*WWR*, Vol. I, 253).

44. Elliott Zuckerman applies this claim about death in music to Wagner's drama: "If the unexpected movement into a remote key is, as Schopenhauer hyperbolically maintains, like death, then the second and third acts of *Tristan* represent (as they should) a continuous dying" (19).

45. *The Birth of Tragedy*, translation by Walter Kaufmann, New York: Vintage Books, 1967, 114.

46. Commenting critically on Schopenhauer's extolling tones over words, Eva Brann makes a similar claim: "What if one's experience is the opposite—that the most passionate music is text-based, composed

as a commentary mostly on sacred texts that are to be treated not as secondary add-ons but as the very meaning of the sound-affect? And what if this verbal-acoustic whole is not an ameliorative emanation from the hell below but an intimating image of the heavens above?" (*Unwilling*, 127).

47. *Summa Theologica* Part I, Question 39, Article 8c. For an excellent discussion of the three formal criteria of beauty, see Umberto Eco, *The Aesthetics of Thomas Aquinas*, translated by Hugh Gredin, Cambridge: Harvard University Press, 1988, 64 ff.

CHAPTER TWO

1. Numbers in parentheses refer to *Sound and Symbol*, translated by Willard R. Trask, Princeton: Princeton University Press (Bollingen Series), 1973.

2. Franz Rosenzweig (1886–1929), from an uncompromising religious perspective, depicts the ideality of music in quite a different way, as an outright evil: "The heinous aspect of music is that it disintegrates real time with ideal times in its desire to be pure. To be absolved from this crime, it would have to allow itself to be conducted out of its Beyond into the here and now of time; it would have to integrate its ideal time into real time" (*The Star of Redemption*, Notre Dame IN: University of Notre Dame, 2008, 360–61). The integration occurs in liturgical music and the "real time of the Church year" (361).

3. The word "dynamic" comes from the Greek noun *dynamis*, which means power, possibility, potentiality, ability, function, and even meaning. In mathematics, it refers to an incommensurable magnitude (like the diagonal in relation to the side of a square). In Greek music theory, a *dynamis* is the function, as opposed to the intervallic distance, of a melodic tone in relation to other tones. Aristoxenus writes: "Our subject-matter then being all melody, whether vocal or instrumental, our method rests in the last resort on an appeal to the two faculties of hearing and intellect [*dianoian*]. By the former we judge the magnitude of the intervals, by the latter we contemplate the functions [*dynameis*] of the notes" (*The Harmonics of Aristoxenus*, translated by Henry S. Macran, Oxford: Clarendon Press, 1902, 189).

4. A similar phrase is used by the musicologist Ernst Kurth (1886–1946). He calls music *das Spiel von Kräften und Regungen*, "the play of forces and impulses" (*Grundlagen des linearen Kontrapunkts*, Berlin: Max Hesses Verlag, 1922, 4). As Zuckerkandl observes, Kurth "interpreted

this dynamic factor as a psychic factor, and even as a creation of the listener's" (61).

5. For a more extensive treatment of this famous melody, see *Man the Musician*, Princeton: Princeton University Press, 1973, 174–78. Zuckerkandl enlists the theory of Heinrich Schenker to shed on light on why the composition of this simple tune caused Beethoven so much trouble.

6. I have said that the melody "lets" $\hat{2}$ resolve. Should I not have said that Beethoven lets it? Zuckerkandl takes up this question in his discussion of time, where he asserts that music, in a sense, "*does* write itself," and that a great musical idea, no less than a scientific breakthrough, is a discovery rather than an invention (223). Every writer knows this from experience, realizes in the grip of composing that the task is to discover where the arc of a story, a line of thought, or an argument "wants" to go. It is anything but self-expression. Zuckerkandl explores composition as a form of discovery in the chapter "Musical Thought" in *Man the Musician* (292 ff.).

7. *The Sense of Music*, Princeton: Princeton University Press, 1971, 22.

8. Plato and Aristotle put forth a corresponding thesis regarding external meaning in the case of the *modes* I touched on in the previous chapter. Various feelings and conditions of character are, for them, present in image-form in melodies themselves. A Dorian melody doesn't merely generate a dignified condition in the soul; it possesses that condition as an inherent form.

9. Erwin W. Straus, "The Forms of Spatiality," *Phenomenological Psychology, Selected Papers*, New York: Basic Books, 1966, 8.

10. Ibid., 9.

11. This deficiency is strikingly apparent in the case of enharmonic equivalents in equal temperament, for example, a C and a B-sharp, which are produced by the same key on the piano. The subject of Bach's fugue in C-sharp minor from Book 1 of the *Well-Tempered Clavier* is a case in point. The woe-filled subject is C-sharp, B-sharp (the raised $\hat{7}$ of the scale), E, D-sharp. No human listener would confuse the dark sound of the diminished fourth between B-sharp and E with the bright major third between C and E, its enharmonic equivalent. The oscilloscope would.

12. In a Zuckerkandlian vein, Roger Scruton writes that music "depends upon, is emergent from, the sequence of sounds. The sounds are 'ontologically prior.' But to hear the music it is not enough to notice the sounds. Music is inaudible, except to those with the cognitive capac-

ity to hear the movement in musical space, orientation, tension and release, the gravitational force of the bass notes, the goal directedness and action-profile of melodies, and so on" (*The Soul of the World*, Princeton: Princeton University Press, 2014, 39).

13. See Hermann Helmholtz, *On the Sensations of Tone*, translated by Alexander J. Ellis, New York: Dover Publications, 1954.

14. The emergence of the diatonic pattern for the ancient Greeks had its origin in the tetrachord, a perfect fourth divided into two whole tones and a half tone. The scale was regarded as the joining of two such tetrachords by a whole tone. In the case of the Ionian mode, this would be C-D-E-F and G-A-B-C′.

15. It is also the only scale in which the tritone, located uniquely between $\hat{4}$ and $\hat{7}$, resolves through half steps to $\hat{3}$ and $\hat{8}$ (or $\hat{1}$), respectively. In other words, it is the only scale in which the tritone, which is present in every diatonic scale, affirms rather than subverts the $\hat{1}$ and the mode. (See my Chapter One, p. 18.)

16. The raising of $\hat{7}$ entailed a corresponding raising of degree $\hat{6}$ in order to avoid an awkward augmented second. The result was the now-familiar "melodic minor" scale, in which degrees $\hat{6}$ and $\hat{7}$ are raised as the scale ascends and lowered as it descends.

17. To quote Scruton again: "These things we hear in music are not illusions: someone who fails to hear them does not hear all that is there to hear, just as someone who fails to see the face in a picture fails to see all that is there" (op. cit., 39).

18. The famous music critic Eduard Hanslick—Wagner's nemesis and champion of Brahms—famously took up arms against the emotive theory of music in his book *On the Musically Beautiful* (1854). The content of music, he affirmed, was not feeling but rather "tonally moving forms" (*tönend bewegte Formen*) (translated by Geoffrey Payzant, Indianapolis: Hackett Publishing Co., 1986, 29). Zuckerkandl mounts a critique of Hanslick's "formalism" in his essay "Words and Tones in Song" in *Man the Musician* (translated by Norbert Guterman, Princeton: Princeton University Press, 1973, 31–51).

19. Drums can of course be tuned to various pitches, which, however, do not typically form melodies.

20. Zuckerkandl revisits this exclusion of rhythm as music's "prime mover" in *Man the Musician*: "motion in music can be accounted for solely on the basis of the audible relations between successive tones, a species of motion peculiar to music and perceived by hearing alone" (162).

21. One wishes Zuckerkandl had said more about why the tonal forces of tonal harmony go hand in hand with bar-line and measure—why, in short, tonal dynamism and rhythmic dynamism imply each other.

22. The glissando plays a crucial, demonic role in Thomas Mann's *Doctor Faustus*, the subject of a later chapter.

23. In this context Zuckerkandl helpfully recalls the *Phaedo* passage in which Socrates distinguishes a genuine cause (*aition*) from that without which a cause would never be a cause (99B3–4). Pitch is the latter: the material condition for a musical tone.

24. In *The Sense of Music*, Zuckerkandl discusses the "preferred meaning" of intervals outside a musical context: When we hear a fifth—nothing but that—like a signal, we will always hear $\hat{1}$-$\hat{5}$; a fourth, under the same conditions, will be $\hat{5}$-$\hat{8}$; a major third, $\hat{1}$-$\hat{3}$; a minor third, $\hat{1}$-$\hat{3}$ minor third; a major second, $\hat{1}$-$\hat{2}$; a minor second, $\hat{7}$-$\hat{8}$" (78–79).

25. The tonal field, we must note, is not there before the tones that are its states of tension. On the contrary, the tones induce the field. This is analogous, as we shall see, to the induction of a rhythmic field by the relative time-values of tones. Zuckerkandl does not address this question of how exactly a musical field is induced, or how we are to understand the circularity of tones as meaningful only in the context of a field that they themselves induce. No doubt, the field, the dynamic context, becomes apparent more quickly in some pieces of music than in others. In the Ode to Joy, the tonal-rhythmic field is almost immediately evident.

26. In *The Sense of Music*, Zuckerkandl explains why $\hat{5}$ functions as a "counter-pole" (26). If the scale were drawn as a circle, the counter-pole would be at the opposite end of the diameter connecting it to $\hat{1}$: "All tonal action can be said to take place between the extremes $\hat{1}$ and $\hat{5}$."

27. The force-inversion that occurs at $\hat{5}$ recalls the similar inversion that Dante experiences when he moves from the Garden of Eden at the top of Mt. Purgatory to the physical heavens. The downward, tragic pull of Earth is transformed into the upward, comic pull of Heaven.

28. For a fuller account of harmony as the movement of chords, see *The Sense of Music*, Chapter V, 171–217.

29. Zuckerkandl points out that a cadence, which means "fall" (from the Latin *cadere*), is not really a fall in tonal space but receives its correct, dynamic meaning as a "going to," "the arrival at the center of gravity" (114).

30. *The Sense of Music*, 191–95. The fifth, the closest harmonic step, is the building block for the ever-helpful "circle of fifths."

31. In *The Sense of Music*, Zuckerkandl calls the major triad "the holy chord of our music" (177).

32. *The Sense of Music*, 176.

33. Zuckerkandl reaches this conclusion by posing a question only he would think to ask: "*Where* is the chord?"

34. The continuity is unimpeded by the presence of a rest in a melodic phrase, as Zuckerkandl shows in the case of a Bach fugue subject (121).

35. This idea of tonal motion fits Aristotle's definition of motion or change (*kinêsis*) as the "actuality of the potential as such" (*Physics* 2, 1, 201a10–11). Aristotle would insist, however, that all motion presupposes a moveable—an *ousia* or substantial *thing*.

36. Hegel's account of music may be found in his *Lectures on Fine Art*, Vol. 2, Oxford: Clarendon Press, 1975, 888 ff. Music is "the complete withdrawal, of both the inner life and its expression, into subjectivity" (889).

37. Gabriel responds by making the scene and his wife into a painting, thereby displacing the musical intimacy and personal meaning of what he is witnessing.

38. This apparently holds in the case of purely rhythmic phenomena, which had been excluded from the realm of "real" music: "Rhythm is not a specifically musical phenomenon" (76). Zuckerkandl's third stage seems very much indebted to Bergson's *élan vital*, the vital impulse that is the heart of all becoming. See *Creative Evolution*, New York: Dover Publications, 1998, 88–97. At one point, Bergson seems to provide the metaphysical foundation for Zuckerkandl's dynamic qualities: "There are no things, there are only actions" (ibid., 248). In the same passage, Bergson defines God as "unceasing life, action, freedom."

39. In *Man the Musician*, in response to Susanne Langer's notion of music as "our myth of the inner life," Zuckerkandl asserts that if music is "the myth of the soul, it is the myth of the world soul, the myth of the world's inner life" (154). The context for the claim about myth and inner life is the distinction between *symbol* and *object*. See *Philosophy in a New Key*, Cambridge Mass.: Harvard University Press, 1979, 245. Langer follows the usual inner/outer dichotomy, according to which the external, objectively true is relegated to the physical sciences. The symbolism of music is confined to the inner psyche.

40. Zuckerkandl seems to have derived this view from Bergson: "*All*

reality is . . . tendency, if we agree to call tendency a nascent change of direction" (*Introduction to Metaphysics*, in *The Creative Mind*, New York: Carol Publishing Group, 1992, 188). For Bergson, however, the dynamic core of the world is cognized by "an effort of imagination" (159), an active intuition that is "the *sympathy* by which one is transported into the interior of an object in order to coincide with what is there unique and consequently inexpressible" (161). "By an effort of intuition," Bergson writes, "one has the feeling of a certain well-defined tension, whose very definiteness seems like a choice between an infinity of possible directions" (185). The crucial word, here, is "effort." From Zuckerkandl's perspective, Bergson fails to pay sufficient attention to music, which provides immediate perceptual access to the external world as tension or force.

41. *Religio Medici* (1642), Pantianos Classics, 65.

42. The passage quoted can be found, in an alternate translation, in *The World as Will and Representation*, Vol. 1, translated by E. F. J. Payne, New York: Dover, 1969, 264.

43. "Music is not a language of emotion—the language of joy, grief, despair, fear, exaltation, rapture, of a feeling I have or someone else has" (*Man the Musician*, 152). Zuckerkandl excludes feelings from what is primary about music but not feeling in the singular: "'Feeling' [in music] denotes a singular for which there is no plural—self-feeling, pure spontaneity, something no one 'has' but everyone 'is,' not something that is originally attached to a self, rather something to which the self attaches itself, something which is 'everything,' as Goethe says. 'Feeling is everything'" (op. cit.). The reference is to *Faust* (l. 3456).

44. Zuckerkandl discusses the communal nature of music and man as the "musical animal" in *Man the Musician*, Chapter 1: "The Two Concepts of Musicality" (7–20).

45. For Aristotle's notion of the divine intellect as an atemporal "thinking of thinking," see *Metaphysics* 12. 9.

46. *Aeneid* IV, 175.

47. The American twelve-tone composer George Rochberg praises this passage in "The Concepts of Musical Time and Space" in *The Aesthetic of Survival*, Ann Arbor: The University of Michigan Press, 2004, 93–4. Zuckerkandl's account of "circle" versus "arrow" in music may be found in *The Sense of Music*, 83–97.

48. In discussing our temporal apprehension of a melody, Husserl makes a similar point: "it is not merely a matter of presentations of the tones simply persisting in consciousness. Were they to remain unmod-

ified, then instead of a melody we should have a chord of simultaneous notes or rather a disharmonious jumble of sounds such as we would obtain if we struck all the notes simultaneously that have already been sounded" (*The Phenomenology of Internal Time-Consciousness*, translated by James S. Churchill, Bloomington: Indiana University Press, 1971, 30).

49. Wolfgang Köhler, one of the founders of Gestalt psychology, cautions against treating a Gestalt as a mere attribute. In Gestalt psychology, a Gestalt is rather "a concrete entity *per se*," that is, "a specific object" (*Gestalt Psychology, An Introduction to New concepts in Modern Psychology*, New York: Liveright Publishing Corp., 1975, 177–78).

50. Zuckerkandl discusses (and critiques) Gestalt psychology at length in *Man the Musician*, 102 ff.

51. Oliver Sacks quotes this sentence and the above passage as explaining why one of his patients, a musician, was able to sing, play, and conduct music, even though he had amnesia (*Musicophilia, Tales of Music and the Brain*, New York: Vintage Books, 2007, 228).

52. Bergson's account of time as duration recalls Augustine's definition of time as a distention of the mind (*distentio mentis*) in the *Confessions* (11, 26).

53. Susanne Langer makes a very similar claim: "*Music makes time audible, and its form and continuity sensible*" (*Feeling and Form*, New York: Charles Scribner's Sons, 1953, 110).

54. The self-negating nature of time is perfectly captured in Hegel's *Philosophy of Nature*, where time is defined as "that being which, inasmuch as it *is*, is *not*, and inasmuch as it is *not*, *is*; it is Becoming directly intuited" (Hegel's *Philosophy of Nature*, translated by A. V. Miller, Oxford: Clarendon Press, 1970, 34).

55. Zuckerkandl's identification of being with motion, time, and change recalls Bergson: "There do not exist things made, but only things in the making, not states that remain fixed but states in process of change" (*The Creative Mind*, 188).

56. The phrase occurs in *Man the Musician*, 10.

57. Zuckerkandl is quoting from Straus's book, *Von Sinn der Sinne*. The title (*On the Sense of the Senses*) echoes Zuckerkandl's title, *The Sense of Music*.

58. The passage is from "Gibt es einen Hörraum?" ("Is there an Audible Space?") (1937).

59. The idea of *fliessender Raum* is developed in Palágyi's *Neue theorie des Raumes und der Zeit* (1901).

60. Faraday's broader formulation, inspired by Boscovitch, is that so-called atoms are in fact non-extended centers of force ("A Speculation touching Electric Conduction and the Nature of Matter," 1844 (*Experimental Researches in Electricity*, Vol. 2, Santa Fe: Green Lion Press, 2000, 284–293). Speaking of the gravitational field, Bergson, whom Zuckerkandl cites, gives a good description of Faraday's speculation on atoms: "For Faraday the atom is a centre of force. He means by this that the individuality of the atom consists in the mathematical point at which cross, radiating throughout space, the indefinite lines of force which really constitute it: thus each atom occupies the whole of space to which gravitation extends and all atoms are interpenetrating" (*Matter and Memory*, translated by Nancy Margaret Paul and W. Scott Palmer, New York: Dover Publications, 2004, 265). For Faraday, atoms, in short, are like tones in a tonal field.

61. The passage Zuckerkandl quotes can be found on page 370 of the Dover edition. The whole of *Sound and Symbol* may be read as an attempt to refute Helmholtz's view of music as explicable in terms of vibrating bodies and the physiological structure of the ear.

62. Zuckerkandl knows that in all this talk of a field, we have thought of a field for the most part as on its own and not necessarily inhering in space as a medium. To this, he reasonably responds: "We are only following the procedure of the physicists [like Faraday] if we do not here make a sharp distinction between dynamic field and space" (316).

63. Von Uexküll bases his account on Kant's transcendental idealism. Hence his frequent reference to the subjective origin of the order found in organisms: "All reality is subjective appearance. This must constitute the great, fundamental admission even of biology" (*Theoretical Biology*, New York: Harcourt, Brace & Co., Inc., 1926, xv). Zuckerkandl rejects the Kantian perspective. For him, externality is real, and space and time are not pure forms of sensibility.

64. Ibid., 270–71.

65. See *Principles of Nature and Grace, Based on Reason* in *Philosophical Essays*, translated by Roger Arlew, Indianapolis: Hackett Publishing Co., 1989, 206–213.

66. One of the most fascinating ideas in von Uexküll's biology is the *Umwelt* or surrounding world. It is something like a biological field of resonance. In a striking parallel with Zuckerkandl's "third stage," the *Umwelt* is a "third world, the *world of action*" (ibid., 127). It is the organic field for all mutual interaction between an organism and the world

beyond it. It is a *third* world because, in addition to the world that is external to an animal, there is also the animal's subjectivity: "Every animal is a subject. . . . The animal itself, by the very fact of exercising such direction [self-guidance], creates a world for itself, which I shall call the *inner world*" (126). This inner world is, in effect, the world of the animal's psyche.

67. Tone color and pitch, for Zuckerkandl, have nothing to do with musical meaning. Their functions in a musical work are unequal: "if we call pitch a garment, then tone color is an overgarment" (353).

68. This is the opening line of *Hyperions Schicksalslied* ("Hyperion's Song of Fate"): "Ihr wandelt droben in Licht/Auf weichem Boden, selige Genien!"

69. The passage occurs, in an alternate translation, in "The Age of the World Picture" in Martin Heidegger, *The Question Concerning Technology*, translated by William Lovitt, New York: Harper & Row, 1977, 119.

70. *The Soul of the World*, Princeton: Princeton University Press, 2014, 166. In the same passage, Scruton quotes from his fictional work, *Perictione in Colophon*: "Music is a movement of nothing in a space that is nowhere, with a purpose that is no-one's, in which we hear a non-existent feeling the object of which is nobody."

71. For an excellent summary of the critique of force in modern physics, see Max Jammer's *Concepts of Force*, New York: Dover Publications, Inc., 1999, 200 ff. Maupertuis (1698–1759), who was strongly influenced by Hume, calls force "a word that serves only to hide our ignorance" (ibid., 209). A more recent critic of force in physics is Ernst Mach.

72. Zuckerkandl's formulation recalls that of Socrates in the *Republic*. If music is to play its correct role in turning the soul toward dialectic, it must, Socrates says, turn away from the embodied *sound* of intervals in order to study their pure ratios and in this way "rise to problems" (7, 531C).

73. "The Origin of the Work of Art," in Martin Heidegger, *Poetry, Language, Thought*, translated by Albert Hofstadter, New York: Harper & Row, Publishers, 1975, 74–75.

74. *Timaeus* 35B–36B; 53C–55C. The geometric construction of the regular solids requires the use of incommensurable magnitudes. These are lines whose lengths have no common measure and cannot be expressed as the ratio of a number to a number. The most famous instance is the incommensurability of the side of a square and its diagonal. For more on Timaeus's construction of the cosmic soul and body, see my

edition of the *Timaeus* (Second Edition, Indianapolis: Hackett Publishing Co., 2016, Appendix, 157–169).

75. Heinrich Schenker, Zuckerkandl's teacher, writes the following about the overtone series: "Nature's help to music consisted of nothing but a hint, a counsel forever mute . . . This hint, then, was dropped by Nature in the form of the so-called 'overtone series.' This much-discussed phenomenon, which constitutes Nature's only source to draw upon, is much more familiar to the instinct of the artist than to his consciousness" (*Harmony*, edited and annotated by Oswald Jonas, translated by Elisabeth Mann Borgese, Chicago: University Chicago Press, 1968, 20).

76. For a very different view, see Edward Rothstein's *Emblems of the Mind: The Inner Life of Music and Mathematics* (Chicago: University of Chicago Press, 2006). Rothstein draws on Zuckerkandl's insights regarding tone and motion, but unlike Zuckerkandl he points to the deep connection between music and mathematics, which, he claims, "share certain techniques, uses of forms, ways of thinking" (133). For him, both disciplines pursue the beauty of truth.

77. The rules of counterpoint govern the local rather than global directedness in a piece of music. Their classic formulation is found in Gioseffo Zarlino's *Art of Counterpoint* (1558), translated by Guy A. Marco and Claude V. Palisca, New York: Norton Library, 1976. Zarlino grounds his presentation of the rules of counterpoint in Pythagorean number theory and Aristotle's *Physics*: "In this, as in everything we do, we should follow nature" (107). The later, better known account is that of Johann Joseph Fux (*The Study of Counterpoint: Gradus ad Parnassum*, 1725, translated by Alfred Mann, New York: Norton Library, 1971).

CHAPTER THREE

1. See Christoph Wolff, *Johann Sebastian Bach, The Learned Musician*, New York: W. W. Norton & Co., 2000, 288–303.

2. I have used the old numbering of the Edition Peters vocal score (1967, edited by Kurt Soldan and Siegfried Ochs) rather than that of the New Bach Edition.

3. Vocal scores for the aria and its preceding recitativo may be found in the Appendix.

4. Philipp Spitta makes a highly interesting remark that underscores Bach's fusion of voices and instruments. Commenting on the chorale that most invites the omission of instruments—the one that appears

right after Jesus's death—Spitta writes: "Bach's chorale settings can produce their special effects only by that peculiar colouring which results from the mixture of human voices with the organ and the tones of instruments. The instruments have besides, in Bach's hands, so much to say of their own individuality that they constitute an intelligible symbolism when they come in unanimously with the four parts" (*Johann Sebastian Bach*, translated by Clara Bell and J. A. Fuller-Maitland, New York: Dover Publications, 1951 [originally published in 1889 by London: Novello], Volume 2, 550, note 632).

5. Wolff observes: "Picander's allegorical dialogue and lament, 'Kommt, ihr Töchter,' is set by Bach in the manner of a French tombeau, as a funeral march for the multitude of believers who ascend to Mount Zion and the holy city of Jerusalem" (ibid., 302). In Picander's original version, the opening number called for a single soprano, the Daughter of Zion, who engaged in musical dialogue with the chorus. The vestige of this soloist is preserved in the use of the singular pronoun: "Come, you Daughters, help *me* lament." For a discussion of this point, see Albert Schweitzer, *J. S. Bach*, English translation from the 1908 German edition by Ernest Newman, London: Breitkopf und Härtel, 1911 (reprint 1955), 211.

6. Whereas the adult choruses consist of questions, answers, and imperatives, the boys' choir is theologically declarative in their address to Jesus: "All sins hast Thou borne, else we needs must have despaired."

7. An amazing example of the musical dialectic at work in this opening chorus can be seen in Bach's use of chromaticism in the opening melody, where the G-natural becomes a G-sharp, thus suggesting E major. The D-sharp and C-sharp in the supporting lines further suggest the fleeting presence of E major. The exotic chromaticism of the opening of the *Passion*, in other words, results from a weird bimodality of major and minor.

8. Wolff, 298–299.

9. His real name was Christian Friedrich Henrici.

10. See Wolff, 296–299.

11. The hymn-tune the chorus sings at this point is used three times in the work, each time with a different harmonization. In #3, the very first chorale of the *Passion*, the chorus asks what Jesus could possibly have done to deserve so harsh a judgment (*Urteil*); in #25, where the chorale is woven into the tenor recitative, the chorus asks what the cause (*Ursache*) of Jesus's woes could be; and here in #55, the chorus, in an

apparent intensification of its earlier questions, expresses wonder at the sentence (*Strafe*) that has been passed on Jesus. It seems clear from the words "judgment," "cause," and "sentence" that Bach intends the three occurrences of the hymn to be heard as a three-fold meditation on the marvel of Jesus's innocence.

12. See the Appendix for the score of the Recitativo and Aria.

13. Elke Axmacher calls the pair of verses—"He has done good for us all" and "Apart from this my Jesus has done nothing"—"poetically surely one of the most beautiful parts of Picander's libretto." See *"Aus Liebe will mein Heyland sterben": Untersuchungen zum Wandeln des Passionsverständnisses im frühen 18. Jahrhundert* (Neuhausen-Stuttgart: Hänsler Verlag, 1984), 177.

14. In addition to *"Aus Liebe,"* the preceding crucifixion fugue, and Jesus's death on the cross, A minor music in Bach's *Passion* includes the tenor aria about patience (*"Geduld,"* #41) and the final appearance of the "Passion chorale" right after Jesus' death (*"Wenn ich einmal soll scheiden,"* #72).

15. In an earlier version of Picander's libretto, the aria was in the first person singular: Jesus himself was to sing. His words were as follows:

> Out of love I am willing to suffer everything,
> Out of love I die before the world.
> Out of love and not for being guilty,
> Am I the ransom for sin.

For a discussion of this fascinating transformation of the text, see Axmacher, 167 and 177–178.

16. The technical term for this sort of upper-register continuo was *bassetchen* or "little bass." See Eric Chafe, *Tonal Allegory in the Vocal Music of J. S. Bach* (Berkeley and Los Angeles: University of California Press, 1991), 350, note 27. Chafe observes that the *bassetchen* "probably represents God's love (as it does in a number of cantatas and, above all, in 'Aus Liebe' from the *St. Matthew Passion*)" (168).

17. Another moment in which Bach conveys an almost terrifying sense of breath withheld occurs in the tenor recitative, #40, just before the aria about patience. Here, too, Bach uses oboes.

18. The overflowing gaiety of this aria makes one wonder how Spitta could have asserted that in the arias of the *St. Matthew Passion*, "every sentiment of joy in its various shades is wholly excluded; they are all based on the emotions of sorrow" (ibid., 558).

19. The overall pattern of phrases is that they ascend through leap and descend through step. The stepwise sinking of phrases is especially evident in measures 5–7. Note the gradual harmonic descent in the accompanying oboes, which sink slowly in thirds. The most eloquent moment in this harmonic descent is the appearance of the B-flat in measure 6.

20. Fermatas also appear in #61, *"Können Tränen meiner Wangen nichts erlangen,"* the next aria after *"Aus Liebe,"* but they are not as arresting and prominent as in the latter aria.

21. Commenting on the similarity between this aria and the F-sharp minor prelude from Book 2 of the *Well-Tempered Clavier*, the harpsichordist Wanda Landowska writes: "When tenderness is overwhelming, Bach suspends the melodic flow under a fermata" (*Landowska on Music*, collected, edited, and translated by Denise Restout, assisted by Robert Hawkins, New York: Stein and Day, 1981, 203). The occasion for Landowska's comparison is the gorgeously prepared fermata in m. 29 of the Prelude to the F-sharp minor fugue.

22. For an illuminating discussion of the musical thinking that went into Bach's choice for the flute at this point, see Victor Zuckerkandl, *Man the Musician*, Princeton: Princeton University Press, 1973, 295–97. Zuckerkandl observes that in Bach's day the transverse flute could not produce the low C that would have been the logical terminus of the flute's descending C-minor scale. Bach solves the problem, not with the flute's going to an E-flat instead (which would have been a correct but bland solution), but by having the flute leap up to a B-natural before resolving to the higher C: "to a composer like Bach a mechanical obstacle like this served as a springboard to his genius" (296).

23. It is interesting, in this respect, to contrast Bach's aria with the first aria from the *Bachianas Brasileiras* by Villa-Lobos. In this aria, a soprano sings of a rising moon that "awakes cruel memories of laughter and tears." The haunting opening of this dreamy nature music seems to have been inspired by Aria 58. The Brazilian composer grounds his aria in a luscious sounding surge of cellos and invests it with an overwhelming sensuality. It is like the sound of *"Aus Liebe"* shorn of its chastity and made into something carnal and erotically anguished. It is the voice of the Earth rather than the voice of Heaven.

24. For a discussion of how Bach, in his *St. Matthew Passion*, gives musical expression to St. Anselm's doctrine of redemption as the pay-

ment of a debt, see Jaroslav Pelikan, *Bach Among the Theologians* (Philadelphia: Fortress Press, 1986), 100–101.

25. The teaching that the Incarnation is most precisely understood as a divine *kenosis* or emptying occurs in Paul's *Letter to the Philippians*, where Paul writes that Jesus "did not count equality with God a thing to be grasped, but emptied himself [*heauton ekenôsen*], taking the form of a servant, being born in the likeness of men" (2:6–7).

26. In his final moments on the cross, as Jesus utters his last words of abandonment—"My God, my God, why have you forsaken me?"—Bach removes the halo of strings that has surrounded Jesus's words up to this point. Bereft of this timeless-sounding halo, Jesus appears as thoroughly mortal. The withdrawal of strings is as brilliant as it is heartrending.

27. The half-diminished seventh chord is a diminished fifth (tritone) with a major third on top. It occurs naturally on the seventh degree of the major scale. The full diminished seventh chord is a diminished fifth with a *minor* third on top. It is, in other words, two interlocked tritones.

28. This aria is not the usual *da capo* aria, which has a straightforward ABA structure. *"Aus Liebe"* is in fact closer to so-called sonata form—the form cultivated by the classical composers (Haydn, Mozart, and Beethoven). It is a form in which three structural parts have a tighter, more organic relation than the ABA structure that we hear in most of the other arias in the *Passion*. Another instance of this quasi-sonata form occurs in Aria 47, *"Erbarme dich."*

29. The crucifixion fugue returns, but not in the earlier key. Originally in A minor, it now appears a step higher, in B minor. The raised key brings Jesus closer to the actual raising of the cross.

30. As Friedrich Smend aptly puts it, the aria *"Aus Liebe"* is the *Herzstück* of the entire work—its heart and core ("Bachs Matthäus-Passion," *Bach-Jahrbuch* 25 [1928], 29–300. For references to Smend's idea of the *Herzstück* in relation to *"Aus Liebe,"* see Chafe, ibid., pp. 350 and 380. It was Smend, according to Chafe, who first saw that the ten *turbae* or crowd sequences in Part 2 of Bach's *Passion* form a symmetrical series. At the center of this series stands the aria *"Aus Liebe,"* flanked by the two appearances of *"Lass ihn kreuzigen,"* "Let him be crucified." For Smend's symmetrical arrangement, see Chafe, ibid., 381.

31. This claim is discussed at length in Zuckerkandl's essay "Words and Tones in Song" (*Man the Musician*, 31–43). Zuckerkandl's example is the German folksong, *Reaper Death*.

32. For more on this subject, see Jaroslav Pelikan, *Bach Among the Theologians*, Philadelphia: Fortress Press, 1986.

33. *Selected Writings of Paul Valéry*, (New York: New Directions Publishing Corporation, 1950), 148.

34. See *Confessions* 10. 33.

CHAPTER FOUR

1. The vocal score for the aria may be found in the Appendix.

2. For an exhaustive study of the Masonic elements in Mozart's opera, see Jacques Chailley, *The Magic Flute, Masonic Opera*, trans. Herbert Weinstock (New York: Knopf, 1971). Chailley finds Masonic meaning even in the number of notes used in individual phrases.

3. See Victor Zuckerkandl, "Words and Tones in Song," Chapter 3 of *Man the Musician*, Princeton: Princeton University Press, 1973, 31–43.

4. The lecture can be found in *Paul Valéry, An Anthology*, Bollingen Series, Princeton: Princeton University Press, 1977, 136–165.

5. "Beethoven's Instrumental Music," in *E. T. A. Hoffmann's Musical Writings*, edited by David Charlton, translated by Martyn Clarke, Cambridge: Cambridge University Press, 1989, 98. In a letter to his father regarding a harmonic progression in *The Escape from the Seraglio*, Mozart writes: "music, even in the most terrible situations, must never offend the ear, but must please the listener, or in other words must never cease to be music" (quoted in *The Classical Style*, Charles Rosen, New York: W. W. Norton & Company, 1997, 307).

6. The continued E-flat puts the IV-chord in its second inversion, the least stable position of the triad. The effect is to make the move from I to IV into a mild departure from the E-flat triad. It is more of an inflection than a chord change.

7. *Wagner on Music and Drama*, selected and arranged by A. Goldman and E. Sprinchorn, New York: Da Capo Press, 1964, 214.

8. It is beyond the scope of this chapter to discuss modulation or change of key. This crucial phenomenon is often taken, erroneously, as the replacement of the previous key for another, subsequent key. For a more musical (because more organic) account of modulation, see Felix Salzer's *Structural Hearing, Tonal Coherence in Music*, New York: Dover Publications, 21. For Heinrich Schenker (Salzer's prime influence), modulation is a mere surface phenomenon that does not account for the primordial level at which a piece of music unfolds. Edward Rothstein puts this succinctly: "In Schenker's view, the very concept of modulation—

of a shift into another tonal region—is unimportant; it is a filigree on a space more fundamentally defined" (*Emblems of Mind: The Inner Life of Music and Mathematics*, Chicago: University of Chicago Press, 2006, 127).

9. Papageno's wistful G-major aria also ended with the desire for rest—with the image of a wife who would sleep by his side "*wie ein Kind*," "like a child."

10. The movement $\hat{3}\rightarrow\hat{2}\rightarrow\hat{1}$ constitutes what Schenker calls the "*Urlinie*" or primordial line. See his *Free Composition*, translated by Ernst Oster, New York: Longman, 1979, 3–9. For a clear summary of Schenker's theory, see Victor Zuckerkandl, *Man the Musician*, Princeton: Princeton University Press, 1973, 169–216.

11. See note 8.

12. *Opera as Drama*, New York: Random House, Vintage, 1956, 125.

13. Kerman cites this sublime passage to support the following general observation about the opera: "Mozart can hardly resolve a dominant seventh chord without shedding on it a light that no other composer has ever comprehended" (ibid., 126).

14. The rising sixth functions as a leitmotif in the opera. Its other crucial appearance is in the Finale of Act I, in the interchange between Pamina and Sarastro. Pamina sings the interval twice in referring to the tender feelings she has for her mother: "The sound of my mother's name is sweet to me. It is she, it is she. . . ." The first sixth is from F up to D, the second from B-flat up to G, the tones of Tamino's opening sixth. Pamina no doubt wants to say: "It is she who gave birth to me, nurtured me, loved me." But Sarastro completes her sentence in his own way: "And a proud woman! A man must lead your heart, for without him every woman will walk outside her proper sphere." On the words "without him [a man]," Sarastro repeats, in his low range, Pamina's sixth from F to D, as if to redirect the chord's tenderness to its proper object. At this very moment, Monostatos drags in Tamino, the sight of whom prompts Pamina to sing "It is he!" Tamino responds in kind: "It is she!" The play of sixths in the exchange between Pamina and Sarastro, coupled with Pamina's shift from the feminine to the masculine pronoun once Tamino arrives, paves the way for the meeting of the lovers in the Finale of Act II.

15. As sometimes observed, Pamina recalls Miranda ("she who is to be wondered at") in Shakespeare's *Tempest*, and Tamino Ferdinand. Both pairs of lovers undergo trials that initiate them into the shared trials of life and marriage. It is not difficult to see Sarastro as the counterpart

of Prospero. In both works, there is the shared theme of magic put to a good and noble use.

16. Reconciliation is explicitly celebrated as the prime feature of the sacred Order in Sarastro's radiantly consoling aria in E major. Within this realm's sacred halls and walls, there is no vengeance against human beings who fall but only forgiveness and a helping hand.

CHAPTER FIVE

1. After his discovery of Schopenhauer, Wagner wrote the following to Liszt: "When I think back on the storms that have buffeted my heart and on its convulsive efforts to cling to some hope in life—against my own better judgement—, indeed, now that these storms have swelled so often to the fury of a tempest, —I have yet found a sedative which has finally helped me to sleep at night; it is the sincere and heartfelt yearning for death; total unconsciousness, complete annihilation, the end of all dreams—the only ultimate redemption!—" (*Selected Letters of Richard Wagner*, translated and edited by Stewart Spencer and Barry Millington, London: J. M. Dent & Sons LTD, 1987, 323).

2. The influence was so strong that Wagner changed the end of the *Ring* cycle to reflect a Schopenhauerian view of the world. Instead of a tribute to love, Brünnhilde would sing: "Grieving love's / profoundest suffering / opened my eyes for me: I saw the world end." This is the shift that Nietzsche mocked in his *Case of Wagner* (section 4). Ultimately, Wagner returned to his initial idea, in which Brünnhilde's final profession of love for Siegfried ("In bliss your wife greets you!") balances and corrects Wotan's grim resignation and provides the right closing note for the whole cycle. Schopenhauer was dear, but the demands of art were dearer. See *Wagner's Ring of the Nibelungen: A Companion*, Stewart Spencer and Barry Millington.

3. David Cartwright, *Schopenhauer: A Biography*, Cambridge: Cambridge University Press, 2010.

4. The story of the doomed lovers was given a second literary life when the French medievalist Joseph Bédier composed his beautiful *Roman de Tristan et Iseut* (1900).

5. *Love in the Western World*, tr. Montgomery Belgion, Princeton: Princeton University Press, 1983, 218.

6. "In writing *Tristan*, Wagner transgressed the taboo. He *said* everything—admitted everything, not only in the words of his poem, but still more in the notes of his score. He sang of the Darkness of the

dissolution of forms and beings, of the release of desire, of desire become anathema, and of the tremendously plaintive and blessed twilit glory of the spirit after it had been rescued at the price of a fatal wound inflicted on the body" (ibid., 228).

7. Quoted in *Prelude and Transfiguration from Tristan and Isolde*, ed. Robert Bailey, New York: Norton Critical Scores, 1985, 47.

8. Joseph Kerman, *Opera as Drama*, New York: Vintage Books, 1956, 194.

9. Quoted in Dieter Borchmeyer, *Richard Wagner: Theory and Theatre*, Oxford: Clarendon Press, 1982, 367.

10. Bailey, 131.

11. See my discussion of the Tristan chord in Chapter One (27) and Chapter Two (44–45). The chord is usually described as a half-diminished seventh chord, that is, a seventh chord in which a major third sits above two minor thirds. A full diminished seventh chord is composed of all minor thirds, that is, two interlocking tritones. For a different interpretation of the chord, see Bailey, 122–25.

12. *Selected Letters*, 486.

13. *The World as Will and Representation*, translated by E. F. J. Payne, New York: Dover Publications, Inc., Vol. 2, 538.

14. *Wagner on Music and Drama*, 270.

15. Rougemont, 229.

16. "Of the two sexual climaxes that are unmistakably depicted in the orchestra, one is interrupted by the entry of Kurvenal on an unnamable discord, and the other occurs after Tristan has been dead for twenty minutes" (Elliott Zuckerman, *The First Hundred Years of Wagner's Tristan*, New York: Columbia University Press, 1964, 22).

17. Rougemont emphasizes the influence on medieval courtly love of the gnostic heresy known as Catharism (from the Greek adjective *katharos*, clean or pure). According to the Catharists, who adopted the Persian-Manichean dualism of Good and Evil, the material world was the work of Satan rather than God (p. 79). Rougemont sees Catharism at work in Wagner's *Tristan*, whose second act "is the passion song of souls imprisoned in material forms" (229).

18. *Wagner on Music and Drama*, 214. In the very first sentence of his book on Wagner's *Tristan*, Ernst Kurth, a devotee of Schopenhauer's metaphysics of will, writes: "Harmonies are reflexes from the Unconscious" (*Romantic Harmony and its Crisis in Wagner's Tristan*, Berlin: Max Hesses Verlag, 1920).

19. Tristan makes this clear in Act 2: "The frightful drink with the torment it gave, I myself—I myself brewed it!"

20. See Borchmeyer, 338. As Carl Dahlhaus writes, "unlike the fatal potion in *Götterdämmerung* it [the potion in *Tristan*] changes nothing but simply brings into the open something which already exists but has not previously been admitted" (*Richard Wagner's Music Dramas*, Cambridge: Cambridge University Press, 1959, 151).

21. *Selected Letters*, 475. Dahlhaus adds: "No less than *Tristan, Parsifal* is governed by Wagner's 'art of transition'" (152).

22. *The Wagner Operas*, Princeton: Princeton University Press, 1949, 196.

23. Newman writes: "the bulk of the opera would make an organic musical whole if played through by the orchestra without the voices" (202).

24. *Ecce Homo* 6.

25. *The Birth of Tragedy* 21, translated by Walter Kaufman, New York: Vintage Books, 1967, 126–27. Wagner writes the following in a letter to Nietzsche: "But 'Tristan' will certainly be of interest to you: only spectacles off! You must hear nothing but the orchestra" (*Selected Letters*, 810).

26. Schopenhauer distinguishes sharply between real life and listening to music. In real life, "we are the vibrating string that is stretched and plucked" (*WWR*, Vol. 2, 451). Julian Young writes: "Whatever . . . the differences between music and life, in musical experience, too, we *are* the 'vibrating string.' What leads Schopenhauer into this phenomenological mistake is, I think, his restriction of his account of the relation between music and emotion to the language of 'representation'" (*The Philosophies of Richard Wagner*, Lanham MD: Lexington Books, 2014, 82).

27. *WWR*, Vol. 1, 196.

28. *On Music and Drama*, 188–89.

29. See Borchmeyer, 365–366. Wagner started his unfinished letter by telling Schopenhauer why he wanted to persuade him of the redemptive potential of sexual love: "You alone give me the material of the concepts through which my views become communicable along philosophical lines" (quoted Curt von Westernhagen in his *Wagner: A Biography*, Cambridge: Cambridge University Press, 1978, vol. 1, 254). Wagner's anti-Schopenhauerian view of Love is clearly summed up by Liébert in Schopenhauerian terms: "It is not by renouncing the longing that makes the will objective that Tristan and Isolde know absolute peace, but by

intensifying it to the point where they cease to be separated individuals and meet in the universal will" (149).

30. In keeping with Nietzsche's criticism of "infinite melody," Elliott Zuckerman writes: "Wagner deprives one of the intellectual pleasures of music—a pleasure, Nietzsche might have added, for which there is no substitute in the recognition and tracing of leitmotifs" (78).

31. Quoted in Borchmeyer, 366. Empedocles was the Sicilian philosopher who leaped into Mt. Etna in order to prove that he was a god.

32. At an early stage of his work on *Tristan*, Wagner had contemplated having Parsifal visit the love-tormented Tristan in order to charm away his suffering with a strain of magical music.

33. In his book on Wagner, Martin Geck, writes the following: "[Wagner] needed the third act to articulate his thoughts on the 'curse of love' to which he refers in one of his sketches for the later libretto" (*Richard Wagner: A Life in Music*, Chicago: University of Chicago Press, 2013, 239).

34. On this point, Geck cites Ernst Bloch's opinion that Isolde's "beatific transfiguration" is nothing more than "a concession to the world of the theater" (ibid., 239). According to Geck, Wagner started out intending to write a monument to the love-happiness he confessed to Liszt he had never experienced and only later decided to dwell on love's extreme torment (233).

35. *Selected Letters*, 456–57.

36. ". . . although *Tristan and Isolde* cannot be salvaged as a coherent philosophical work, we are under no obligation to rescue it in this way. Unlike the *Ring*, the fascination it exudes rests not on the depiction of a baleful system but on an underlying message we would do best not to examine too closely" (Geck, 244).

37. Newman says something similar about the concert version of *Tristan*: "The selection from *Tristan* known in the concert room as the Prelude and Liebestod . . . makes an admirably rounded whole, musically and psychologically" (204).

38. Love as the destruction of individuality recalls Aristophanes's myth in Plato's *Symposium*. According to the myth, human beings were once prodigious, godlike circle-beings, who, in their hybris, assaulted Olympus (190B–C). To keep them in line, Zeus cut them in half, thus producing the metaphysical *wound* that is Eros. Lovers seek happiness in a return to their original union through sex. But such union is temporary and incomplete. As Aristophanes observes, what lovers want

but cannot put into words is complete and eternal fusion. The desire of lovers is "to become a one out of two by coming together and being fused together with the beloved" (192E), (translation by Brann, Kalkavage, Salem, Indianapolis: Hackett Publishing, 2017). This coveted fusion would entail the destruction of human beings in their current condition and, it seems, could only occur after death. The erotic teaching of Plato's Aristophanes is, in several aspects, a harbinger of Wagner's *Tristan*. It also foreshadows Schopenhauer's tragic sense of life—life as endless desire and therefore endless suffering.

39. According to Rougemont, Gnosticism is inherent in Gottfried's original tale: "*Tristan* is far more profoundly and indisputably Manichean than the *Divine Comedy* is Thomist" (135). For a full discussion of Gnosticism, see Hans Jonas, *The Gnostic Religion*, Boston: Beacon Press, 1958. Especially interesting is the Epilogue: *Gnosticism, Existentialism, and Nihilism*. The most eloquent poetic statement of Gnosticism occurs in Paul Valéry's *Ébauche d'un serpent*, where the serpent from Genesis calls the created universe *un défaut / Dans la pureté du Non-être*, "a flaw in the purity of Non-being." His long soliloquy ends, fittingly, with the word *Néant*, "nothingness."

40. *Hymns to the Night* 1, translated by Dick Higgins, New York: McPherson & Co., 1988, 11.

41. ". . . Tristan did not love Iseult for herself, but only on account of the love of Love of which her beauty gave him the image. He, however, did not know this, and his passion was naïve and strong" (223). ". . . Tristan is not in love with Iseult, but with love itself . . . [Iseult] is but a lovely pretext" (309) "Let us remember, however, that the passion of love is at bottom narcissism, the lovers' self-magnification, far more than it is a relation with the beloved" (260). See also Zuckerman on this point: "The lovers, in short, are in love not with each other but with love itself. Their quest is not for transitory fulfillment but for the obstacles that prolong passion—ultimately for the final obstacle, death, which is paradoxically the only permanent fulfillment" (24).

42. *Inferno* 5. Tristan is among the "carnal sinners who subjected reason to desire" (l. 67).

43. *WWR*, Vol. 2, 507.

44. As Roger Scruton observes, "erotic love is individualizing: its intentional object is the irreplaceable incarnate subjectivity of the other, as he is in himself, irreducible to his attributes or to any characteristic

that he might share" (*Death-Devoted Heart: Sex and the Sacred in Wagner's Tristan and Isolde*, Oxford: Oxford University Press, 2004, 130).

CHAPTER SIX

1. In the passage from the *Inferno* (Canto 2, 1–9), Dante invokes both the Muses and his *alto ingegno*, his lofty ingenuity or genius. Ingenium will play a central role in Mann's novel.

2. Zuckerkandl gives a clear description of the path from tonality to so-called suspended tonality to atonality, of which serialism is a special case: "Towards the end of the 19th century the disintegration of tonality begins. The first link to be cut is that between the changing keys and the super-key [the key governing the whole piece]: music is written in keys but not in a key. The foundation is no longer stability; it is change. Later, key dissolves, the moving centers cut themselves loose from the common point of reference. Finally, the ever more rapid succession of changes of center put the notion of center itself in doubt; the diatonic order disappears, and with it all tonal relations as we have known them. This is *atonal* music, the product of our century; in the perspective of tonality the purest negation; in its own perspective a search for new kinds of tone relations" (*The Sense of Music*, Princeton: Princeton University Press, 1971, 55–56).

3. Schoenberg invented twelve-tone technique in 1921. His first piece composed entirely in this style, the *Piano Suite* (Opus 25), appeared in 1923. Another Austrian composer and theorist, Josef Matthias Hauer (1883–1959), claimed to have been the first to discover "the law of the 12 notes." Schoenberg's criticism of Hauer's theories may be found in in *Style and Idea, Selected Writings of Arnold Schoenberg*, edited by Leonard Stein and translated by Leo Black, Berkeley: University of California Press, 1975, 209–214.

4. Schoenberg's most famous atonal work is the expressionist monodrama *Erwartung (Expectation)* (1909). In this work, an anxious woman recalls what is perhaps a dream in which she searches for her lover only to find his dead body. The goal of the drama, Schoenberg writes, "is to represent in *slow motion* everything that occurs during a single second of maximum spiritual excitement, stretching it out to half an hour" (*Style and Idea*, 105).

5. The quartet, written in 1936–38, was Webern's last published work. Lasting under eight minutes, it perfectly illustrates Schoenberg's obser-

vation that the new music combined "extreme expressiveness" with "extraordinary brevity" (ibid., 217).

6. Reference to the chromatically named Bach was popular among the serialists. In this, they were following Bach himself, who used his name as a subject in *The Art of Fugue*. The BACH theme enters almost toward the end of the final fugue, shortly before it ends in midstream, perched on an unstable 6/4 chord. In the Preface to the Philharmonia Pocket Score of Webern's quartet, we read the following: "[The minute paraphrases of the B-A-C-H theme] make the quote the object of a magic reflection. In the multiple echoes of the paraphrased name, the reference comes to have the nature of an invocation" (Vienna: Philharmonia Partituren, iv).

7. All three tetrachords are built on the seminal half-step with which the row begins, B-flat to A. The idea or theme of the row is therefore present in the opening two tones. Another feature is that the inversion of the row is identical with its retrograde. This is characteristic of Webern's gift for compression and economy.

8. Theodor W. Adorno, *Philosophy of New Music*, Minneapolis: Minnesota Press, 2006, 51. "The tone that recurs too soon, as well as the tone that is 'free'—fortuitous vis-à-vis the whole—becomes taboo" (ibid., 52). Adorno's phrase about the "free" note will appear in Mann's novel.

9. *Style and Idea*, 218.

10. Ibid., 246.

11. Zuckerkandl describes the new musical world as follows: "The interval becomes absolute, stands wholly on its own, and expresses nothing but the relation between two tones of different pitch" (*Man the Musician*, Princeton: Princeton University Press, 1976, 118). He makes the further remark that "the patterns of twelve-tone music," based as they are on pitch, are, unlike the patterns of tonal music, "fully consistent with the teachings of Gestalt psychology" (op. cit.). He means that twelve-tone patterns are not temporal but merely "pseudo-temporal Gestalten" that treat music as if it were nothing but a matter of acoustical intervals, along the model of visual patterns in space.

12. *Style and Idea*, 216.

13. In his series of lectures on the rise of the new music (1932–33), Webern describes the major and minor modes as two different "genders" (*The Path to the New Music*, translated by Willi Reich, Bryn Mawr: Theodor Presser Co., 1963, 27 and 36). He quotes Schoenberg as having

said that "double gender" [major and minor modes] has given rise to a higher race" (ibid., 37). The new music will be, in its way, transgender. The approving reference to a "higher race" is unsettling.

14. "The true beneficiary of twelve-tone technique is unquestionably counterpoint . . . [T]welve-tone technique is contrapuntal in its origin—for all the simultaneous notes in it are equally independent, given that they are integral components of the row" (Adorno, 70–71). The polyphonic potential of twelve-tone music is best exemplified by the music of Anton Webern, who wrote his doctoral thesis on the music of the Netherlands polyphonist Heinrich Isaac (1450–1517).

15. Commenting on the diminished seventh chord, Adorno writes: "Even the dullest ear perceives the shabbiness and tiredness of the diminished seventh chord" (ibid., 32). This chord, which is "correct and filled with expression at the beginning of Beethoven's Sonata opus 111," has "lost its weight" through the historical process (ibid., 33).

16. On the subject of twelve-tone melody, Adorno writes: "the melodic coherence becomes dependent on extramelodic means: a rhythmics that has acquired a life of its own" (ibid., 59).

17. Adorno is helpful on this point: "Music, contracted to a moment, is true as an eruption of negative experience. It touches on real suffering" (ibid., 34–35). Adorno continues in a Freudian vein: "Passions are no longer faked; on the contrary, undisguised, corporeal impulses of the unconscious, shocks, and traumas are registered in the medium of music" (ibid., 35). He concludes: "With the negation of semblance and play, music tends toward knowledge" (ibid., 36).

18. As I noted in Chapter Two, tonal music is a non-verbal form of narration. Tones all by themselves tell a story. They can do so only if dynamic qualities are in play. In their absence, other means must be used for dramatic settings. In several early atonal works of Schoenberg, the jarring music mirrors a psychic fragmentation that is both a breaking out and a breaking down. Examples are the monodrama *Erwartung* (described in note 4) and the expressionist drama *Die glückliche Hand* (*The Lucky Hand*), in which a man loses the woman he loves, then regains her only to lose her again. Adorno praised the latter (which dramatizes an event in Schoenberg's own life) as especially successful in hitting upon "the social character of loneliness" (ibid., 38).

19. See *Schoenberg*, Malcolm McDonald, Oxford: Oxford University Press, 2008, 30, 121.

20. *Style and Idea*, 141–42.

21. *Serial Composition and Atonality*, Berkeley: University of California Press, 1962, 3.

22. In twelve-tone music, complementary intervals (intervals that together fill out the octave) are considered identical.

23. "In the first works in which I employed this method, I was not yet convinced that the exclusive use of one set would not result in monotony . . . But soon I discovered that my fear was unfounded; I could even base a whole opera, *Moses and Aron*, solely on one set" (Schoenberg, *Style and Idea*, 224).

24. There is no theoretical preference for the set's prime or original statement, which may equally be regarded as a permutation of any of the other versions of itself.

25. *Style and Idea*, p. 215.

26. *Path to the New Music*, 40.

27. The translation is suggested by Willi Reich, Webern's translator (ibid., 57). The Latin is ambiguous and can be rendered in various ways, including "The Sower Arepo holds the wheels by work (or effort)."

28. As Willi Reich observes, the magic square "clearly shows the basic principle of twelve-tone technique: the equal status of basic set, inversion, cancrizan [retrograde] and inverted cancrizan" (ibid., 57).

29. Ibid., 55. Webern connects this saying with Goethe's *Urpflanze* or "archetypal plant." This is the self-same principle from which all plant differentiation proceeds. See *The Metamorphosis of Plants* in *Goethe: The Collected Works*, Vol. 12, *Scientific Studies*, translated by Douglas Miller, Princeton: Princeton University Press, 1995, 96–97 and note 27 (328–29).

30. Webern claimed that tonality was "really dead" (*Path to the New Music*, 47). The claim is eloquently refuted by Robert Reilly in his *Surprised by Beauty, A Listener's Guide to the Recovery of Modern Music* (revised and expanded edition), San Francisco: Ignatius Press, 2016. Among the many gems in Reilly's book is an interview with George Rochberg, the American composer who turned away from twelve-tone composition in the mid 1960s, back toward tonality. Another champion of tonality and critic of "sonic" music, John Borstlap, comments on the problem of meaning in Webern's magic square: "A unifying structure in itself is no guarantee for a meaningful communication, be it in terms of language or music . . . If anything, the 'magical square' shows that the more thoroughly and regularly a structure is organized at the material level, the less differentiation in terms of meaning it can produce" (*The Classical*

Revolution, Thoughts on New Music in the 21st Century, New York: Dover Publications, Inc., 2017, 30).

31. Adorno offers an apt critique of the serialists' number-fetish: "The arithmetical play of twelve-tone technique and the constraint that it exercises is reminiscent of astrology. . . . As a closed system in itself and at the same time self-opaque, twelve-tone rationality—in which the constellation of means is immediately hypostasized as goal and law—verges on superstition" (ibid., 53). He continues: "The question that twelve-tone composition poses to the composer is not how musical meaning can be organized but rather how organization can become meaningful" (ibid., 54).

32. *Thomas Mann, The Ironic German,* Cambridge: Cambridge University Press, 1981, 261.

33. Commenting on the difficulty of translating the novel into English, Heller observes that "even the full title is untranslatable" (ibid., 260). The word translated as "composer" is the archaic *Tonsetzer,* literally "tone-setter." Archaism is one of the novel's central themes, and the order obsessed Leverkühn is a true *Tonsetzer:* he puts tones in their place.

34. Serenus plays the viola d'amore (6). The instrument perfectly fits Serenus's moderate nature: the viola steers between the emotional extremes of the violin and the cello.

35. The Faust figure is an alter ego of Mann himself as a composer of musically inspired prose. Serenus, too, is an alter ego, "a parody of myself," as Mann wrote in a letter (quoted in *Faust as Musician, A Study of Thomas Mann's Doctor Faustus,* Patrick Carnegy, New York: A New Directions Book, 1973, 16). "Zeitblom is that part of him which felt that the world had been turned upside down, yet found it difficult to live as though this were the case or even to recognize the possible implications" (op. cit.). Serenus also embodies Mann's own love for Adrian: "I never loved a creature of my imagination . . . as I did Adrian" (*The Story of a Novel, The Genesis of Doctor Faustus,* translated by Richard and Clara Winston, New York: Knopf, 1961, 88).

36. Ibid., 276.

37. *The Story of a Novel,* 32.

38. In a letter to the Hungarian philologist Karl Kerényi, Mann calls *Faustus* his "Nietzsche novel" (*Letters of Thomas Mann,* selected and translated by Richard and Clara Winston, New York: Knop, 1971, 490).

39. For an account of the Mann/Schoenberg controversy, see Carnegy, 37–54.

40. *The Story of a Novel*, 45. As Carnegy notes, Schoenberg's "subjection of music to rigorous rational analysis, for Adorno, led to the converse of rationality and a casting back of the art into the dark, mythological realm" (*Faust as Musician*, 13).

41. Ivan's conversation with the devil occurs in Part 4, Book 11, Chapter 9: "Ivan Fyodorovich's Nightmare."

42. Numbers in parentheses refer to the English translation by John E. Wood, *Doctor Faustus*, New York: Vintage Books, 1999.

43. *Historia von D. Johann Faustus*, Berlin: Holzinger, 2013, 15.

44. Elsbeth embodies an aspect of Mann's own sense of music. According to his daughter Monika, Mann feared that if he had pursued a career in music, its inarticulateness "would have corrupted him and delivered him to the devil." She goes on to say that music for her father was "necessarily somehow linked with sin." The passages are quoted in *Music and Thomas Mann* by Ethel E. Caro, Stanford: Stanford Honors Essays in Humanities, Number II, 1959, 3.

45. See note 8.

46. Adorno cites Stravinsky's *Rite of Spring* as a prime example of the ultimate identity of old and new: "Nothing perhaps demonstrates so clearly how in Stravinsky modernism and the archaic are two sides of the same thing" (*Philosophy of New Music*, 118).

47. "Sensuousness in its elemental originality is the absolute theme of music" ("The Immediate Erotic Stages" in Part 1 of *Either/Or*, translated by Howard V. Hong and Edna H. Hong, Princeton: Princeton University Press, 1987, 71).

48. Mann, via Kretzschmar, brilliantly compares music to Wagner's Kundry, "who does not wish to do what she does and yet flings soft arms of lust around the neck of the fool [Parsifal]" (68).

49. Kretzschmar's father, we are told, heard this heavenly singing as a young man. Kretzschmar himself was born in Pennsylvania of German-American parents and migrated to the Old World (53).

50. "The analysis of the row system and the criticism of it that is translated into dialogue in Chapter 22 of Faustus is entirely based upon Adorno's essay" (*The Story of a Novel*, 46).

51. In appropriating Schoenberg's method, Mann departed from it in crucial ways. For an astute summary of these departures, see Patrick Carnegy, *Faust as Musician, A Study of Thomas Mann's novel Doctor Faustus*, New York: A New Directions Book, 1975, Chapter Four, "Schoenberg and Leverkühn," 37–54. Gunilla Bergsten suggests that the falsification

of the method "stems from Mann's use of musical terminology to illuminate a literary problem; he sometimes has to twist the terminology to make it fulfill its symbolic function" (*Thomas Mann's Doctor Faustus, The Sources and Structure of the Novel*, translated from the German by Krishna Winston, Chicago: University of Chicago Press, 1969, 74).

52. Nietzsche writes about the event in a letter to Paul Deussen (see Deussen's *Erinnerungen an Friedrich Nietzsche*, Leipzig, 1901). In his late essay, "Nietzsche's Philosophy in the Light of Recent History," Mann narrates Nietzsche's two visits to a brothel: "one year after he had fled from the house in Cologne he returned—without diabolic guidance [from an unknown man whom Nietzsche asked to lead him to a good restaurant]—to some similar place and contracted the disease (some say deliberately, as self-punishment) which was to destroy his life but also to intensify it enormously" (Thomas Mann, *Last Essays*, translated by Richard and Clara Winston and Tania and James Stern, New York: Knopf, 1970, 145–46).

53. Adrian's pronouncements, "*Beziehung ist alles*" and "*Organisation ist alles*," recall Faust's utterance in Goethe's poem: "*Gefühl ist alles*," "Feeling is all" (3456). Mann's Faust figure is the inversion of Goethe's. Adrian scorns feeling. For him, it is all about the intellectualism of the magic square.

54. Mann gets this claim from Adorno: "This is why Bach is truly what Goethe said he was: a 'harmonist'" (*Philosophy of New Music*, 72). Adrian's preference for the older, northern counterpoint is echoed by the obnoxious philosopher of culture, Chaim Breisacher, whom we meet in Chapter 28. Breisacher, to the shock of his conservative colleagues, rejects Palestrina, an icon of musical conservatism, as too progressive, smooth, and prone to "harmonic chords" (296).

55. The formulation is that of Adorno (*Philosophy of New Music*, 45).

56. The poem's first line is *Die Welt war mir zuwider*, "The world was hateful to me." Each of its eleven stanzas ends with the refrain *O lieb Mädel, wie schlecht bist du!* ("O dear girl, how bad you are!"). The poet recounts how, despite all the suffering he has endured from his "bad girl," he continues to love her desperately. He forgives her having poisoned him and has no regrets.

57. Mann was theoretically at home with twelve-tone music but did not enjoy or love it. His musical tastes ran more to Schubert and Wagner. According to Carnegy, Mann may even have regarded the twelve-tone method as "in its own way as much an aberration as the totalitarian principle in politics" (*Faust as Musician*, 142).

58. It seems fitting that the Manardi house, where Adrian is staying, is haunted by a recent event: the hallucinations of a Russian lodger, a prince, who thought he saw ghosts, at whom he sometimes fired his pistol in his bedroom (227). Not long after the incident, the Manardi's simple-witted daughter Amelia formed the habit of asking her spoon, "*Spiriti? Spiriti?*"

59. Carnegy, *Faust as Musician*, 79.

60. E. M. Butler criticizes Mann on this point: "this is one of the sweeping statements [in the novel] which lacks the sanction of universal truth . . . And even if it were true, where is the parallel with Germany? Leverkühn and Germany are very strikingly represented as victims of dark and demonic forces; but an artist's fate is something much too individual to symbolize a nation's destiny. The attempt to do so here would result in a laying the blame for the tragedy Germany brought about and suffered at the door of her musical gifts, or in regarding her as in some special sense the artist among nations" (*The Fortunes of Faust*, Cambridge: Cambridge University Press, 1952, 336).

61. Commenting on this passage, Heller writes: "Such is the thoroughness with which Thomas Mann 'unwrites' Goethe's *Faust*. For with Goethe it is Mephistopheles who is all critique, irony, and mockery, and Faust himself the enthusiastic creator" (ibid., 274). The reversal derives from Mann's rejection of Goethe's optimism, his positing a pre-established harmony between self and world, man and cosmos. Whereas for Goethe, our faculties are in harmony with the cosmic order, Leverkühn's faculties "are deeply at odds with the architecture of the world which, even if comprehended, might be found wanting in wonder. For its discovered truths are certainly of little use to the soul" (275).

62. Adorno criticizes "the work" at the very beginning of his *Philosophy of New Music*: "Under the constraint of its own objective logic, music critically canceled the idea of the consummate artwork and severed its tie with the public" (29). Mann slyly avoids the charge that his Faustus novel is a finished work through the relentless self-criticisms of Serenus. As Heller observes, Mann's *Doctor Faustus* is "its own critique . . . There is no critical thought which the book does not think *about itself*" (ibid., 279). On the problematic nature of the musical work, see Carl Dahlhaus, "On the decline of the concept of the musical work" in *Schoenberg and the New Music*, Cambridge: Cambridge University Press, 1988, 220–33.

63. Carnegy rightly calls this passage "a direct indictment of the Third Reich" (ibid., 91). "Blessed Messengers" is the name of the phar-

macy that belonged to Serenus's father. It is where Adrian's father bought the chemicals for his osmosis experiments (23).

64. On this point, see E. M. Butler's comment, quoted in note 60.

65. Adrian's attempt to outwit the devil recalls Guido da Monte-feltro, who is mentioned in the *Inferno* in connection with the town of Palestrina. Guido tries to outwit the devil by claiming to have received, through confession, pardon for his handing over the town to Pope Boniface. The devil who comes to fetch Guido schools him in the theology of contrition and tells him: "Perhaps you didn't think I was a logician" (*Inferno* 27, 122–23).

66. As Michael Beddow observes, Adrian's conversation with the devil "has the full impact of a living and waking experience" (Thomas Mann, *Doctor Faustus* in *Landmarks of World Literature*, Cambridge: Cambridge University Press, 1994, 72).

67. Is Serenus saying that the monstrosities of the cosmos were not created by God, or that God created monsters that ought not be admired? His devotion to humanism, the strongest element in his personality (apart from his love for Adrian), outweighs any thoughts he may have about the theology of creation, in which he seems to have no interest. He is no speculative Catholic.

68. See Heinrich Kleist, *Selected Writings*, edited and translated by David Constantine, Indianapolis: Hackett Publishing Co., Inc., 2004, 416.

69. *The Story of a Novel, The Genesis of Doctor Faustus*, 151.

70. In his late essay on Nietzsche, Mann says the following of Sorel: "Nowadays the phrase 'powerful illusions' reminds us of Sorel and his book *Sur la violence*, where no differentiation is yet made between proletarian syndicalism and fascism, and mass myth, quite independent of truth or falsehood, is pronounced the indispensable motive force of history" ("Nietzsche's Philosophy in the Light of Recent History," *Late Essays*, translated by Richard and Clara Winston and Tania and James Stern, New York: Knopf, 1970, 155).

71. The phrase "blond beast" is from Nietzsche's *On the Genealogy of Morals*, I. 11, translated by Walter Kaufmann, New York: Vintage Books, 1969, 40. The image refers to the hidden beast that is in the soul of "noble races," the "hidden core that needs to erupt from time to time." It came to be the epithet of the Nazi officer, Rheinhard Heydrich.

72. Serenus here speaks for Mann, who in the late essay cited above harshly criticizes Nietzsche's Overman. This is the all-daring heroic

individual who embodies the triumph of the aesthetic over the moral and rational ("Nietzsche's Philosophy in the Light of Recent History," 141–177). Mann quotes the Novalis passage that appears as an epigraph to this chapter (165–66): "What Novalis calls the ideal of aesthetic greatness is nothing more or less than Nietzsche's superman" (166).

73. The Four Horsemen are described in *Revelation* 6 and are variously interpreted, often as representing Conquest, War, Famine, and Death. Only Death (*Thanatos*) is named. Adrian's composition (at least from what Serenus describes) seems to omit several scenes from the book and from Dürer's depiction: the adoration of the Lamb (who opens the Seven Seals), Michael's defeat of the Dragon, and the pregnant Woman clothed in white. *The Book with Seven Seals*, an oratorio by the Catholic Austro-Hungarian composer Franz Schmidt, was a more comprehensive depiction. A thoroughly tonal work, it was first performed in 1938. Mann seems to have been unaware of it. In any case, a tonal piece of music would hardly have suited his purposes.

74. In the Preface to the *Phenomenology of Spirit*, Hegel refers to the act of dwelling with the negative as the *Zauberkraft*, the magic force, that converts non-being into being (A. V. Miller translation, Oxford: Clarendon Press, 1977, 19).

75. Adrian's use of Rudi as his surrogate is taken from the life of Nietzsche, who used his friend Paul Rée to offer marriage proposals to Lou Andreas-Salomé (*Story of a Novel*, 33).

76. Rudi woos Adrian in a room that has been darkened to accommodate one of Adrian's migraines (367). Taking advantage of the darkness, Rudi says of the desired concerto, "I'd be its mother, and you would be its father—it would like a child between us, a platonic child" (369).

77. Mann describes Schoenberg's string trio and its depiction of the composer's illness and medical treatment in *The Story of a Novel*, 217.

78. In the German original, this appears in italics: *es soll nicht sein*.

79. *The World as Will and Representation*, translated by E. F. J. Payne, New York: Dover Publications, Inc., 1969, Vol. 1, 326.

80. Serenus refers to his fellow countrymen as "children of the dungeon" who "dreamt of a song of joy." In Beethoven's opera *Fidelio*, which celebrates freedom and marriage, Leonore disguises herself as the prison guard Fidelio in order to liberate her husband Florestan from a political prison.

81. The repetition simultaneously echoes and negates the "*Freude! Freude!*" from the Ode to Joy.

82. The undynamic nature of lament recalls Vergil's Andromache, who in the *Aeneid* weeps continually beside the empty tomb of fallen Hector (Book 3). There is no future for her, only the eternal return of grief.

83. Serenus's reference to language recalls Jonathan Leverkühn's search for meaning in the tiny markings of the conch shell. Adrian's formal art, unlike mute nature, *succeeds* as communication.

84. In *The Story of a Novel*, Mann reports that Adorno instructed him, justly in Mann's opinion, to tone down the optimism of the original ending: "I had been too optimistic, too kindly, too pat, had kindled too much light, had been too lavish with the consolation" (ibid., 222–23). Mann reveals his optimism regarding the future of Germany in a letter to the novelist Walter von Molo: "Let us not in any way suggest that the devil has now collected the soul of Germany. Grace is stronger than any pact signed in blood. I believe in grace, and I believe in Germany's future, however desperate her present may look, however hopeless the destruction seems to be" (*Letters*, 484).

85. "Thomas Mann the Musician," The Thomas Mann Commemoration at Princeton University, Princeton: Princeton University Library, 1965, 13.

86. Ibid., 15.

87. Ibid., 15.

88. *Doctor Faustus*, Chapter 15, 142–43. The description occurs in a letter to Serenus. It is a mocking diatribe against composers who seek to produce "beauty." Adrian at this point has not yet thrown himself into the arms of music, which he longs for and which longs for him (143).

89. "Thomas Mann the Musician," 29.

90. Ibid., 29.

91. Ibid., 29.

92. Ibid., 29.

93. Ibid., 29–30.

94. Ibid., 30. Zuckerkandl further develops his notion of ideal reality in "Mimesis," an unpublished lecture given at St. John's College in 1955. There, Zuckerkandl distinguishes between image and *mimêma* as the product of artistic imitation. An example of the former is the physical cosmos in the *Timaeus*. The cosmos, as image, is derivative from a more real being: the eternal archetype after which the cosmos is fashioned. Timaeus's likely story itself is, by contrast, not the image of an original but an originary producer of meaning. It is a word construct in which

mythic elements (e.g., the demiurge) are related to other mythic elements (e.g., the musical scale). The story is a *mimêma*—a poem and piece of music—that sheds light, in some mysterious and perplexing way, on the cosmos whose divine order Timaeus wishes to celebrate.

95. *Doctor Faustus*, Chapter 8, 63.

96. "Thomas Mann the Musician," 31. The definition is from Mann's "Germany and the Germans," a lecture Mann gave at the Library of Congress in 1945.

97. Ibid., 32.

98. Ibid., 32. As Erich Heller observes, Mann undercuts the novel's formal perfection through the relentless self-criticisms of Serenus (see note 62). Nevertheless, these self-criticisms are integral to the novel's ironic artistry.

CHAPTER SEVEN

1. For a helpful description of the various recordings of the opera, see Robert R. Reilly, *Surprised by Beauty: A Listener's Guide to the Recovery of Modern Music*, Revised and Expanded Edition, San Francisco: Ignatius Press, 2016, 267–68. The context is Reilly's gem-like discussion of Poulenc's opera and the equally moving *Stabat Mater*.

2. The title of the English version is *The Song at the Scaffold*, translated by Olga Marx, San Francisco: Ignatius Press, 2011. Von le Fort's novel was based on a chronicle written by Marie of the Incarnation, one of the sisters who was in Paris on personal business at the time of the arrest. For a detailed account of the historical events and personages, see William Bush, *To Quell the Terror: The True Story of the Carmelite Martyrs of Compiègne*, Washington, D.C.: ICS Publications, Institute of Carmelite Studies, 1999.

3. William Bush wrote his book in order to tell the true story of the sisters of Compiègne and to put the spotlight back on the sisters as united in a common purpose. That purpose was to pray, and ultimately offer their lives, for those who sought to destroy the Church.

4. The film was eventually made in 1960 but with unfortunate changes to Bernanos's text.

5. For an illuminating account of the changes Bernanos made to the novel, see Robert Speaight, *Georges Bernanos, A Study of the Man and the Writer*, New York: Liveright, 1974, 265–66. Most interesting is the change regarding Blanche's fate: "With Gertrud von le Fort there is no question of Blanche's salvation, but for Bernanos she must run the Christian risk,

and run it to the end. Only a miracle of grace can save her; and where in the novel her personality is dissolved almost to its roots, in the play her response to the Divine invitation is active and conscious" (265).

6. Poulenc's earlier opera was *Les Mamelles de Tirésias* (*The Breasts of Tiresias*), an *opera buffa* based on a surrealist play by Apollinaire. The outlandish story is about reversed sexual roles in marriage. The farcical events had a serious goal: to promote the repopulation of France after the devastations of the recent war. Comparing Poulenc's two operas, Wilfrid Mellers writes: "*Les Mamelles de Tirésias* . . . was and is physically life-enhancing. *Dialogues des Carmélites* is metaphysically death-celebrating, and forms a complement, as well as polar opposite, to *Les Mamelles*" (*Francis Poulenc*, Oxford Studies of Composers, Oxford: Oxford Universithy Press, 1993, 102).

7. *Echo and Source, Selected Correspondence*, translated by Sidney Buckland, London: Victor Gollancz, 1991, 387.

8. *Francis Poulenc*, translated by Edward Lockspeiser, New York: Grove Press, Inc., 1959, 81. Hell is referring to the six Strauss operas based on plays by Hugo von Hoffmansthal, Debussy's *Pelléas et Mélisande*, and Alban Berg's twelve-tone opera *Wozzeck* (which Poulenc very much admired). Debussy's opera exerted a strong influence on Poulenc's *Dialogues*.

9. In a letter to Stéphane Audel, Poulenc wrote: "I am crazy about my subject, to the point of believing that I have actually known these women" (*Selected Correspondence*, 206). In another letter (to Dodo Conrad), he expressed himself even more colorfully: "I am obnubilated (lovely word) with my *Carmelites* . . . I can think of nothing else, I live for nothing else" (ibid., 211).

10. Ferroud was hit by a car and decapitated when he was walking along a road in Hungary. After Ferroud's death, Poulenc made a penitential pilgrimage to the shrine of the Black Virgin at Rocamadour in Southwestern France. On his return home, he composed his first religious piece, *Litanies à la Vierge Noir*, scored for three-part children's or women's voices and organ.

11. Of this work Mellers writes: "Although, for obvious reasons, the *Sept Répons* will never be as popular as the *Gloria*, it is probably Poulenc's greatest religious work" (157–58). The *Répons* had its premiere in April of 1963, roughly three months after the composer's death. Several of Poulenc's sacred works were written in response to a death. The *Stabat Mater* was composed in response to the death of Poulenc's painter-friend

Christian Bérard. The *Dialogues* was written while Poulenc's lover, Lucien Roubert, was dying of cancer. When writing the *Répons*, the composer knew that his own end was not far off.

12. Poulenc did use the resources of twelve-tone music when he deemed them emotionally appropriate. A good example occurs in the third of the *Répons* on the words *Caligaverunt oculi mei a fletu meo* ("My eyes are darkened by my weeping"). Mellers observes that the passage "could not have happened had Poulenc been entirely ignorant of Schoenberg" (155).

13. The letter to Henri Sauget is quoted by Roger Nichols in *Poulenc, A Biography*, New Haven: Yale University Press, 2020, 222.

14. Commenting on the close connection with Monteverdi, Mellers writes: "Monteverdi, speaking of his *Orfeo*, said that it mated recitative, which is speaking while singing, with arioso, which is singing while speaking. This applies to Poulenc's opera which, given his empathy with the human voice and command of French prosody, relates character both to the inner life of the psyche and to action in the world" (104).

15. Poulenc wrote the following to Pierre Bernac: "If I am to succeed with this work it will only be through the music identifying absolutely with the Bernanos *spirit*. Very light orchestration to allow the text to come through" (*Selected Correspondence*, 206). As Henri Hell observes, Bernanos's literary style in the *Dialogues* "is noticeably simpler than that of his novels and pamphlets which is often inclined to be highly rhetorical," no doubt because the work was intended for the screen (80).

16. French composers were very good at melding the old and new worlds. The most impressive example is Maurice Duruflé's *Quatre Motets sur des thèmes grégoriens* (1960).

17. The historical sisters' last song as they ascended the scaffold was in fact Psalm 117, *Laudate Dominum omnes gentes*, "which proclaims the mystic truth couched at the heart of the Christian experience of salvation: God's mercy is at the center of all things, even of being guillotined" (Bush, 14–15). The crucial line is "For His mercy is confirmed upon us."

18. Nichols, 237.

19. The Réveillon riots signaled the first stirrings of revolution. They were prompted by the mistaken opinion that Réveillon, a wallpaper manufacturer, had advocated lower wages. Some wordplay is involved here. Réveillon's name derives from the verb *réveiller*, to wake up or to rouse. The riots were a wakeup call to the sleepy aristocracy. *Réveillon* also refers to Christmas or New Year's Eve supper.

20. *Joy*, translated by Louise Varèse, Providence RI: Cluny Media, 2020, 165. This reflection on fear is uttered by Abbé Chevance and addressed to the pure but troubled Chantal, the novel's central character.

21. According to Mellers, this is traditionally a key of benediction (108).

22. Honor was central to Bernanos's life and thought. In his book on Bernanos, Hans Urs von Balthasar writes the following: "[Honor] was not for him one important value among other possible ones; rather honor was something like the absolute ethical foundation that imparts personal dignity, moral splendor, sublimity, and divine likeness to all the commandments and the fulfillment of the commandments" (*Bernanos, An Ecclesial Existence*, translated by Erasmo Leiva-Merikakis, San Francisco: Ignatius Press, 1996, 551).

23. As Mellers observes, the latter key will later be associated "negatively with revolutionary violence and positively with the New Prioress" (115). B-flat minor in Poulenc's music signals not only darkness and fear but also mystery. It is the key of the motet, *O magnum mysterium*, where B-flat minor expresses wonder at the mystery of the Incarnation.

24. Since the work consists mostly of female voices, Poulenc had to be scrupulous about voice range and quality. In the present scene, Blanche's soprano contrasts beautifully with the Prioress's contralto, the lowest female range.

25. Letter to Pierre Bernac, *Selected Correspondence*, 206.

26. Voltaire was certainly of this opinion regarding monks and nuns: "They eat, they pray, they digest" (quoted by Nichols, 234).

27. Bernanos died at the age of fifty-nine.

28. Mellers offers an insightful comment on Sister Constance: "After Blanche and the Old Prioress, Constance is the most significant character in the opera, since her child-like innocence is to prove the agent of Blanche's belated redemption" (110).

29. Letter to Pierre Bernac, in *Selected Correspondence*, 214.

30. The sounding of the English horn recalls the analogous opening of Act 3, Scene 1 of *Tristan and Isolde*, the scene that depicts Tristan's suffering and journey to death.

31. Poulenc believed that the suffering of Lucien Roubert was for the sake of the composer's escape from a suspected cancer (Nichols, 243). In a letter to Simone Girard, Poulenc writes: "I have finished [the opera]: Monsieur Lucien will die now" (*Selected Correspondence*, 236).

32. The chord is formed by two minor thirds with a major third on top. It suggests transcendence rather than anguish.

33. As Constance's *qui* (the relative pronoun for "who") makes clear, we are entering in the middle of the Office for the Dead, which is very long. The phrase sung by Constance is in fact a *response* to a preceding verse from Job, and Blanche's phrase is the next *verse*. Poulenc's choice of the only Lazarus reference in the Office was perhaps suggested by the Prioress's "bad death." Like Lazarus, the Prioress will be "called forth" from the bodily death that she morbidly feared.

34. It is tempting to interpret the framing device of the clock along metaphysical lines. The doctrine of sacrificial substitution points to the work of grace within the realm of time and is part of time's providential structure.

35. Nichols quotes Bishop Varden's interesting assessment of the choice of Mme. Lidoine as the new Prioress: "There is more than a hint in Bernanos's play that the election of Madame Lidoine was a matter of temporizing on the nuns' part: might this bourgeoise save them from the revolutionaries' fury? That the new Prioress is sensitive to this possibility is implicit when she invites Sister Marie to conclude her own inaugural address, as if admitting that she occupies a place that should have been Mother Marie's by right. And yet: Madame Lidoine shows herself, for all her commonness and talk of cabbage, able to rise to mystic levels, assuming the other sisters' vow in extremis, thus displaying a purity of faith that, in Mother Marie's case, is contaminated by self-will" (236). Mme. Lidoine's rise to mystic levels occurs in a later scene, when the sisters are in prison.

36. Nichols, 237.

37. Letter to Henri Hell, *Selected Correspondence*, 216.

38. Mellers writes helpfully: "the violence of the music [in scene 3] is explained by the fact that the old world's seductiveness cannot but perturb Blanche in being illusory; certainly this third tableau intensifies the seductions the past had offered her in the first act" (116).

39. Nichols observes that the Chevalier's eight measures echo Puccini, whose music Poulenc loved and admired (237).

40. In Bernanos's screenplay, the interchange goes on. CHEVALIER: "Without being a Sorbonne theologian, I would reply that it would be likewise here or elsewhere." BLANCHE: "No, my brother, it is here that I feel myself most at His mercy." (*Dialogues of the Carmelites, The Heroic Face of Innocence, Three Stories by Georges Bernanos*, translations by R.

Batchelor, Pamela Morris and David Louis Schindler, Jr., and Michael Legat, Grand Rapids: William B. Eerdmanns Publishing Co., 1999, 93.)

41. In Bernanos's text, Marie adds: "But one should not contort oneself in an effort to become humble, like a cat trying to force itself into a rat-hole. True humility is first of all a propriety [*une décence*], a balance [*un equilibre*]" (*Dialogues*, 95).

42. Blancard will get the sisters arrested for continuing to meet. His name recalls that of Blanche, "white." Mellers suggests that Blancard's name may not be ironic, since "the sisters' ultimate salvation is their martyrdom" (120). Like Judas, Blancard has his part to play in the unfolding of providence. His act of betrayal is the first step toward the saintly purity of martyrdom, especially the miraculous martyrdom of Blanche.

43. The *Ça ira* ("It'll be fine") was the official song of the Revolution. In the Revolution's more violent stages, additional verses called for the lynching of aristocrats and clergy: "It'll be fine!"

44. The sarabande, one of the standard movements in a Baroque suite, is a dignified slow-to-medium-tempo dance in 3/4 time. Its defining rhythmic gesture is a strong accent on the second beat. Famous examples include the sarabande from Handel's harpsichord Suite No. 11 in D minor and the final movement from Bach's *St. Matthew Passion*, where a double chorus sings to Jesus: "We sit down in tears and call to Thee in the grave: 'Rest gently, gently rest!'" Examples from Poulenc's music include "*Fac ut portem*" from the *Stabat Mater* and the penitential motet *Timor et tremor*, both in A minor. The former resembles the *Tempo de Sarabande* from the *Dialogues* in its use of (French) double-dotted figures. Its trochaic text provides a thematic connection: "*Fac, ut portem Christi mortem, / Passionis fac consortem, / Et plagas recolere*" ("Make me of thy death the bearer, / In thy Passion be a sharer, / Taking to myself thy pain.").

45. Bernanos's screenplay further clarifies Marie's meaning: "It would be . . . a grave and gross lack of propriety [*décence*] to inflame ourselves with big words and big gestures, like soldiers who take alcohol before the assault" (*Dialogues*, 127).

46. In Bernanos's screenplay, the nuns leave the convent *en civil*, that is, wearing civilian clothes. Poulenc rejected this idea. Nichols cites a letter in which Poulenc comments critically on the Milan production, apparently because the sisters in this scene were not wearing their habits: "making the Carmelites into individuals was a mistake. Until

Constance's arrival, they should be a flock with a single reaction: confidence" (239).

47. The music is taken from the Andante of Poulenc's Sonata for two clarinets.

48. The slow instrumental transition, which features the family theme, was added after the vocal score was published. As Nichols observes, the insertion makes up for the odd exclusion of the theme from the original faster transition that follows (240)—odd because the scene shows us Blanche back home.

49. The spectacle of two nuns kneeling in front of a stove is surreal.

50. The saying echoes Montaigne: "the most barbarous of our maladies is to despise our own being" ("Of Experience," *Essays, The Complete works of Michel de Montaigne*, translated by Donald M. Frame. New York: Knopf [Everyman's Library], 2003, 1039.)

51. In Bernanos's list of characters, Rose Ducor is referred to as an actress.

52. The address has special meaning for the story: *2 Rue Saint Denis*. Saint Denis was a third-century saint, martyr, and bishop of Paris. He was decapitated under the reign of the emperor Decius and is often depicted holding his head in his hands.

53. The instrumental interlude replaces an omitted scene, which was spoken. Two old women and an old gentleman meet Blanche on a street near the Bastille. Blanche is returning from her grocery shopping. One of the women asks Blanche if she has relatives in Compiègne, the woman's hometown, and reports that just yesterday the sisters of Carmel were arrested. "Perhaps you have relatives there?" the woman asks. "Oh no, madame!" Blanche responds. "Besides, I've never been to Compiègne. I arrived in Paris with my employer only eight days ago from Roche-sur-Yon." Here, Blanche reenacts Peter's denial of Christ. Cf. Nichols, 240. Omitting the scene was a wise choice, since spoken words would have disrupted the opera's lyrical flow.

54. Mellers calls E minor Bach's key of crucifixion (123). He is thinking of the *Crucifixus* from the *Mass in B Minor*.

55. Mellers, 123. The Prioress's sublime song of consolation suggests that the former Prioress was right to choose Mme. Lidoine as her successor over Mother Marie.

56. Poulenc took this part of the Prioress's address from an earlier scene in Bernanos's screenplay. It is uttered by Sister Marthe (*Dialogues*, 117).

57. The Tristan chord, which we met in Chapter 5, is the most famous example of a half-diminished seventh chord. It is formed by two minor thirds with a major third on top. The darkly tense full diminished seventh chord is a stack of three minor thirds: two interlocked tritones.

58. The screenplay makes clear that they celebrated Mass clandestinely on Good Friday (*Dialogues*, 111).

59. Marie's high B-flat echoes that of Mme. Lidoine in the previous scene. It suggests that this is yet another instance of transferred grace. The new Prioress dies in place of Mother Marie.

60. Sister Constance was, in historical fact, the *first* to die (Bush, 11).

61. Poulenc worried about the timing of the thumps: "It is horribly difficult to work out a plausible moment for the beheading of the poor nuns that does not coincide with the beginning and ending of phrases. I will solve it eventually, but it is like a puzzle. . . . So I am now resorting to instinct" (letter to Pierre Bernac, *Selected Correspondence*, 234).

62. Poulenc set the chant to music in the darkly lulling motet from 1941.

63. It is reported that as Constance mounted the scaffold singing, she was as radiant "as a queen going to receive her diadem" and waved aside the usual assistance from the executioner and his valet (Bush, 213). Mme. Lidoine presided over the sacrifice of her fifteen daughters and was the last to die (op. cit.).

64. Robert R. Reilly comments insightfully on the causality at work in Blanche's redemption, which is, dramatically, a deus ex machina: "Yet, in this case, the deus ex machina adds to, rather than detracts from, the drama of the work, because it operates on the same plane of grace that is the premise of the whole work" (*Surprised by Joy*, 266).

65. "This makes a point, for what has been slaughtered is not only a community of nuns but also an ancestral way of life. The final tolling of bells is a requiem for a world, as well as for the souls of the decapitated nuns" (Mellers, 125).

66. Letter to Rose Dercourt-Plaut, *Selected Correspondence*, 230.

67. *Selected Correspondence*, 390.

68. Cf. Bush, 228–233.°

Bibliography

Adorno, Theodor W. *Philosophy of New Music*. Trans. Robert Hullot-Kentor. Minneapolis: University of Minnesota Press, 2006.

Alighieri, Dante. *The Divine Comedy*. Trans. John D. Sinclair. New York: Oxford University Press, 1961.

Anon. *Historia von D. Johann Fausten*. Berlin: Holzinger, 2013.

Aristotle. *Politics*. Trans. Joe Sachs. Indianapolis: Hackett Publishing Co., 2012.

Aristoxenus. *The Harmonics of Aristoxenus*. Trans. Henry S. Macran, M.A. Oxford: Clarendon Press, 1902.

Augustine, Saint. *Confessions*. Trans. John K. Ryan. New York: Doubleday, 1960.

Bailey, Robert. *Wagner: Prelude and Transfiguration from Tristan and Isolde*. New York: W. W. Norton & Co., 1985.

Balthasar, Hans Urs von. *Bernanos: An Ecclesial Existence*. Trans. Erasmo Leiva-Merikakis. San Francisco: Ignatius Press, 1996.

Beddow, Michael. *Mann: Doctor Faustus in Landmarks of World Literature*. Cambridge: Cambridge University Press, 1994.

Bergson, Henri. *Creative Evolution*. Trans. Arthur Mitchell. New York: Dover Publications, Inc., 1998.

———. *The Creative Mind: An Introduction to Metaphysics*. Trans. Mabelle L. Andison. New York: Citadel Press, 1992.

———. *Matter and Memory*. Trans. Margaret Paul and W. Scott Palmer. Mineola NY: Dover Publications, Inc., 2004.

Bernanos, Georges. *Dialogues of the Carmelites*. Trans. Michael Legat. *The Heroic Face of Innocence: Three Stories by Georges Bernanos*. Trans. R. Batchelor, Pamela Morris, David Louis Schindler, Jr., and Michael Legat. Grand Rapids: William B. Eerdmans Publishing Co., 1999.

———. *Dialogues des Carmélites*. D'après une nouvelle de Gertrud von Le Fort et un scenario du R. P. Bruckberger et de Philippe Agostini. Édition du Seuil, 1996.

Borchmeyer, Dieter. *Richard Wagner, Theory and Theatre*. Trans. Stewart
    Spencer. Oxford: Clarendon Press, 1991.
Borstlap, John. *The Classical Revolution: Thoughts on New Music in the
    21st Century*. Mineola NY: Dover Publications, Inc., 2017.
Brann, Eva. *Un-Willing: An Inquiry into the Rise of Will's Power and an
    Attempt to Undo It*. Philadelphia: Paul Dry Books, 2014.
Bush, William. *To Quell the Terror: The True Story of the Carmelite Martyrs
    of Compiègne*. Washington D.C.: ICS Publications, 2013.
Butler, E. M. *The Fortunes of Faust*. Cambridge: Cambridge University
    Press, 1979.
Carnegy, Patrick. *Faust as Musician: A Study of Thomas Mann's Novel
    Doctor Faustus*. New York: New Directions, 1973.
Caro, Ethel E. *Music and Thomas Mann*. Stanford: Literary Licensing,
    1959.
Cartwright, David E. *Schopenhauer: A Biography*. Cambridge: Cambridge
    University Press, 2010.
Chailley, Jacques. *The Magic Flute, Masonic Opera*. Trans. Herbert Wein-
    stock. New York: Knopf, 1971.
Dahlhaus, Carl. *Richard Wagner's Music Dramas*. Trans. Mary Whittall.
    Cambridge: Cambridge University Press, 1979.
———. *Schoenberg and the New Music*. Trans. Derrick Puffett and Alfred
    Clayton.Cambridge: Cambridge University Press, 1988.
Dostoevsky, Fyodor. *The Brothers Karamazov*. Trans. Richard Pevear and
    Larissa Volokhonsky, New York: Vintage Books, 1991.
Faraday, Michael. "A speculation touching Electric Conduction and the
    Nature of Matter," in *Experimental Researches in Electricity*, Vol. II.
    Santa Fe NM: Green Lion Press, 2000.
Fux, Johann Joseph. *The Study of Counterpoint: Gradus ad Parnassum*,
    1725. Trans. Alfred Mann, New York: Norton Library, 1971.
Goethe, Johann Wolfgang von. *Faust*. Trans. Walter Kaufmann. New
    York: Anchor Books, 1961.
———. *The Collected Works*, Vol. 12, *Scientific Studies*. Trans. Douglas
    Miller. Princeton" Princeton University Press, 1995.
Hanslick, Eduard. *On the Musically Beautiful*. Trans. Geoffrey Payzant.
    Indianapolis: Hackett Publishing Co., 1986.
Hegel, G. W. F. *Hegel's Aesthetics: Lectures on Fine Art*, Vols. I and II. Trans.
    T. M. Knox. Oxford: Clarendon Press, 1998.
Heidegger, Martin. *Poetry, Language, Thought*. Trans. Albert Hofstadter.
    New York: Harper Colophon Books, 1971.

————. *"The Question Concerning Technology" and Other Essays*. Trans. William Lovitt. New York: Harper Torchbooks, 1977.

Heller, Erich. *Thomas Mann: The Ironic German*. Cambridge: Cambridge University Press, 1981.

Helmholtz, Hermann. *On the Sensations of Tone*. Trans. Alexander J. Ellis. New York: Dover Publications, Inc., 1954.

Hoffmann, E. T. A. *E. T. A. Hoffman's Musical Writings*. Trans. Martyn Clarke. Cambridge: Cambridge University Press, 1989.

Husserl, Edmund. *The Phenomenology of Internal Time-Consciousness*. Trans. Calvin O. Schrag. Bloomington: Indiana University Press, 1971.

Jammer, Max. *Concepts of Force*. New York: Dover Publications, Inc., 1999.

Jonas, Hans. *The Phenomenon of Life: Toward a Philosophical Biology*. Chicago: Chicago University Press, 1966.

————. *The Gnostic Religion*, 2nd ed. Boston: Beacon Press, 1963.

Joyce, James. "The Dead," *Dubliners*. New York: W. W. Norton & Co., 2006.

Kalkavage, Peter. "Plato's *Timaeus* and the Will to Order." *The St. John's Review*, Vol. 47, Number 1, 2003.

————. "Music and the Idea of a World." *The St. John's Review*, Vol. 57, Number 2, 2016, 25–46.

Kerman, Joseph. *Opera as Drama*. New York: Random House, Vintage Books, 1956.

Kierkegaard, Søren. *Either/Or*. Trans. Howard V. Hong and Edna H. Hong. Princeton: Princeton University Press, 1987.

Kleist, Heinrich von. *Selected Writings*. Trans. David Constantine. Indianapolis: Hackett Publishing Co., 2004.

Köhler, Wolfgang. *Gestalt Psychology, The Definitive Statement of the Gestalt Theory*. New York: Liveright, 1992.

Kurth, Ernst. *Romantische harmonik und ihre Krise in Wagner's 'Tristan.'* Berlin: Max Hesses Verlag, 1920.

————. *Grundlagen des linearen Kontrapunkts*. Berlin: Max Hesses Verlag, 1922.

Langer, Susanne K. *Philosophy in a New Key: A Study in the Symbolism of Reason, Rite, and Art*. Harvard: Harvard University Press, 1979.

Le Fort, Gertrud von. *Die Letzte am Schafott*. Stuttgart: Reclam, 1983.

————. *The Song at the Scaffold*. Trans. Olga Marx. San Francisco: Ignatius Press, 2011.

Liébert, Georges. *Nietzsche and Music*. Trans. David Pellauer and Graham Parkes. Chicago: Chicago University Press, 2004.

MacDonald, Malcolm. *Schoenberg*. Oxford: Oxford University Press, 2008.

Mann, Thomas. *Doctor Faustus*. Trans. John E. Woods. New York: Vintage Books, Random House, Inc., 1999.

———. *The Story of a Novel: The Genesis of Doctor Faustus*. Trans. Richard and Clara Winston. New York: Knopf, 1961.

———. *Essays*. Trans. H. T. Lowe-Porter. New York: Vintage Books, 1957.

———. *Last Essays*. Trans. Richard and Clara Winston and Tania and James Stern. New York: Knopf, 1970.

Mellers, Wilfrid. *Francis Poulenc* (Oxford Studies of Composers). Oxford: Oxford University Press, 1995.

Newman, Ernest. *The Wagner Operas*. Princeton: Princeton University Press, 1991.

Nichols, Roger. *Poulenc: A Biography*. New Haven: Yale University Press, 2020.

Nietzsche, Friedrich. *The Birth of Tragedy and The Case of Wagner*. Trans. Walter Kaufmann. New York: Vintage Books, 1967.

———. *Untimely Meditations*. Trans. Daniel Breazeale. Cambridge: Cambridge University Press, 2003.

Novalis. *Hymns to the Night*. Trans. Dick Higgins. New York: McPherson & Co., 1988.

———. *Philosophical Writings*. Trans. Margaret Mahony Stoljar. New York: SUNY Press, 1997.

Pelikan, Jaroslav. *Bach Among the Theologians*. Philadelphia: Fortress Press, 1986.

Perle, George. *Serial Composition and Atonality*. Berkeley: University of California Press, 1962.

Plato. *Republic*. Trans. Allan Bloom. New York: Basic Books, 1968.

———. *Phaedo*. Trans. Eva Brann, Peter Kalkavage, Eric Salem. Indianapolis: Hackett Publishing Co., Inc., 1998.

———. *Timaeus*, 2nd ed. Trans. Peter Kalkavage. Indianapolis: Hackett Publishing Co., 2016.

Poulenc, Francis. *Francis Poulenc, 'Echo and Source,' Selected Correspondence 1915–1963*. Trans. Sidney Buckland. London: Victor Gollancz LTD, 1991.

Reilly, Robert R. with Jens F. Laurson. *Surprised by Beauty: A Listener's Guide to the Recovery of Modern Music* (revised and expanded edition). San Francisco: Ignatius Press, 2016.

Révész, Geza. "Gibt es ein Hörraum?" *Acta Psychologica* (The Hague), III, 1937.

———. *Introduction to the Psychology of Music.* Trans. G. I. C. de Courcy. New York: Dover Publications, Inc., 2001.

Rochberg, George. *The Aesthetics of Survival: A Composer's View of Twentieth-Century Music.* Ann Arbor: University of Michigan Press, 2004.

Rosen, Charles. *The Classical Style* (expanded edition). New York: W. W. Norton & Co., 1998.

———. *Arnold Schoenberg.* Chicago: University of Chicago, 1996.

Rothstein, Edward. *Emblems of the Mind: The Inner Life of Music and Mathematics.* Chicago: University of Chicago Press, 2006.

Rougemont, Denis de. *Love in the Western World.* Trans. Montgomery Belgion. Princeton: Princeton University Press, 1983.

Sacks, Oliver. *Musicophilia, Tales of Music and the Brain.* New York: Vintage Books, 2008.

Salzer, Felix. *Structural Hearing, Tonal Coherence in Music.* New York: Dover Publications, Inc., 1982.

Schenker, Heinrich. *Free Composition.* Trans. Ernst Oster. New York: Longman Inc., 1979.

———. *Harmony.* Trans. Elisabeth Mann Borgese. Chicago: University of Chicago Press, 1968.

Schoenberg, Arnold. *Style and Idea.* Trans. Leo Black. Berkeley: University of California Press, 1984.

Schopenhauer, Arthur. *The World as Will and Representation,* Volumes I and II. Trans. E. F. J. Payne. New York: Dover Publications, Inc., 1969.

———. *Parerga and Paralipomena,* Volumes I and II. Trans. E. F. J. Payne. Oxford: Clarendon Press,1974.

———. *The Fourfold Root of the Principle of Sufficient Reason.* Trans. E. F. J. Payne. LaSalle, Illinois: Open Court Publishing Co., 1974.

Scruton, Roger. *Death-Devoted Heart: Sex and the Sacred in Wagner's Tristan and Isolde.* Oxford: Oxford University Press, 2004.

———. *The Soul of the World.* Princeton: Princeton University Press, 2014.

Shakespeare, William. *Love's Labour's Lost,* London: The Arden Shakespeare, 1998.

———. *The Tempest,* London: The Arden Shakespeare, 1999.

Sorel, Georges. *Reflections on Violence.* Trans. Thomas Ernest Hulme, with revisions by Jeremy Jennings. Cambridge: Cambridge University Press, 2012.

Speaight, Robert. *Georges Bernanos: a Biography*. New York: Liveright, 1974.

Stevens, Wallace. *Collected Poetry and Prose*, New York: The Library of America, 1997.

Strassburg, Gottfried von. *Tristan*. Trans. A. T. Hatto. London: Penguin Books, 2004.

Straus, Erwin W. *Phenomenological Psychology*. Trans. Erling Eng. New York: Basic Books, Inc., 1966.

Uexküll, Jakob Johann von. *Theoretical Biology*. Trans. D. L. Mackinnon. New York. Harcourt, Brace & Co., Inc., 1926.

Valéry, Paul. "Poetry and Abstract Thought" (trans. Denise Folliot) in *Paul Valéry: An Anthology*. Selected and introduced by James R. Lawler. Princeton: Princeton University Press, Bollingen Series, 1977.

Wagner, Richard. *Wagner on Music and Drama: A Compendium of Wagner's Prose Works*. Selected and arranged by Albert Goldman and Evert Sprinchorn. Trans. H. Ashton Ellis. New York: Da Capo Press, 1988.

———. *Selected Letters of Richard Wagner*. Trans. Stewart Spencer and Barry Millington. London: J. M. Dent & Sons LTD, 1987.

Webern, Anton. *The Path to the New Music*. Trans. Willi Reich. Bryn Mawr: Theodore Presser Company, 1963.

Wolff, Christoff. *Johann Sebastian Bach, The Learned Musician*. New York: W. W. Norton & Co., 2000.

Zarlino, Gioseffo. *The Art of Counterpoint* (Part Three of *Le istitutioni harmoniche*, 1558). Trans. Guy A. Marco and Claude V. Palisca. New York: Norton Library, 1976.

Zuckerkandl, Victor. *The Sense of Music*. Princeton: Princeton University Press, 1971.

———. *Sound and Symbol: Music and the External World*. Trans. Norbert Guterman. Princeton: Princeton University Press, 1973.

———. *Man the Musician (Sound and Symbol: Volume Two)*. Trans. Willard R. Trask. Princeton: Princeton University Press, 1976.

Zuckerman, Elliott. *The First Hundred Years of Wagner's Tristan*. New York: Columbia University Press, 1964.

Index

ABA form, 87–88, 214, 273n28
absolute music, Wagner, 21, 59
accompaniment, 87, 89, 91, 108, 115
acoustical pitches, 45, 67, 142, 144
acoustics-approach to musical experience, 68
active listening, 37
Adorno, Theodor, 142, 148–49, 153, 158–59, 163, 165, 282n8, 283nn15–18, 285n31, 286n40, 286n46, 287n54, 288n62, 291n84
Aeneid (Virgil), 51, 291n82
Aeolian scale, 33, 34–35
aesthetic contemplation, 14–15, 133–34
aestheticism, 154, 172–73
aisthêton (object of musical perception), 40, 73, 104, 109
Alberti bass, 116
Alighieri, Dante, 25, 102, 137–38, 140, 167, 172, 263n27, 281n1
Allesch, Gustav von, 36
A-major Polonaise (Chopin), 49–50
ambiguity, 152, 161, 169, 183–84
An die Musik (Schubert), 28
anticipation, 53–55, 116
Apocalypsis cum figuris oratorio in *Doctor Faustus*, 158, 167, 170–71, 173–76, 177, 180
applied dominant, 111, 113, 117
appoggiaturas, 18, 90, 92, 109–10, 112–19, 137, 143, 182
archaism, 285n33

arias. *See* "*Aus Liebe will mein Heiland sterben*"; *Bachianas Brasileiras* (Villa-Lobos); "*Dies Bildnis ist bezaubernd schön*"
arioso, 194, 198, 210–12, 294n14
Aristotle, 5–6, 16, 24, 47, 261n8, 264n35, 269n77
Aristoxenus, 260n3
arkhê (source), 72
arpeggiated chords, 201
arpeggio, 98, 197, 231
arrival, 40, 43, 52–53, 66, 69
arrow of time, 50, 67, 144
arrow symbol, 41–42, 67
artificiality, 162–63
artistic imitation, 291n94
artistic unity, 174
Art of Counterpoint (Zarlino), 269n77
The Art of Fugue, 282n6
asceticism, 135, 148, 153–54, 156, 168
associationism, 31, 34–36
astronomy, 9–10, 13, 241
atoms, Faraday, 267n60
atonality, 141, 258n33, 281n2
atonal music, 182, 281n2, 281n4
audible/auditory space, 60–72
Aufhebung, 48, 189–90
augmented second, 262n16
Augustine, Saint, 102, 137, 266n52
aura, 43
"*Aus Liebe will mein Heiland sterben*," 81–102, 194, 272n21, 272n23, 273n28, 273n30

307

Peter Kalkavage is the author of *The Logic of Desire: An Introduction to Hegel's Phenomenology of Spirit* (Paul Dry Books, 2007). He has translated the *Timaeus* and co-translated the *Sophist, Phaedo, Statesman, Symposium,* and *Meno*—all for Hackett Publishing Company. Kalkavage has been teaching at St. John's College in Annapolis, Maryland for over forty-five years, and for the last thirty years, he has been the director of The St. John's Chorus, which regularly performs sacred music from the Renaissance to the present.